Praise for *The Business of Healthcare*

"The editors and writers of *The Business of Healthcare* have created a compelling and highly informative set of books that merge various disciplines and perspectives to create a comprehensive look at the challenges facing the healthcare industry. These books should prompt valuable discussion and, hopefully, action that will strengthen and advance the U.S. health system."

Craig E. Holm, FACHE, CHE
Health Strategies & Solutions Inc. Philadelphia

"Thoughtful and provocative, *The Business of Healthcare* is a clearly articulated exploration of critical issues facing healthcare leaders today."

C. Duane Dauner
President, California Hospital Association

"Just when the pressures and challenges on healthcare practitioners and organizations seem unbearable, Cohn and Hough have skillfully assembled this work which offers advice and comfort, not only on how to cope with today's climate, but how also to take advantage of the opportunities that abound while not abandoning the call to serve humanity."

Robert A. Reid, M.D.
Director of Medical Affairs, Cottage Health System,
Santa Barbara, California
Past president, California Medical Association

"Now, more than ever, this three-volume set is necessary and important. The format and breadth of content is impressive; rather than a prescriptive set of how-tos, I come away with an expanded vision of 'want to' and 'able to.'"

Leonard H. Friedman, Ph.D., MPH
Professor and Coordinator Department of Public Health,
Oregon State University

# The Business of Healthcare

## Volume 2: Leading Healthcare Organizations

EDITED BY
KENNETH H. COHN, MD
DOUGLAS E. HOUGH, PhD

PRAEGER PERSPECTIVES

Westport, Connecticut
London

**Library of Congress Cataloging-in-Publication Data**

The business of healthcare / edited by Kenneth H. Cohn, Douglas E. Hough.
    p. cm. — (Praeger perspectives)
    Includes bibliographical references and index.
    ISBN 978–0–275–99235–4 (set : alk. paper)
    ISBN 978–0–275–99236–1 (v. 1 : alk. paper)
    ISBN 978–0–275–99237–8 (v. 2 : alk. paper)
    ISBN 978–0–275–99238–5 (v. 3 : alk. paper)
  1. Medical care—United States.   2. Medical offices—United States—
Management.   3. Medical care—United States—Quality control.   4. Health
services administration—United States.   5. Health care reform—United
States.   I. Cohn, Kenneth H.   II. Hough, Douglas E.   III. Series.
    [DNLM:   1. Delivery of Health Care—organization & administration—
United States.   2. Leadership—United States.   3. Practice Management,
Medical—United States.   4. Quality of Health Care—United States.
W 84 AA1 B969 2007]
RA395.A3B875   2008
362.1068—dc22          2007031135

British Library Cataloguing in Publication Data is available.

Library of Congress Catalog Card Number: 2007031135
ISBN: 978–0–275–99235–4 (Set)
        978–0–275–99236–1 (Vol. 1)
        978–0–275–99237–8 (Vol. 2)
        978–0–275–99238–5 (Vol. 3)

First published in 2008

Praeger Publishers, 88 Post Road West, Westport, CT 06881
An imprint of Greenwood Publishing Group, Inc.
www.praeger.com

Printed in the United States of America

The paper used in this book complies with the
Permanent Paper Standard issued by the National
Information Standards Organization (Z39.48–1984).

10 9 8 7 6 5 4 3 2 1

# Contents

# Preface

The healthcare system in the United States is a mass of paradoxes. We lead the world in the creation and application of technology for the clinical practice of medicine; yet the United States lags behind the rest of the developed world in basic health indicators (e.g., infant mortality rate, life expectancy). We provide some of the highest quality care in some of the premier health institutions that are the envy of the world; yet 45 million Americans cannot take advantage of these benefits because they lack health insurance. We outspend every other country on healthcare; yet almost no one is satisfied with the results: patients may get unparalleled quality care, but they pay a lot for that care and access can be erratic; payers are frustrated that they (and their customers) are not receiving good value for their growing outlays; and providers are feeling harassed by payers and regulators and unappreciated by patients.

Some claim that healthcare is being ruined by the intrusion of business interests, which put the bottom line ahead of the appropriate care of patients and denigrate the professionalism of those sworn to care for the sick. They worry that these interests are making healthcare no different than any other "industry" in this country. Others argue that the problems of inconsistent quality, sporadic access, and high and rising costs can only be solved by imposing the discipline of the market. To these observers it is business thinking and processes that can transform the current system.

The editors of *The Business of Healthcare* believe that the issue is not professionalism *or* business in healthcare, but professionalism *and* business. We believe that the healthcare system in the United States needs the perspectives and expertise of physicians and economists, nurses and accountants, technicians and strategists. We have organized this three-volume set for Praeger Perspectives to demonstrate how these mutual viewpoints can yield innovative solutions to our healthcare conundrum.

In designing *The Business of Healthcare,* the editors recognized that the solutions to the challenges facing the U.S. healthcare system will not come from one source. Rather, the solutions must address both the micro and the macro aspects of the system. Individual medical practices, as the foundation of healthcare delivery, must be operated as efficiently as possible. Healthcare organizations of all types must be led in ways to maximize the effectiveness of both human and financial resources. Finally, attention must be paid to the systems currently in place that affect all aspects of the healthcare sector.

To that end, we have organized *The Business of Healthcare* into three volumes that address each of these levels of the healthcare system in the United States. Volume 1 *(Practice Management)* focuses on those areas critical to the successful operation of physician practices: the process of joining and leaving a practice; promoting a practice; and managing the human and financial resources of a practice. It addresses the current structure of physician practices (including the continuing viability of solo practice) as well as the very future of the physician practice itself.

Volume 2 *(Leading Healthcare Organizations)* shifts the focus to the complex tasks of leading in healthcare. The chapters in this volume illustrate that leadership involves the integration of relationship management (such as the appropriate involvement of physicians in healthcare organizations), new modes of care (including such disparate areas as biotechnology, complementary and alternative medicine, and pastoral care), and operations (informatics, clinical supplies, liability risk management).

Volume 3 *(Improving Systems of Care)* widens the lens to consider how systems in healthcare can be transformed to resolve the paradoxes that we noted above. The chapters in this volume address systems to improve clinical quality and safety, development systems (e.g., for moving scientific ideas from the lab to the market, for developing medical technologies), operational systems (e.g., disaster response, information technology, and end-of-life care), and financial systems (such as the new "Massachusetts Plan" to cover all members of society). The volume also includes the voice of the patient in improving systems of care.

We are grateful to all of our chapter authors who volunteered scarce time to write about aspects of healthcare about which they are passionate. Our goal has been to provide works by experts that will engage stakeholders in discussions of issues important to our nation's health and economy. We hope that we have succeeded.

## VOLUME 1: PRACTICE MANAGEMENT

It used to be that physicians could graduate from medical school, complete a residency, and be confident that they could start a practice that was financially and professionally successful almost from the first day. Those halcyon days are long gone, with the advent of constrained reimbursements, increased regulation, and real competition for patients. Today, physicians must run their practice as if it was a business—because it is. Although many physicians may be accidental business people, they must pay attention to the most critical operational aspects of their practice if they are to achieve their professional goals.

To that end, we asked our authors to bring forward the issues that they see from their experience as those most critical to the operational success of the medical practice. They responded with eight focused and insightful chapters on how to:

- Manage the continuing opportunities and challenges of solo practice
- Join and leave a practice
- Measure performance in a medical practice
- Build a culture of accountability in a practice
- Manage difficult physicians
- Promote a practice
- Create a practice marketing plan
- Manage the revenue cycle

In addition, two authors took a broader look at the environment of medicine, one exploring the potential and realities of the new pay-for-performance and the other considering the future of the medical practice.

In all, these chapters should provide physicians and practice administrators with the most up-to-date practical thinking on the effective management of physician practices.

## VOLUME 2: LEADING HEALTHCARE ORGANIZATIONS

Leadership is the art of instilling in people the desire to strive together to create a better future. Leaders listen, observe, provide direction and meaning, generate and sustain trust, convey hope, and obtain results through their influence on other employees. The challenge is to energize people to push themselves beyond what they thought they could do (Cohn, Cannon, and Boswell 2006).

Nowhere are these principles more evident than in the chapters in Volume 2, where nationally known authors discuss the need for and evidence of leadership in healthcare. Diane Dixon begins this volume with an analysis of six healthcare leaders who embraced a positive, can-do mindset that enabled them to transform their institutions. Drs. Waldman and Cohn describe ways to transcend the adversarial relations that traditionally accompany physician-hospital relations and the dividends to patient care of engaging physicians in clinical priority setting, which Jayne Oliva and Mary Totten build on by describing the dual opportunity and responsibility of physicians serving on hospital boards.

The final six chapters highlight the need for and benefits of leadership in specific sectors of healthcare, including biotechnology, informatics, complementary and alternative medicine, supply costs, risk management, and pastoral care.

In healthcare, as in other fields that serve the public welfare, dedicated professionals prefer being inspired to being supervised. Through their influence on business strategy and especially on organizational culture, effective leaders:

- Create a safe environment for reflection and learning
- Improve the practice environment and hence practice outcomes
- Help people reconnect with the values that attracted them to healthcare in the first place

The purpose of this series and of Volume 2 in particular is to create a nurturing environment that stimulates further reflection, discussion, and action, resulting in improved healthcare for our communities. Only then can we consider our efforts successful.

## VOLUME 3: IMPROVING SYSTEMS OF CARE

The imperative for improvement is clear for everyone who works in healthcare. Through breakthrough studies championed by the Institute of Medicine, we have learned that inadequate systems of care jeopardize the health and recovery of hundreds of thousands of patients annually, adding billions of dollars of expense to an unsustainable healthcare budget.

For people inside and outside the nonsystem of fragmented U.S. healthcare, the complexity can be overwhelming. A framework that treats a patient or healthcare processes as a number of mechanical parts, without paying attention to interactions of human beings with other human beings, is likely to fail.

We are fortunate in Volume 3 to have chapters written by experts who have created a platform for learning and discussion that can inform the healthcare debate, point out the choices we need to make, and help us maintain optimism about our future. Carl Taylor provides practical and organizational insights that can guide us in meeting the needs of patients, families, and healthcare workers during the next man-made or natural disaster. Michael Doonan and Stuart Altman use the recently enacted Massachusetts health plan to discuss a way forward for dealing with the needs of the uninsured and underinsured. Philip Buttell, Robert Hendler, and Jennifer Daley define quality and safety in operational metrics that permit tracking, improvement, and cultural change. Jack Barker and Greg Madonna analyze the similarities and differences between aviation and healthcare and offer promise that simple practical steps like briefing, debriefing, coaching, and team training can enhance skill sets in communication and improve safety outcomes, as they did in aviation nearly three decades ago.

Hospitals' success increasingly relies on sharing information to prevent adverse outcomes in medication administration and proactive disease management, as seen in the next three chapters on informational technology solutions, medical technology, and improving outcomes and reimbursement. In the final four chapters, Donald McDaniel, Anirban Basu, David Kovel, and Ian Batstone argue that despite the expense of our poorly coordinated (non)system of care, healthcare creates high-wage, high-tech, and high-touch jobs that form the backbone of the American economy. Rudy Wilson Galdonik, who has been a caretaker and a patient, offers practical suggestions for improvement of systems of care from a humanistic perspective. Lynn Johnson Langer notes the rapid uptake that accrues when scientists translate the results of their research to the business community to serve the interests and needs of society. Finally, Kenneth Fisher and Lindsay Rockwell point out the tremendous cost of care in the last year of life and the billions of dollars that could be freed to support systems improvement if we instituted practical changes in the way that we provided terminal care.

Although change may feel like failure when we are in the middle of it, we have reached a critical time when we can move from individual "blame-storming" to ways to ameliorate systems of care. This volume and indeed the entire three-volume series will only be successful if the insights contributed by our authors inspire us to create an environment conducive to questioning our past assumptions and learning new ways to study and improve patient care.

Kenneth H. Cohn, MD, MBA
Douglas E. Hough, PhD

## REFERENCE

Cohn, Kenneth H., S. Cannon, and C. Boswell. 2006. "Let's Do Something: A Cutting-Edge Collaboration Strategy." In *Collaborate for Success! Breakthrough Strategies for Engaging Physicians, Nurses, and Hospital Executives*, ed. Kenneth H. Cohn, 76–77. Chicago: Health Administration Press.

# CHAPTER 1

# Perspectives on Leading Complex Healthcare Delivery Systems

Diane L. Dixon

There is hope for the future of healthcare delivery systems. We read and hear a great deal about all that is wrong with hospitals, nursing homes, physician practices, and other types of healthcare organizations. Numerous articles, books, and documentaries have described what needs to be fixed. The intent of this chapter is not to duplicate what has already been done, but rather to convey positive perspectives on leading complex healthcare delivery systems. There are many hard working leaders who are demonstrating every day that it is possible to transform an ailing system. There are no fancy models or quick fixes. Hope for delivering quality care lies within hopeful leaders who are committed to service and people. This chapter will share examples of six leaders who have achieved performance excellence by leading with a bold vision for better quality care and igniting leadership in the people who knew best how to make that vision a reality. They faced the same challenges that everybody else deals with such as quality, patient safety, financial restraints, staff shortages, and care for the uninsured to name a few. But they did not let these challenges become barriers to excellence. What makes them different? One of the key differences is that these leaders did not let conventional practices block their openness to engage in different ways of thinking and being. They embraced a positive mindset that enabled them to make progress in unstable and difficult times. These leaders understand the traditional, mechanistic, organizational paradigm and its potentially negative impact on their leadership. This understanding helped them to embrace different worldviews that influence how they lead.

## EMBRACING DIFFERENT WORLDVIEWS

The manner in which leaders see organizations and their relationships to them directly impacts how they lead. A machine metaphor has been descriptive of the traditional organizational paradigm that has its foundation in Newtonian scientific principles.[1] When the machine metaphor dominates thinking about organizations and management, it becomes a filter through which leaders determine how they manage.[2] Seeing an organization as a machine suggests that the whole is the sum of its parts. Translated into a hospital or nursing home setting, this would mean individual departments are the focus and that understanding the organization is dependent upon looking more closely at departments separately. Silos dominate the landscape, creating boundaries that impede interaction. This thinking is well aligned with long-established hierarchies that have traditionally controlled healthcare delivery systems. In the mechanistic worldview, things are rational, predictable, and controllable. There is a basic assumption of stability and order. So the command and control management technique works well in this context.

## SOCIOLOGY OF REGULATION

This way of thinking has been influenced by a worldview of Western society that asserts the need for regulation in human affairs as a means of holding the society and institutions within it together. To further comprehend the power of the traditional paradigm and its impact on healthcare leadership, it is important to understand the "sociology of regulation."[3] The sociology of regulation is characterized by concern with the status quo, social order, cohesion, and what is actual as a way of understanding society. One can posit a relationship between this point of view and mechanistic thinking. If an organization functions like a machine, regulations will ensure that the parts will be cohesive, and the status quo and order will be maintained to keep the machine running smoothly. And, from a health policy and governmental standpoint, regulations have been the key manner in which healthcare institutions have been managed. The regulation mindset has often constrained the thinking of healthcare leaders. This accepted pattern of assumptions about how organizations behave in the context of our larger society has influenced how leaders lead and manage for a long time. These mechanistic viewpoints have collectively formed the foundation of the traditional organizational paradigm for healthcare organizations.

Challenges to this worldview are very evident in a fast-paced, highly turbulent, unpredictable, and continuously changing world. According to Burrell and Morgan, there is another very different sociological construct or way of understanding society and its institutions. The "sociology of radical change" has to do with seeking explanations for radical change, entrenched structural conflict, forms of domination, and contradiction.[4] This view of society purports liberation from structures that limit potential for human and organization development. There is a focus on what is possible rather than maintaining the status quo. Given the current state of healthcare and the turbulent environment in which it exists, this perspective seems more aligned with the reality of care delivery systems in need of radical change to adapt to the demands of society.

Related to the sociology of radical change is a different viewpoint of organizational behavior. For example, rather than seeing a hospital or nursing home as machines to be regulated, we can see them as complex adaptive living systems.[5] This viewpoint is informed by complexity science which is an emerging science that embraces a combination of theories and concepts including physical, biological, quantum, chaos, and social science. A complex adaptive system is a nonlinear system comprised of numerous connections and interdependence between diverse elements and independent agents that have the capacity to learn and adapt from experience.[6] As these diverse agents, which may be departments within a delivery system, interact with each other, they have the capability to self-organize without external intervention. Within a complex adaptive system, relationships and connectedness are more important than individuality. The whole system and its interdependent elements become the focus for leaders. So if leaders accept that healthcare delivery organizations are complex adaptive systems in an environment on the verge of radical change, then leading becomes a process of facilitating change by building relationships and collaboration. Leadership is guided by core values and mission that act as simple rules in an unpredictable and uncontrollable environment.

Embracing new worldviews requires leaders to change their mindsets so that they are open to and can discover new ways of thinking. To do this, leaders need to be aware of their mindsets; those assumptions, beliefs, and values that act as filters.[7] They need to know what they think, why they think the way they do, and how their thinking affects their behavior. This is how leaders break the cycle of implementing new approaches the old way, a familiar pattern in healthcare. The leadership examples shared in this chapter demonstrate how healthcare leaders can really change and improve care delivery systems when they break this mechanistic cycle.

## LEARNING FROM LEADERSHIP CASES

The six leadership cases are presented as sources of learning and reflection rather than best practices. They are intended to inspire deeper inquiry about the leadership capabilities required to transform healthcare delivery systems. While each case is different, the leaders share some common leadership characteristics and practices. The examples are based on conversations with each of the featured leaders and a review of supplemental material describing their organizations.

### Christy Stephenson, RN, MBA, Former President and Chief Executive Officer, Robert Wood Johnson University Hospital Hamilton

Christy Stephenson, RN, MBA, retired in December 2006 as president and CEO of Robert Wood Johnson University Hospital Hamilton (RWJUHH) after serving in that position since 1998. Prior to becoming chief executive officer (CEO), she was the chief operating officer for six years. Her entire career has been in healthcare, beginning as an aide, then becoming licensed as a registered nurse (RN) and attaining a masters in business administration. She has served in many different positions in seven hospitals. One of these experiences included two and a half years with a for-profit ambulatory care company. Ms. Stephenson has learned a great deal about leadership over the years. Her most recent experiences at RWJUHH define her leadership with many markers of success.

RWJUHH is located in Hamilton Township, Mercer County, New Jersey. It is a private, not-for-profit, acute-care hospital serving more than 350,000 residents in the region. The hospital is part of Robert Wood Johnson Health System and Network and is affiliated with the University of Medicine and Dentistry of New Jersey-Robert Wood Johnson Medical School. There are over 1,750 employees and more than 600 physicians representing more than 30 medical specialties.[8]

Ms. Stephenson's leadership approach resulted in the emergence of leaders throughout the hospital on all levels during her tenure. The leadership team led RWJUHH to earn many notable achievements. The success of RWJUHH demonstrates that healthcare delivery can provide high quality care in a challenging environment. The hospital was awarded the Malcolm Baldrige National Quality Award in 2004. This is the highest honor an organization in the United States can accomplish for quality management and performance excellence. They are one of a few hospitals to receive this mark of distinction. In 2006 and 2007, the hospital attained the Distinguished Hospital for Clinical Excellence Award from HealthGrades, Inc. This designation ranks the hospital's clinical excellence among the top five percent in the nation.

*Voice of the Customer*

Leaders at RWJUHH have focused their attention on achieving excellence through service for three primary customer groups—patients, employees, and community. According to Ms. Stephenson, the leadership team continuously listens to the Voice of the Customer. They developed a database that captures customer needs and anticipates future trends. Community surveys provide valuable data as well. Employee opinions are also solicited, and their recommendations are a foundation for improving customer service. Providing excellent service means that the leadership team sees the hospital as a system that links all functions together as a whole and does not work in silos. Continuous cycles of improvement, measurement, and evaluation are the foundation of excellence through service.

Ms. Stephenson believes that employee satisfaction has been integral to patient satisfaction. This is why there are daily briefings with staff at RWJUHH. Each executive management team member shares critical information and answers questions that enable the frontline staff to do their jobs better. Ms. Stephenson also participated in these briefings. Every employee is only three steps away from organizational goals. Organizational goals are prioritized, and the top five organizational goals cascade down so each department of the hospital has a goal linked to the top organizational goals. The departmental goals further cascade down to each individual employee. For example, a hospital goal is 7 percent RN vacancy rate or lower. The human resources (HR) departmental goal is to reduce time to hire RNs to below 30 days. An HR staff person's goal is to reduce 90 day turnover for RNs.

Each individual carries an E-3 card (*Engage Every Employee*). The E-card reminds employees of their role in achieving organizational objectives. The inclusiveness and involvement of employees has improved their satisfaction to over 90 percent from 78 percent. Another key factor contributing to satisfaction is employee teamwork and interdepartmental collaboration. The "Walk in My Shoes" process gives employees the opportunity to work in departments other than their own. This process has several benefits that include cross training, sharing information, and gaining valuable insights.

*Five-star service standards* are the signature of patient satisfaction, according to Ms. Stephenson. These standards consist of commitments to customers and coworkers, courtesy, etiquette, and safety awareness. They are used to recruit, train, and evaluate employees. An example is the 15/30 Program in the emergency department. The program guarantees that every patient will see a nurse within 15 minutes and a physician in 30 minutes. Standards like these serve as the operating agreement for how patients will be treated at RWJUHH. Because of this unified commitment to patient service, the hospital has consistently improved patient satisfaction. Patient satisfaction, specifically with nursing and physician care, has remained above the 92nd percentile for several years.

An integrated information technology system helps employees and physicians serve patients more efficiently. RWJUHH has been engaged in an "IT Innovation Journey" for several years. They have pioneered technologies such as fully digital radiology, bar coding of medications, electronic patient medical records, and computerized physician order entry systems. Technology, particularly computerized patient records, are more accurate, legible, and can be reviewed by more than one health practitioner at the same time. In 2006, RWJUHH received an award from *Hospitals and Health Networks* for being one of the most technologically advanced hospitals, incorporating wireless applications.

### Team Leadership

Leadership has been the key ingredient to success at RWJUHH. When asked about her leadership, Ms. Stephenson points out that it was not only about her as a leader, it was a team effort. She stated, "We accomplished great things because of our teamwork." Her job was to set the direction and engage everybody in the process of achieving the vision "to passionately pursue the health and well-being of patients, employees, and the community."[9] Stephenson believes effective leaders see the best in each person and are successful when they tap into the passion that brought them into healthcare in the first place. Her passion about the vision and mission helped to ignite passion in others. She thinks leadership is not about position or education, but rather about attitude. Her positive mindset greatly contributed to her leadership approach. Stephenson always wanted the best and aimed higher. This positive outlook transcended the organization and sparked others to be more motivated to achieve common goals. For example, at a staff meeting prior to Ms. Stephenson's retirement, an employee who had come back to the hospital five years ago after 18 years at another local hospital, credited

Ms. Stephenson's leadership as being the driving force in helping her find fulfillment in her work.

However, a positive outlook will only go so far in leading a hospital system in a competitive, constantly changing environment. The decision to embrace the Baldrige Health Care Criteria for Performance Excellence Framework as a guide for transformational change helped leaders at RWJUHH to create an environment in which the vision and values cascade throughout the organization on all levels.[10] This means that every employee understands the vision and values and how important their role is to bringing them to life. In this way, staff become leaders of service through excellence. Employees work in a culture in which suggestions are encouraged on how the hospital can improve patient care and action is taken when suggestions come forward. Staff closest to the patient know what needs to be improved to enhance service delivery. The role of leaders is to remove roadblocks that get in the way of quality improvement and to provide the staff with the resources to do their jobs well. Ms. Stephenson believes that this is how leaders embed performance improvement into the culture so that it can be sustained. This philosophy is a departure from traditional thinking in healthcare that typically focuses on financial health. In focusing on performance improvement grounded in high involvement and engagement of all staff working toward shared goals as an interdisciplinary team, financial health is achieved. Dialogue, listening, and communicating effectively are essential for building relationships paramount for teamwork and connecting all stakeholders in an interdependent process of performance excellence.

Ms. Stephenson has demonstrated that healthcare leaders who have a vision of excellence and know how to foster leadership in everyone through passionate pursuit of vision and values can make a difference.

### John H. Tobin, DMan, MPH, President and CEO, Waterbury Hospital

John H. Tobin is president and CEO of Waterbury Hospital, located in Waterbury, Connecticut. He has been CEO of this mid-sized community and teaching hospital for 28 years. Licensed for 357 beds, Waterbury Hospital serves approximately 15,000 inpatients and more than 21,000 outpatients. It is the second largest employer in the city with a workforce of approximately 2,000 employees. Waterbury Hospital faces the challenges of providing healthcare to the underserved and indigent along with those who have health insurance. Financial resources are continuously strained in an effort to balance competing values of business and a social mission whose guiding principle states, "Caring makes a world of difference."

What makes John Tobin like most of his peers, in many ways, yet different? How does his leadership approach make a discernable difference? John Tobin will tell you that his experience as a chief executive does not mirror that of the traditional image of top leaders. That is, he does not see himself as a powerful charismatic figure who uses prestige of an elite to influence stakeholders to embrace visions that have the potential to create sweeping change. He is not the enigmatic strategist who uses singular authority to move board decisions throughout the organization. Rather, John Tobin talks about his world as one of groups of people in collaboration. He describes the Waterbury Hospital world as an intricate tangle of interdependence in which consistent, purposeful behavior in word and action over time with appropriate use of restraint and tact are more influential than charisma. Tobin states that his world is one of "shifting patterns of leading, of constant interplay between my role in the formal structure of the hospital and the roles that emerge in social interaction."[11] He states that strategies often do not emerge from linear articulations of intent but may emerge in patterns within a stream of messy conversations, short-term plans, and prudent decisions made in a moment in time when they are most practical. Tobin believes that the potential for sweeping change is possible in these less structured contexts, although it rarely occurs. More often, change happens as an evolving process that may not always be evident in the midst of action, but becomes clearer upon reflection.

This is a fundamental shift in thinking for Tobin who, early in his career, was educated and mentored to be a traditional healthcare administrator. Healthcare administrators are typically trained to be effective managers and transactional leaders who focus on planning, organizing, controlling, and managing performance through contingent rewards like pay for performance in a hierarchical structure that assumes vertical power dynamics as a means for achieving organizational goals.[12] How does a leader move from this traditional framework of leadership to one that embraces social interaction, empowerment of staff, emergence of ideas in a nonlinear context, and the power of groups and group process? In John Tobin's case, the impetus was his introduction to the work of Dr. Ralph D. Stacey who is a professor of Management and director of the Complexity and Management Centre at the Business School of the University of Hertfordshire in England.

### Complex Responsive Processes

Dr. Stacey explains that what is going on in organizations is "complex processes of relating."[13] This construct suggests that during a typical day in a hospital, for instance, there is a continuous interchange of verbal and nonverbal interactions, a series of gestures which form a complex, nonlinear, dynamic interplay of thought and spoken word. Leader and follower relationships are an example of how these patterns of social interactions flow in an organization.[14] According to Tobin, leading is fundamentally a social process that has no meaning without interaction with followers. To deepen his understanding of this perspective, Tobin completed a doctorate of management from the University of Hertfordshire. For Tobin, understanding complex responsive processes of relating h as reshaped how he sees himself as a leader.

Traditional leaders tend to think in terms of what "I" want to happen rather than what "we can do to make things happen." Leading is more than a list of characteristics, behaviors, and practices. Tobin stated that "the way I think of who I am, how I got to be what I am, and how I function in groups has a major impact on my behavior as a leader."[15] He believes that engaging in group interaction as more of a participant rather than just an authority figure affects his behavior in subtle ways. He balances his role as an executive leader and the positional power to influence with being a participant in the process. For example, meetings once seen as time wasters are now appreciated as time for human collaboration. The format of department director meetings has changed significantly by shifting rows of chairs into an open circle so that all participants can see each other. This circle format also helps to equalize the power dynamic so that the CEO is not the only influencer in the group. Tobin's role is both facilitator and leader of the meeting process. The meeting is a balance of structured agenda items and open conversation enabling topics to arise based on the interests of the group. Rather than just reporting a list of events or actions, issues are discussed making the meeting more interactive and dynamic.

### Group Process

The appreciation of group process and its impact on Mr. Tobin has affected other processes at Waterbury Hospital. Planning is a collaborative social process involving not just the executive team but individuals in various levels of the organization, including the medical staff and department directors. Group process and collaboration have also played a key role in developing a healing environment in which staff work together across departmental boundaries. Interdisciplinary teamwork has been an essential aspect of this organizational development process as well as quality improvement processes. The scope of issues that are addressed by interdisciplinary teams and a wider circle of involvement including physicians have greatly enhanced outcomes. Tobin, as chief executive, is not separate from these processes, but is actively immersed as a full participant.

For example, at a directors' off-site meeting that Tobin facilitated along with the executive team, discussion of the hospital information technology project was used as a process for director development and learning. This project is a large-scale system change targeted to speed transfer of information, reduce errors, and enhance communication with an end goal of improving patient care. As a team, the executives and directors engaged in dialogue about the positive experiences that the directors had working on this project. The intention was to identify what could be replicated and applied to other projects. Directors indicated that the project provided an integrative structure that forced them to work across departmental boundaries to solve software and implementation problems. In the emergency department, for example, they discovered that it was essential for clinical and administrative staff to understand the needs, interests, and perspectives of each other. Another important lesson was the value of conflict in bringing issues to the surface and that questioning behaviors that get in the way of progress can be a source of creativity. They also learned that the mutual accountability for producing results motivated staff to work together, reach accommodations, and make collective decisions. Collaboration and shared leadership have advanced project implementation. The overall impact of this project is still being measured, but indicators suggest that the information technology upgrade is on the path to achieving the intended results.

*Twenty-First Century Leadership*

John Tobin believes leading successfully in twenty-first century healthcare delivery systems requires leaders to be receptive to groups and the value of relationships. Understanding the role of working in a group of interacting human beings as a coordinator and facilitator of the process rather than an authoritarian boss will significantly enhance the teamwork needed to improve quality of care delivery. He thinks that the group collaborative experience is an excellent context for ethical leading which means leaders hold themselves accountable for their actions and take into account the needs, interests, and feelings of others. And one of the most important things healthcare leaders can do is to continuously learn and reflect on what will help them to think differently. Tobin believes that the way leaders think will have a significant impact on leading healthcare delivery systems now and in the future to meet the evolving needs of their communities.

## Dr. Anthony J. Cusano, MD, Staff Physician, Waterbury Hospital, Assistant Clinical Professor, Yale School of Medicine

Dr. Anthony J. Cusano, MD, is a nephrologist and an assistant clinical professor at the Yale School of Medicine who works as a staff physician in private practice at Waterbury Hospital in Waterbury, Connecticut, and is one of the teaching faculty for the hospital residency program. As a member of the Medical Staff Quality Committee at the hospital, he has led efforts to transform traditional medical practices in an effort to prevent medical errors. In September 2004, Dr. Cusano listened to a presentation given by Jerry Sternin, the director of the Positive Deviance Initiative at Tufts University in Boston. John Tobin, president and CEO of Waterbury Hospital, invited Sternin to share perspectives on positive deviance with hospital administrative staff and department heads so that they could learn about this approach. Positive deviance focuses on finding people in the organization who are using different approaches to common problems and achieving better solutions.[16] As a result of participating in this meeting, Dr. Cusano was intrigued with how positive deviance could be applied to improving medical practices.

*Positive Deviance Approach in Action*

After some discussion, the group that participated in the meeting with Jerry Sternin decided to focus on communication as an area for improvement. Dr. Cusano recognized that communication was an important aspect of medication reconciliation at the time of hospital discharge. When patients are discharged, there may be changes in their medication regimens. Sometimes these changes are not accurately transferred to the medical record, and the physician may not reconcile the changes in the discharge instructions for the patient. Also, Dr. Cusano noted that on occasion, physicians may write generic names or preferred brand substitutions that might be different from what the patient was taking prior to hospitalization. A patient may be told to resume their original medication at the time they leave the hospital and then become confused when the medication name is different. The problem can be compounded if the patient is required to either taper medication dosage or use variable dosage regimens. He decided that this was a problem that needed further investigation.

Dr. Cusano led the effort to study medication reconciliation along with Bonnie Sturdevant, RN, nurse manager for quality improvement. By March of 2005, they formed a multidisciplinary team that decided to use the positive deviance approach to address this issue. The team developed a survey tool to review 20 randomly selected medical records of discharged patients. These patients received a telephone call within 48 hours after discharge to determine whether they were taking their prescribed medications properly. This process helped the team to identify problems that patients may have confronted with their medication regimen as well as learn how discharge instructions and other information were communicated by healthcare professionals. The survey results indicated that 49 percent of the patients were not taking their discharge medications as prescribed.

Typically, when healthcare leaders identify problems, they either look outside of the group to find best practices or engage in some kind of problem-solving process. Rather than do this, which targets healthcare providers who did not successfully advise patients, Dr. Cusano and his team applied the positive deviance approach. They studied the 51 percent of patients who did not experience problems with their medical regimens and the staff who advised patients appropriately. Successful practices were discovered that could be replicated such as using a written communication sheet to list the medications with specific instructions for complex regimens and follow-up phone calls after discharge. It was important to share these findings at noon teaching conferences and departmental ground rounds in a collaborative education and engagement process. Staff were asked for their reactions to the findings and, later, as many as 25 to 30 healthcare providers volunteered to call patients to collect additional data on their discharge regimens and compliance. This raised awareness throughout the hospital about the need to communicate medication regimens appropriately at discharge. Widespread engagement and involvement of staff increased ownership for improvement. The result was that six months after beginning the collaborative education and engagement process, 78 percent of the healthcare staff used written communication tools for discharge instructions and 66 percent of patients were more likely to use their medications without diffculty.[17]

### Lessons Learned from Positive Deviance Process

Dr. Cusano reflected on his leadership and what he learned from the positive deviance process. Here are several key lessons:

- *Involvement.* Facilitate the group so that they can embrace the problem. Leaders need to do this knowing that there are people in the group who are successfully solving the problem. It is important that leaders develop confidence in the people who are closest to the issues. A top-down approach coming from senior leaders who think they know all the answers either impedes solution discovery or stops it. The discharge medication problem was identified by the group of professionals who were responsible for solving it.

- *Self-Discovery*. The process of self-discovery can enable staff to act as owners. Leaders inhibit staff when they give solutions to problems that they have not experienced directly. It was important for the staff to experience the problems and dilemmas that providers and patients faced with medication regimens at the time of discharge. Involvement in surveying patients and reviewing records that were successfully completed helped staff to discover solutions firsthand. Self-discovery motivated staff to become more engaged in championing solutions.

- *Continuous Learning*. By engaging staff in collaborative education about solutions to medication reconciliation at discharge, collective learning was enhanced. Learning was embedded in the action of staff experiencing the problem and inquiry associated with identifying solutions. This was an action-learning process. Action learning is a group process that involves learning as problems are being solved and implementing system-wide solutions.[18] An important aspect of this process is developing leadership skills and self-awareness. Leaders such as Dr. Cusano were facilitating learning by continuously asking staff what they were learning as they were working on solutions. Dr. Cusano believes that this is a good example of the positive deviance principle, "acting their way into a better way of thinking, rather than to think their way into a better way of acting."[19]

- *Organizational Culture Change*. Interdisciplinary collaboration and the collective learning process helped to change the organizational culture at Waterbury Hospital. Developing solutions for improved medication recognition and reconciliation engaged staff in a whole new way of working together. Because of this experience, staff now approach other problems using positive deviance principles that encourage tapping the wisdom within the group. For example, one of the surgical chief residents is using a positive deviance approach to improve the practices for diagnosing and treating acute appendicitis. Another group of physicians, nurses, dieticians, pharmacists, and patient educators and advocates have begun using positive deviance to engage and improve the care of hospitalized patients who have diabetes mellitus.

- *Enlarging Networks by Enabling Self-Organizing*. The collaborative manner in which discharge medications were managed engaged stakeholders across the entire hospital. Relationships were enhanced and the positive energy from working together ignited self-organizing networks of new relationships seeking to improve practices in the hospital.

Dr. Cusano has demonstrated that physician leadership is essential for performance excellence in healthcare delivery systems.

### Linda Rusch, RN, MS, APN; Vice President, Patient Care Services, Hunterdon Medical Center

Linda Rusch has been vice president of patient care services for 14 years at Hunterdon Medical Center in Flemington, New Jersey. Hunterdon Medica Center is a 180-bed nonprofit community hospital providing acute and preventive care. Ms. Rusch describes the work environment as a place where people thrive and positive energy is focused on providing the best care to the patients they serve. The best care is measured by benchmarking such factors as falls, decubiti prevalence, central line infections, and patient satisfaction. At Hunterdon, patient satisfaction is in the 90th percentile and the nursing retention rate has been approximately 97.5 percent for 10 years.[20] At one point in 2005, there was actually a precedent-setting waiting list of nurses who wanted to work for this hospital. This is quite unusual considering the national nursing shortage. What makes Hunterdon different? Ms. Rusch attributes their success to her people, because she believes that "you are only as good as your people." It is also evident that leadership has played a significant role.

Leadership does not just reside in the vice president's office, but rather cascades throughout the patient services division. The organization chart looks like a reverse pyramid in that patients and families are at the top of the chart in the center surrounded by a circle of caregiver staff that include RNs, licensed practical nurses, patient care assistants, unit coordinators, and technicians. Staff members are empowered to be leaders of caregiving and their work is coordinated by a management council, education council, nurse practice council, and performance improvement/research council. A coordinating council synchronizes the work of the multiple councils. This shared governance approach has been one of the hallmarks of Hunterdon's success. Senior leadership is comprised of the vice president of patient care services who is assisted by a director of staff development and director of patient care services. This dynamic organization structure demonstrates the true meaning of transformational leadership as leaders are developed on all levels and engaged in a shared mission of providing quality care.

#### Complexity Science at Hunterdon

Ms. Rusch believes she leads with a complexity science lens. Complexity science bridges multiple disciplines such as biology and social sciences to address questions about living systems.[21] Contrary to Newtonian scientific principles that are grounded in stability and predictability, complexity science principles embrace the dynamism and unpredictability inherent in today's healthcare delivery systems. The traditional machine metaphor has limitations because the focus is on understanding each part of a system separately. This construct limits and influences our thinking about how organizations behave. Seeing the healthcare world through a complexity lens helps to clarify and explain organizational behavior. Ms. Rusch believes a complexity lens helps her to see Hunterdon as a whole organization comprised of interdependent relationships. Change in any part of the system affects other parts of the system. The synergy of interconnectedness of relationships is a key component to maximizing positive outcomes in patient services. Authenticity, communication, effective dialogue, and mutual respect are the guideposts of healthy relationships. It is through nurturing these relationships and observing, asking questions, and discovering new emerging patterns that Ms. Rusch makes sense of the complex world of patient service delivery. This is the work of a transformational leader in a new age.

The process for selecting new patient beds is a good example. A variety of bed vendors were identified. During a specific time frame, beds were brought to the hospital and placed in several patient rooms so that evaluation and assessment would be convenient during the selection process. Nurses and other staff who were directly involved with patient beds, such as housekeeping and maintenance, were engaged in evaluating and rating them. They collectively selected the best beds for Hunterdon. This high involvement process appreciated the great diversity of perspectives that, through a complexity lens, enables creative ideas to emerge. Bed selection in this context was built on a foundation of interdependent relationships and simple rules of openness, creativity, mutual respect, and what would work best for patients.

Another example of complexity-informed leadership is the hospital process that Hunterdon calls "transforming care at the bedside." All departments that nursing depends on to provide patient care are involved. Ms. Rusch believes that diversified teams minimize hierarchy because the focus is on shared purpose and achieving mutual outcomes. She posits that diversity fuels the energy for change. Leaders should enter the change process with no assumptions or preconceived ideas. They need to ask questions rather than have all of the answers. In this example, focusing on positives such as, "What is working well with regard to providing patient care at the bedside?" sets the discovery path for transformation in the right direction. Another important question was, "What would give minutes back to nurses so that they can be more vigilant about taking care of their patients?" Simple rules were followed such as, "Tell the truth no matter how hard it is," And, "Work with the patient in mind." These rules guided staff through this complex process. Keeping the rules simple enables the team to self-organize and, as the flow of the process unfolds, creative ideas emerge that lead to transformation.

Shared governance meetings are an important aspect of the process. But these are not the typical meetings we experience in healthcare settings that are often focused on getting through a standard agenda with little time for interaction. Meetings in patient services are opportunities for free-flowing ideas and creativity. At Hunterdon, the agendas include time to have conversations about house issues and lessons learned.[22] Ms. Rusch thinks it is important for leaders to provide unstructured open space in meeting agendas to allow spontaneous dialogue to emerge. When this dialogue is facilitated in a "no blame culture," the truth about problems and mistakes such as medical errors can be revealed without fear. Then, as a team, the staff can solve problems constructively. This open space is also a time for appreciative inquiry that enables staff to reflect on what is going well and what they are learning.

### Transformational Leadership with a Complexity Worldview

Linda Rusch is a transformational leader who has learned to view the world through a complexity science lens, seeing the hospital as a nonlinear complex adaptive system in which diverse agents such as clinical professionals and support staff interact with each other and possess the dynamic capability to spontaneously self-organize. There is evidence of how shared purpose and minimizing hierarchy enables self-organization to thrive and how this approach leads to powerful results. Ms. Rusch accepts that there are many factors inherent to healthcare delivery systems that are fundamentally unpredictable and uncontrollable. Acting on this premise helps her to be more creative as she takes risks and continuously learns from mistakes. Simple rules like those cited in the examples guide the journey on sometimes uncharted and rugged paths. Ms. Rusch develops her staff to become leaders of the vision and mission by involving them and encouraging their participation in continuous improvement processes targeted toward providing quality patient care. They travel the journey together, and she is not separate from the staff, but rather very much immersed in supporting them. By nurturing relationships, she builds a community of trust and mutual respect that enables her staff to work as a team. With this as a foundation, the work of Ms. Rusch has demonstrated that anything is possible.

## Steve McAlilly, President and CEO of Mississippi Methodist Senior Services, Inc., Tupelo, Mississippi

Steve McAlilly has been president and CEO of Mississippi Methodist Senior Services, Inc., for 13 years. This organization provides long-term care services to approximately 1,600 elders on 11 campuses in Mississippi. Mr. McAlilly pioneered the development of the first Green Houses on their Traceway Retirement Community campus in Tupelo. Green Houses are a radically different model of care for elders. The concept was created by Dr. William H. Thomas, MD, a geriatrician who is a thought leader for transforming long-term care. The individual houses are specifically built to provide an enjoyable living environment for 8 to 10 elders. There are private rooms with private baths. A central hearth with an adjacent open kitchen gives elders an opportunity to enjoy community meals and participate in cooking activities. Elders have access to all areas of the house. Pleasant surroundings make it appealing for residents to go outside within full view of the staff. This is a social model of care that is a paradigm shift from the nursing home as a medical institution.

It is not only the physical environment that is dramatically different from a traditional nursing home, but also the organizational structure that greatly influences leadership relationships with staff. Life in a Green House is focused on the needs of the residents, and all decisions are made by those who work closest to the elders. The hierarchical pyramid is transformed into a circle of direct care staff. This self-managed team provides person-centered care to elders living in the Green House. They are called shahbazim, a term Dr. William Thomas created based on the metaphor of the king's falcon that protects people, since direct-care workers protect, nurture, and sustain elders in Green Houses.[23] In essence, they are the leaders of caregiving. A guide supports the team by acting as a coach, providing guidance and monitoring quality of care and quality of life. The guide is a licensed nursing home administrator, but is not in the traditional role. The direct-care team works collaboratively with a clinical support interdisciplinary team that works under the direction of the medical director and director of nursing. Outcomes of their work are monitored by the guide. The higher level of staff involvement greatly influences leadership in Green Houses and shifts the primary decision making about care delivery and the overall well-being of residents to direct care workers. Leading is a shared responsibility in a circle of interrelationships among staff in the house.

### Servant Leadership

Steve McAlilly has learned to lead differently. Leading the development of Green Houses has been a transition for Mr. McAlilly, a lawyer by training. He started as a volunteer for Mississippi Methodist Senior Services. After reading *Servant Leadership*, which was given to him by his father, the need to lead as a servant became more apparent.[24] A servant leader puts service first and leads with that as the central purpose of their leadership. Mississippi Methodist Senior Services was a setting in which he could become a servant leader. When asked to describe his leadership style, he quickly stated, "I do not think leaders can put on a leadership style. It is about who I am as a person."[25] Leading involves doing something that is worthwhile and makes a difference.

### Leading a Paradigm Shift

Mr. McAlilly was asked what it takes to be a leader of the Green House Project and to lead a paradigm shift in long-term care. He indicated that to lead transformational change, leaders have to be able to articulate a vision in a way that captures the essence of where the organization is going. The vision has to be big enough to inspire people to become change agents and to motivate them to want to do everything they can do to achieve it. In the case of Green Houses, the organizational culture is not just being changed, it is being replaced. Everyone had to change their mindset about how care gets delivered and how the relationships among staff work. The old way of thinking that views top leaders as the key decision makers had to be replaced with the new culture in which the direct caregivers are the decision makers because they are the closest to the resident. This significantly changes the role of top leaders.

One of the biggest lessons McAlilly had to learn was to give up power and control. This means continuously balancing shared authority and power with people closest to the residents, yet knowing when to intervene. He had to learn to trust that the staff would do what is right. Building that trust means getting close to staff so that he could develop relationships and learn their capabilities.

McAlilly believes leading is all about relationships with people who share a common goal. As staff were being trained to work in the Green Houses, McAlilly became more deeply engaged with the direct care staff and learned everything he could about their jobs. He put his jeans on and became one of them, participating in the training focused on developing direct care staff to become leaders of caregiving and interdisciplinary team members.

This approach is a departure from the typical healthcare top executive who is removed from the direct care staff and works through the chain of command to learn about issues that impact their effectiveness. McAlilly had to change his CEO mental model of a leader with all the answers to a leader who facilitates inquiry, coaches, and mentors. He believes that each person has an innate desire to do their best and wants to help people grow. However, these beliefs are grounded in a pragmatic understanding that there are some people who are not going to get on the bus. Leaders have to be willing to either let these detractors select themselves out of the new culture or to manage their performance sooner than later to help them move on.

### Insights on Leadership

Leading transformational change required McAlilly to be introspective and reflect more deeply on how to be an effective leader. Letting go of long-held beliefs about the role of top leaders and how they interact with staff was not easy. But his openness to becoming more self-aware and willingness to learn enabled him to grow. He shared several important insights about leadership that helped him.

- Paradigms and mental filters have a great impact on how leaders view themselves and how they lead. The implication is that leaders need to become aware of their thinking and assumptions.
- A positive outlook influences a leader's ability to lead effectively.
- Acknowledge that you do not have all of the answers. A leader cannot become so focused on the needs of their own egos and take themselves too seriously. McAlilly began the Green House Project believing that he had all of the answers. As the change process evolved and he put more faith in his staff, he realized that with support, the staff closest to the elders had important insights. He learned that leaders have to let go of control and accept ideas from staff that may be different from the leaders' own. Differences of opinion and mistakes are learning opportunities.
- Leaders learn to ask the right questions. For example, a key question healthcare leaders need to ask is, "What is wrong with this system that no matter how many regulations we put in place, residents and staff are still not satisfied and results are the same?" By asking questions such as these, leaders can get to the root causes of the problems that impede transformational change in healthcare.

- Accept the uncertainty and ambiguity in transformational change. Embrace ambiguity. McAlilly said, "I don't know what is going to happen on the journey, but I know we have the capacity to get where we are going. I believe the people can do it."[26] It is this trust that enables him to lead his organization and develop staff to become leaders of the change process.
- McAlilly learned that "you cannot lead by remote control." Leaders need to be available so that they can listen, learn, and help staff solve problems and concerns. He believes that leading requires building relationships with those who are transforming the culture, particularly the direct care staff.

Steve McAlilly is an example of a transformational servant leader because service drives his leadership and he engages followers by developing them to become leaders of making the vision a reality. His strong beliefs and values about the quality of life that elders deserve have enabled him to lead the Green House Project. At the end of the interview, McAlilly stated that he is leading because it is the right thing to do.

### David A. Green, Retired President and CEO, Evergreen Retirement Community

David A. Green retired in 2005 as president and CEO of Evergreen Retirement Community in Oshkosh, Wisconsin, after 29 years of service. As a pioneering leader in the field of long-term care, Mr. Green left a legacy that has been sustained. Evergreen is a continuing care retirement community that provides quality living environments for elders ranging from independent homes and assisted living apartments to skilled nursing care. While the development of Evergreen as a nationally recognized community for elders is interesting, the real story is the transformational leadership that facilitated the innovative design of their skilled nursing facilities, Creekview North and Creekview South. Mr. Green exemplifies the quote from Winston Churchill, "We shape our buildings; thereafter they shape us."[27] The Creekview story illustrates how a visionary leader grounded in values of service and relevant knowledge in architectural engineering and long-term care administration radically changed an organization with the help of an expansive circle of involved stakeholders.

*The Creekview Story*

During a presentation at Evergreen Retirement Community in August 2006, David Green gave an overview of the Creekview story.[28] After the presentation he was interviewed to gain further insights about Creekview.

In 1983, Green started thinking about how nursing homes needed to be more person and relationship centered. He had struggled for years with the traditional model of nursing homes that are designed to be extensions of hospitals. But it was not until 1987 that his ideas became more concrete and he envisioned a neighborhood of households rather than a long corridor of isolated residents in rooms. He believed that the skilled nursing facility at Evergreen should be redesigned to become household/neighborhoods in which elders live in the community, and their well-being—physical, emotional, spiritual, and social—would be the central focus. Mr. Green took bold steps to make this vision a reality and did not let financial and regulatory constraints stop him from articulating his picture of the future to those who needed to embrace it. A positive mind-set enabled him to see potential barriers to change as opportunities that could lead to the ideal home for frail elders.

He recognized that if his vision was to become reality, it would require leadership beyond him. Also, he knew that he did not have all the answers but had many questions that others needed to consider. In collaboration with his staff and the board of directors, Green created the Evergreen Health Center Planning Committee to include board members, residents, and staff at every level. They were tasked with the job of further developing a vision of the perfect nursing home. Mr. Green believed it was critical to engage the people who would be directly responsible for implementing the change and that they would need to become leaders. The committee worked hard to widen the circle of involvement to include as many people as possible in the process, including state officials. Green and the committee recognized that state regulators had to become partners in change rather than adversaries. Teamwork and collaboration were essential for success.

The result of these efforts was a household/neighborhood design concept that envisioned elders living in a community with more opportunity for meaningful relationships and activities, as well as more control over their lives. This groundbreaking idea was affirmed by the passing of the Nursing Home Reform Act of 1987, which was part of the Omnibus Budget Reconciliation Act passed that same year (OBRA 87). The legislation established that resident outcomes should be the basis for evaluating nursing homes. Evergreen provided an excellent model for how nursing homes could not only be reformed, but transformed to be resident and relationship centered.

### Prototypes for Change

Mr. Green recognized that this transformational change would be costly in terms of time and money. He decided that it would be wise to conduct a pilot study of this innovative design before investing the resources needed to build a new nursing home. In 1992, an eight-resident section of the existing skilled nursing facility was remodeled as a household with resident rooms opening directly onto a living/dining/kitchen area for those residents. An interdisciplinary team of direct care staff was formed to provide care and to create a positive living environment for the residents. A 30-hour Continuous Quality Improvement training program equipped the staff to function effectively as a self-directed team for the one-year project. Mr. Green believed that it was important to measure resident, family, and staff outcomes so that what they learned from the pilot could be used to plan a new 36-resident household/neighborhood. Data were collected and used to evaluate the quality of life, quality of care, and satisfaction. The results confirmed that the household/neighborhood model improved resident quality of life and satisfaction, as well as family satisfaction and staff fulfillment. The most important indicator of success was the uniform response of the residents, families, and staff involved that all nursing home residents should have the opportunity to live in this kind of environment.

This evidence convinced the Evergreen Board of Directors to approve building the 36-resident household/neighborhood. An estimated $3 million was needed for the project. The combination of a collaborative relationship with the state of Wisconsin, a $1 million capital campaign, and long-term financing enabled the project to be built. In June 1997, 36 residents moved into a household/neighborhood named Creekview because of its proximity to Sawyer Creek. The look and feel of Creekview was positive, with lively neighborhoods comprised of homelike households. The nine residents of each household share a kitchen/dining/living area that looks onto a sunny, protected backyard. A neighborhood center connects the four households, providing space for gathering. The skilled nursing facility was transformed into a warm home where elders can live a quality life while receiving the medical care they need.

Transformational leadership also requires good management. Mr. Green again recognized the need to measure results and document evidence that Creekview improved quality of life, functional health status, family satisfaction, and staff satisfaction. He engaged an external consultant to conduct a year-long evaluation study of the 36 Creekview residents and 56 residents in Evergreen's traditional skilled nursing units. A comparative analysis indicated significant positive changes in each of the areas measured for Creekview residents as compared with individuals in the traditional units.[29]

At the end of one year, the residents of the neighborhood consistently rated higher or better on cognitive, emotional, and behavioral indices, although they were lower on physical functioning. Additionally, these results were highly consistent across all the different instruments, suggesting high validity. This research supported the positive impact of the neighborhood design on the lives and care of a typical nursing home population.

*Building on Success*

The success of Creekview led to the construction of Creekview South and Creekview Center in July 2004. Mr. Green solicited suggestions for improvements from staff who had experience with what is now Creekview North to plan the new facility. Some improvements included more kitchen counter and dining floor space, redesigned work areas for medication administration and documentation, and a more spacious bathing facility. The neighborhood center added features such as a large aviary; a game area; an information area with a computer terminal, books, and reference materials; a music area with a piano; a children's play area; and cozy seating areas around a large stone fireplace. Creekview Center, which connects the north and south buildings, includes a café, aquatic center, fitness center, and aerobics studio which are available to all residents, their families, employees, and community elders. The Creekview model for skilled nursing care is truly a success story, not only because the vision became a reality, but because it has been enhanced and sustained over time.

### Leaving a Legacy—Sustaining Transformational Change

A visit to Creekview in the Summer of 2006 confirmed that David Green left a legacy at Evergreen. One of the biggest challenges with transformational leadership and change is sustaining it. So often when transformational leaders leave an organization, their vision goes with them. But this is not the story at Evergreen. Mr. Green had a keen understanding of the critical role of governance in sustaining transformational change. He believes the CEO is not the future of the organization. The board of directors is the future because the board is "the steward of the organization's moral owners," according to Mr. Green.[30]

The Policy Governance Model™ developed by John Carver greatly influenced his leadership and relationship with the Evergreen Board of Directors.[31] This model of governance recognizes that organization sustainability depends upon the board being the chief guardian of the organization's values. The Evergreen values were embedded into the culture of the organization by leaders at all levels as they worked to design and implement the household/neighborhood model. When values are constant and are the platform on which change is built, transformational change has a better chance of being sustained.

The dedication of Mr. Green to developing several potential successors for his CEO position from the executive team helped to ensure leadership continuity. Succession planning by staff in combination with appropriate governance enabled Evergreen's operational and governance leaders to engage in a thoughtful process which prepared the organization for Green's retirement. The board's selection of an internal candidate with a positive leadership track record in the organization helped to ensure that his legacy lives on. And, because of Mr. Green's development of the leadership team, the internal candidates who were not selected continue as members of the team.

David Green has demonstrated that leaders can challenge conventional systems and shift the traditional healthcare delivery paradigm. He had a bold vision grounded in values of service and competence, and discovered how to achieve collaboration and teamwork among those who would make the vision a sustainable reality.

## LEADERS SHARE COMMON APPROACHES

The leadership examples give us insights into what leaders of complex healthcare delivery systems need to be and do to transform these organizations. It is clear that the featured leaders are not mechanistic thinkers who use regulations as a means to maintain the status quo. Rather, these leaders are change agents who are guided by a deep commitment to service. They understand that their organizations are complex, dynamic systems that need to adapt to an unstable and unpredictable environment. The challenges of delivering healthcare in this environment have not obstructed their bold vision for better quality care and quality of life for all of those served by their organizations. Therefore, the vision and mission of their respective delivery systems are patient/resident and relationship-centered. Passion for achieving that vision provided them with the motivation and resilience needed to lead in tough and turbulent times. They share a positive mindset characterized by a belief that people deserve excellent service and most people who work in care delivery systems want to do their best work. These leaders really care about people. They are authentic leaders who are guided by their beliefs and values. Grounded in a clear sense of purpose, they do not succumb to the whims of the next new fad or model but lead to improve quality patient care for their communities. This focus helps to ensure that the transformational changes they put into practice are sustainable.

The leaders in these examples, while different, share some important leadership approaches. The term *approach* is used rather than *style* because these leaders are being themselves. They did not adopt a textbook leadership style that did not fit their core values, but rather are leading authentically with self-knowledge that enables them to lead with integrity. In fact, a couple of the leaders specifically stated, and the others implicitly indicated, that leadership is not just a list of characteristics and behaviors or a style they put on. Leadership is very much about leaders knowing themselves, being themselves, and not trying to be like somebody else. This does not mean that they did not learn from other leaders, just as readers of their stories will learn from them, but they took the lessons learned from leadership role models and made them their own based on who they are as a people and what makes sense in their situations. Here is what the leaders in the examples share in common:

- *An ability to see the organization as an interdependent whole*

The organizational lens through which the leaders see their delivery systems greatly influences how they lead and build relationships with stakeholders. They do not see a machine image that focuses on individual departments and disciplines, but rather they see an image of a dynamic living system in which interrelationships and interdependence hold the keys to transformation. The vision encompasses the whole system. The silos of the mechanistic organization are transformed into an interconnected network of relationships focused on achieving shared goals.

- *The knowledge that leadership exists within the entire organization*

The leaders believe that central to the success of attaining their vision and living the mission, leaders are developed beyond the executive realm. They have expanded the span of power and influence, particularly to those who directly care for patients. This meant changing the traditional hierarchical pyramid to a circle of inclusion.

Sharing power and control as a CEO means letting go of mindsets and conventional training that suggest administrators of hospitals and nursing homes must tightly control operations, policies, and procedures to comply with regulatory demands. The leaders in the examples see it differently. They recognize that their organizations must be resilient and adapt quickly to a changing environment. To do this, authority and decision making need to be with the people who have the most knowledge and wisdom to do what needs to be done. With a clear mission, vision, shared values, and articulated expectations as the simple guides in a complex system, staff possess the ability to self-organize. Ideas for how to continuously improve will emerge. The leaders know how to balance being close to employees with enough distance to lead effectively.

- *The value of inclusion and involvement*

In each example, it is evident that the leaders believe in the value of inclusion and involvement of staff, physicians, board, and community in transformational change. Key stakeholders were active participants in shaping the vision, and their ideas were used to develop new approaches to delivering quality care. Because these leaders widened involvement and participation, there was less resistance to change, and the natural resistance that did occur was embraced as a source of information for identifying obstacles to the intended changes. These leaders demonstrate that there is more ownership and commitment to change when people who will be affected by the change are involved.

- *The development and facilitation of interdepartmental teamwork and collaboration*

When leaders see their organizations as an interconnected network of interdependent relationships, it is easier for them to facilitate and guide the interdepartmental teamwork and collaboration required for the changes that they need to implement. These leaders not only know how to build teams, but also how to facilitate them. They model teamwork and collaboration by removing the barriers to interdepartmental, multidisciplinary, and interorganizational team development. The leaders featured in this chapter transcended organizational boundaries and made sure they engaged all the people who needed to work together to achieve patient/resident-centered goals.

- *Commitment to effective communication*

Communication is more than sharing information and the expectations for change. The leaders spent a lot of time asking questions and listening. These individuals recognize that they do not have all of the answers. This is counterintuitive to the manner in which many top leaders are trained and socialized to believe that they should know everything. Accepting that they do not know everything is at once humbling and empowering because it frees leaders from an impossible task and enables them to open up to others who are more likely to possess knowledge critical for success, as the leaders in the examples demonstrated. They did this by coming out of their executive offices and engaging in conversations with employees on all levels. Other key stakeholders such as patients, residents, families, and the community were given many opportunities to share their perspectives about targeted changes. The leaders' communication mirrors the image of organizations as a network of interdependent relationships.

- *Understanding the importance of measuring results*

Achieving results begins with a clear shared understanding and commitment to specifically defined outcomes and measures of success. Measurement provides the documented evidence required to determine whether targeted outcomes are being achieved. It is important to note that these leaders did not measure for the sake of measuring or become so consumed with evidence-based data that they missed the point of why they were measuring in the first place. The leaders used the data to learn what needed to be improved, sustained, and replicated. They saw that measurement is a source of learning.

- *Appreciation of continuous learning*

Learning is important to these leaders and has played an integral role in their ability to lead transformational change efforts. Their openness to engage in conversations to learn different perspectives about change and what is going on in the organization demonstrates learning in action. Learning informed their thinking about how to adapt their leadership approaches so they could effectively lead and manage change. Mistakes were a catalyst for deeper learning and inquiry. These leaders also embedded learning into their organizations by providing education and training to help staff learn new ways of approaching organizational challenges and to develop the skills required for change management. Continuous learning was ingrained in their organizational cultures.

## CONCLUSION

The seven leadership approaches that the leaders shared, along with a positive mindset, bold vision, clear values, and enduring purpose grounded in a spirit of humble service helped these leaders to lead and manage significant transformational change in their organizations.

## LOOKING FORWARD

We have learned from the six leaders that authentic transformational change in complex healthcare delivery systems is possible. The business of healthcare is really the business of people and relationships interconnected in a mutual quest for quality care delivery that is affordable and accessible. A bright future requires transformational leaders who are dedicated to people and service. They must be willing to embrace new worldviews that will enable them to genuinely change the traditional paradigm and develop innovative approaches to healthcare delivery. Hope for a better future depends on leadership.

## NOTES

1.  Zimmerman, B., C. Lindberg, and P. Plsek. 1998. *Edgeware: Insights from Complexity Science for Health Care Leaders*. Irving, TX: VHA Inc., 4–5; Wheatley, M. J. 1992. *Leadership and the New Science: Learning about Organization from an Orderly Universe*. San Francisco: Berrett-Koehler Publishers, 25–45.

2.  Morgan, G. 2006. *Images of Organization*. Newbury Park, CA: Sage Publications, 11–26.

3.  Burrell, G., and G. Morgan. 1979. *Sociological Paradigms and Organisational Analysis: Elements of the Sociology of Corporate Life*. Portsmouth, NH: Heinemann Educational Books, Inc., 11–20.

4.  Burrell and Morgan, *Sociological Paradigms and Organisational Analysis*.

5.  Barker, A. M. 2006. "Complexity Science and Change: A Path to the Future." In *Leadership Competencies for Clinical Managers: The Renaissance of Transformational Leadership*, ed. A. M. Barker, D. Taylor Sullivan, and M. J. Emery, 57–75. Sudbury, MA: Jones and Bartlett Publishers.

6.  Zimmerman, Lindberg, and Plsek, *Edgeware*.

7.  Anderson, D., and L. Ackerman Anderson. 2001. *Beyond Change Management: Advanced Strategies for Today's Transformational Leaders*. San Francisco: Jossey-Bass/Pfeiffer, 77–84.

8.  Robert Wood Johnson Hospital Hamilton. n.d. *Robert Wood Johnson Hospital Hamilton*. Available at: http://www.rwjhamilton.org. Accessed August 22, 2006.

9.  Christy Stephenson interview with the author. July–December 2006, via telephone from the author's office in Columbia, MD.

10.  Baldrige National Quality Program. 2006. *Health Care Criteria for Performance Excellence*. Gaithersburg, MD: National Institute of Standards and Technology, United States Department of Commerce.

11.  Tobin, J. H. 2003. "The Practical Side of Complexity: Implications for Leaders." PhD thesis, University of Hertfordshire.

12.  Bass, B. M., and R. E. Riggio. 2006. *Transformational Leadership*. 2nd ed. Mahwah, NJ: Lawrence Erlbaum Associates, 3–4.

13.  Stacey, R. D. 2001. *Complex Responsive Processes in Organisations*. London: Routledge, 5–7.

14.  Tobin, J. H., and J. H. Taylor. 2004. *Complexity as a Management Tool*. Available at: http://www.hhnmag.com/hhnmag_app/jsp/articledisplay.jsp?dcrpath=HHNMAG/PubsNewsArticle/data/040831HHN_Online_Tobin&domain=HHNMAG. Accessed August 24, 2006.

15.  John H. Tobin, interview with the author, July–December 2006, via telephone from the author's office in Columbia, MD.

16.  Pascale, R. T., and J. Sternin. 2005. "Your Company's Secret Change Agents," *Harvard Business Review* 83 (5): 72–81.

17.  Positive Deviance Institute. n.d. *Positive Deviance Makes Its Debut in Healthcare at Waterbury Hospital in Connecticut*. Available at: http://www.positivedeviance.org/projects/waterbury/waterbury_narrative_final.pdf. Accessed August 25, 2006.

18.  Marquadt, M. J. 2004. *Optimizing the Power of Action Learning: Solving Problems and Building Leaders in Real Time*. Palo Alto, CA: Davies-Black Publishing.

19.  Positive Deviance Institute, *Positive Deviance Makes Its Debut in Healthcare*.

20.  Rusch, L. 2006. "Complexity Science in Action." In *Leadership Competencies for Clinical Managers: The Renaissance of Transformational Leadership*, ed. A. M. Barker,

D. Taylor Sullivan, and M. J. Emery, 297–310. Sudbury, MA: Jones and Bartlett Publishers.

21. Zimmerman, Lindberg, and Plsek, *Edgeware*.

22. Rusch, "Complexity Science in Action."

23. Dixon, D. L. 2004. "Changing the Landscape of LTC." *Caring for the Ages* 5 (11): 61–65.

24. Greenleaf, R. K. 1977. *Servant Leadership*. Mahwah, NJ: Paulist Press.

25. Steve McAlilly, interview with the author, July–December 2006, via telephone from the author's office in Columbia, MD.

26. Ibid.

27. Churchill, W. 1960. *Simpson's Contemporary Quotations*. Available at: http://www.bartleby.com/63/83/5583/html. Accessed September 23, 2006.

28. Green, D. A. 2006. "The Creekview Story." Presentation at the Evergreen Retirement Community, Oshkosh, Wisconsin; Green, David A. *The Story of Creekview, Evergreen Retirement Community* brochure, Oshkosh, Wisconsin.

29. Calkins, M. P. 1999. *Creekview: Its History and Evaluation, Final Report*. Cleveland, OH: Innovative Designs in Environments for an Aging Society.

30. David A. Green, interview with the author, July–December 2006, via telephone from the author's office in Columbia, MD.

31. Carver, J. 1997. *Boards That Make a Difference: A New Design for Leadership in Nonprofit and Public Organizations*. San Francisco: Jossey-Bass.

# CHAPTER 2

# Mending the Gap between Physicians and Hospital Executives

## J. Deane Waldman and Kenneth H. Cohn

This chapter explores the relationship between two components of our healthcare system: physicians, representing all providers of direct care, and hospital executives, referring to those with administrative responsibilities, regulatory obligations, and resource control. Currently, there is a wide gulf, or gap, representing an adversarial interaction. Over the past 50 years, there have been dramatic, frankly, revolutionary, changes in the practice of medicine without corresponding or matching adjustments in the healthcare system. As a result, both physicians and healthcare executives are frustrated. The present adversarial tone between healthcare executives and physicians adversely impacts healthcare outcomes.

We discuss data showing differences between physicians and healthcare executives in education, background, work experience, and culture. However, the two share common core values: altruism, service, and love of a challenge. They also have common concerns about the future.

We conclude that the real enemy is not the so-called other—physicians or healthcare executives—but our dysfunctional healthcare system. The common values and concerns shared by physicians and healthcare executives could provide the framework for successful communication leading to a bridge across the gap and a collaborative rather than confrontational relationship. Physicians could teach healthcare executives about clinical priorities, useful new technologies, and scientific methodology, including evidence-based decision making. Healthcare executives could educate physicians about management tools and techniques for planning, implementation, and assessment, especially systems thinking. Together as partners, healthcare executives and physicians could address many of the currently insoluble problems in healthcare.

## INTRODUCTION

If you have not used the tube (subway) transit system in London, you have missed a pleasurable experience. In a place where streets are narrow and wind around buildings, where street names change without notice and are routinely mispronounced by tourists, it would be easy to get lost. The tube helps you get where you need to go. There are, however, places where the subway rails are not flat but cantilevered, forcing the train to be tilted away from the platform edge, creating a dangerous gap into which passengers can fall to injury. At each of these places, when the train comes into the station, a stentorian mechanical voice with a British accent warns: "Mind the gap!" In the following discussion of hospital-physician relations, we have stolen and modified the tube-stop clarion call, writing that we need to *mend* the gap.

During the discussion that follows, we use the words hospital, management, and MGT (management) interchangeably to indicate those within a hospital or healthcare system who have administrative functions and resource responsibility. This includes managers, support staff, billing individuals, all the way up to the chief executive officer (CEO) and the board. We intersperse the terms physician, medicine, and provider to represent all who directly provide care, such as doctors, nurses, therapists of all kinds, social workers, and technologists.

---

### Case Report: Local Newspaper Reports 10-Hour Waits in Emergency Room

The following is a dramatization of an actual meeting in a hospital after the major local newspaper printed a front-page story about how long people waited in the emergency room (ER).

| | |
|---|---|
| Director of public relations: | "You all saw last week headlines. The board is very distressed over the story showing that patients often wait in our ER for 8 to 11 hours. I have called this meeting to see what we can do." |
| Medical director of ER: | "We have real problems. Yes, people do wait a long time in my ER. We need more resources: nurses, bed spaces, and equipment." |
| Vice president of operations: | "We have no additional money. The ER is a money-losing facility. How long can it take to see if the patient is bleeding and sew him up or determine what the child's rash is?" |
| Director of inpatient services: | "We do not have beds to accept patients from the ER, and we frequently are sitting around waiting for the cath lab." |
| Chief of nursing: | "I cannot recruit enough nurses to fill the vacant positions we have in the ICU or the cath lab." |

| | |
|---|---|
| Chief of cardiology: | "It is malpractice to have a patient with an evolving heart attack waiting around in the ER. This cannot go on!" |
| Director of fiscal services: | "Too many ER patients have no insurance or are undocumented or refuse to fill out papers. No one has preauthorization. We just do not get paid for what we do." |
| Chairman of surgery: | "Patients lie in the ICU [intensive care unit] or the wards waiting for surgical times to get into the operating room. We need more rooms and surgeons, or the waiting list just gets longer." |
| Director of Emergency Transport Services: | "Our hospital is the Level I trauma center for the area. I *have* to bring the patients here, and, oh, we lose money on every uninsured patient. We are mandated to transport them but do not get paid." |
| Chairman of Pediatrics: | "During epidemic seasons, we have to house dehydrated or asthmatic children in the ER because there is no other place to put them." |
| Medical Director of the ER: | "We have to do something!" |
| Director of Public Relations: | "We have to do something!" |

Each person was speaking the truth from his or her perspective. No one understood the others' issues. No one was talking *to* anyone else. No one was diagnosing causes of ER flow problems, and no one was suggesting any workable solutions.

## PHYSICIAN-HEALTHCARE EXECUTIVE EXCHANGES

Below are some additional examples of communications between physicians, called white coats, and healthcare executives, nicknamed blue suits. As above, they are actual, recent in-hospital verbal exchanges. Even the jocular names—*white coats* and *blue suits*—suggest opposing teams rather than teammates, much less colleagues, and certainly not brothers.

- Doctor (to receptionist): "Please fax this information immediately to Dr. X."
- Hospital receptionist: "I can't. My name is not on the medical release form."

- Provider (doctor): "How can I talk to my patient when there are no translators?"
- Manager (director of translation services): "Do these doctors think I can print money?"

- Provider (doctor): "I should talk to the patient about the complication."
- Manager (risk management director): "You can't. They might sue, and besides, all discussions at morbidity and mortality conferences are confidential."

- Provider (surgeon): "Where is the family of the patient I just operated on?"
- Hospital (receptionist): "Somewhere in the hallways. There are 22 waiting room chairs for a 72-bed ICU."

- Doctor (surgeon in operating room): "I need a 24-mm Carpentier-Edwards heart valve."
- Hospital (operating room [OR] manager): "We only have 20 and 25 Shiley valves. Those were the only ones I was allowed to order."

- Provider (doctor): "Why must this patient wait four days for the surgery she needs?"
- Manager (OR supervisor): "Because we only have three ORs and they are all booked solid."

- Doctor (department chairman): "We need to recruit Dr. Z as soon as possible."
- Hospital (human resources [HR] director): "It will take 6 to 18 months, approximately seven different forms, at least four committee meetings, compliance with EEOC [Equal Employment Opportunity Commission] regulations, and I have no idea how much it will cost. Oops. She has an H-1 visa. Sorry, we cannot hire her."

- Provider (social worker): "I saw in this morning's paper that our CEO got a 4 percent performance bonus. His 'performance' success means we have fewer translators."
- Hospital (CEO): "I saved the hospital $4 million last year and am underpaid by national standards."

- Provider (respiratory therapist): "Why aren't we using the ventilators with the new servo control?"
- Hospital (unit manager): "If I stay within budget, I get my annual bonus."

- Provider (nurse): "I have had it here. I am moving to Hospital X uptown."
- Hospital (HR manager): "I cannot understand why she left. We gave her a signing bonus."

- Both, separately: *"But we meant well!!"*
- In unison: "You won't believe what *they* just did!?!"

Whether the subject at hand is an individual patient, facilities within the hospital, relations with outside agencies, or outcomes—medical or financial, the providers and managers seem to be shouting at each other rather than having collegial discourse. Relations are either silo type, with one side functioning independently of the other, or frank adversaries, where each side sees the other as the source of its problems.

## ADVERSARIES

Most physicians and nurses simply want to do their work free of hassle, providing high-quality, patient-sensitive care.[1] They see themselves as doing what society *wants*, and therefore expect society to make it easy, rather than difficult-to-impossible. Unfortunately, most experience the opposite: hindrances and hassles due to the plethora of diverse expectations and restrictions placed by organizations, managerial personnel, regulatory agencies, and patients.[2] Not surprisingly, clinicians tend to direct their anger and frustration on immediately available, easily identifiable individuals, such as their own managers, rather than some faceless insurance entity, an unknown regulator, a distant legislator, or global economic pressures.

Healthcare executives are responsible for creating conditions that enable and promote quality care while overseeing limited resources. Ultimately, their administrative decisions impact medical care delivery. However, the complexity of modern medicine presents serious challenges to anyone in hospital management who seeks to create a milieu free from error, strife, dissatisfaction, and constant turnover.[3–5] As the presumed top of the power pyramid, the hospital CEO has come to symbolize the enemy in the minds of many physicians looking for a convenient scapegoat.[6]

A pejorative view by physicians of those in hospital management does little to resolve problems or improve health care outcomes.[7] Such attitudes only exacerbate an already contentious care delivery setting.[8] Moreover, this tendency to stereotype CEOs is inconsistent with evidence-based practice. In many respects, physicians probably know less about the CEOs who lead their hospitals than they do about the neighbor next door.

### Change in Function without Change in System

Consider a hospital in 1950—what was possible, the standards of medical care, roles, and relationships. All these were in the future: heart surgery; drugs affecting specific organs like Viagra, Cardizem, Lipitor, and Zoloft; nonsurgical repairs; CAT (computerized axial tomography) scans; echo studies; computers; and the Internet.

The 1950s hospital was filled with patients convalescing from pneumonia, diarrhea, ear infections, appendectomy, and childbirth (the standard was five days in the hospital postpartum). Almost all modern specialties did not exist, such as cardiology, neonatology, even the ICU. Medicine was incapable of caring for patients with renal failure or premature babies, and therefore such patients were not hospitalized. Older people with heart failure died at home in bed.

The 1950s hospital consisted of a cadre of nurses, some supply personnel, no lawyers on staff, and a very small group of professional managers. Most doctors were in private practice, and many hospitalized patients had their own private duty nurses. Physicians made rounds in the early morning on their hospitalized patients, possibly taught some students, and then went to their private offices. The doctor and the hospital sent separate bills to the patient, invariably a few lines on a single sheet of paper. People paid their own medical bills in cash.

Most patients in modern hospitals are gravely, not mildly, ill, requiring complex technologies and highly trained, specialized teams. Over 80 percent of all the medical care available in your hospital did not exist in 1950. High-acuity patients are extremely resource intensive in terms of equipment, supplies, expertise, personnel, and liability. The 2006 hospital is typically staffed with full-time physicians and hospital-employed nurses. Private duty nurses are not allowed in hospitals, and many office-based physicians delegate in-patient care to the full-time staff. Interestingly, 55 percent of all the people who work in a hospital never see or physically touch a patient![3] The CEO is responsible for an annual budget ranging from $25 million in a small rural hospital to over $1 billion for major metropolitan institutions. The vast majority of all medical bills are paid by third parties rather than out of a patient's wallet.[9]

In 1950, production efficiency was the key to success in any business. The hospital was, after all, a business owned by a political entity, usually the county or the federal government. Reimbursement was "cost plus," meaning a cost was determined, invariably by allocation and calculation, not direct measurement, and a profit margin or predetermined "plus" was added. The more one did, the more one got. Success, for both hospital and doctor, was effectively having all hospital beds filled all the time. In 2006, most reimbursements are fixed price, based on a diagnosis and contractual arrangements. A detailed bill listing what was done and what was used has become almost irrelevant. Success is achieved by having the right types of patients—both diagnosis and insurer—and getting them in and out the hospital as quickly as possible. Since the pot of healthcare dollars is predetermined and fixed, the less you take out, the more that is left over to be profit. Therefore, providing the least care gives the most money.

The entire healthcare paradigm has been radically altered, from the care possible to the finances, from the definition of success to medical impacts on society. Have the roles of managers and doctors radically changed over the past half century? Of course they have. Have the relationships between managers and doctors adapted correspondingly to the changes in their roles and responsibilities? They have not, and the absence of this adjustment is, in large measure, the genesis of the so-called gap.

### The Adversarial Relationship Is Inevitable

Some see the conflict between providers and managers as inevitable, citing the inherent nature of the two sides, somewhat like the Sharks and the Jets in

*West Side Story.* The *West Side Story* analogy has some real merit in our healthcare system with its unsustainable supply/demand ratio: fixed supply of funds, but uncontrolled and apparently limitless demand for services. How would 10 rats or people behave if you only gave them enough food to feed 7?

## Doctors and Healthcare Executives Are Both Frustrated

Both providers and managers feel squeezed and frustrated. For physicians, job satisfaction has decreased because of increased workload, decreased reimbursement, and feelings of powerlessness as well as disenfranchisement.[10] The providers believe that managers belittle, even sometimes distort, what is to them a sacred trust between provider and patient. The physician's role as captain of the team has diminished, and providers, in general, are confused by a system that wants them to do social *good works* but then puts stumbling blocks in their way. They are experiencing "vu jàdé,"[11] where the world itself makes no sense.

Managers are frustrated as well. They were socialized in a collaborative, bottom-line management environment where machines, money, and people (like nurses and doctors) are simply means to an end, generally treated as undifferentiated commodities. They do not understand the doctors' failure to recognize, much less understand, and accept resource constraints. Just as managers are frustrated by their internal environment (and those doctors), so too are they frustrated by the obligations and restrictions placed by the outside world, particularly governmental agencies and insurers. They are required to offer services without adequate resources and follow confusing, often contradictory, rules. Managers, like doctors, feel they are in a no-win position.

An unintended, important, and subtle change in the physician-management relationship has resulted from the intrusion of regulatory and accreditation bodies into the management and delivery of healthcare. Healthcare executives have been forced to become agents of the government, as they are responsible for compliance and for providing mandated services. If their institutions fall out of compliance or fail a Joint Commission on Accreditation of Healthcare Organizations (JCAHO) audit, the hospital loses accreditation and becomes unable to bill Medicare for services. As an agent of government regulations, the healthcare executive comes, by necessity, into conflict with the physicians.

In addition to the dynamic tensions and adversarial interactions that might naturally occur between management and medicine, each has personal and professional frustration that they must vent. Both tend to focus on the nearest convenient target—those egotistical white coats or those bean-counting blue suits. (Amongst doctors, the single word *suits* is used derisively to refer to managers.)

## How They Communicate

Providers of healthcare services are trained rigorously in the knowledge base, judgment, and technical skills necessary to be providers. In the past, physicians did not receive training in communication or in cross-cultural relationships that could improve communication capabilities between medical people and management people. The only *process* that the providers see is their interaction with the patient, rather than a broader process of healthcare. If providers could master process skills, such as communication, team building, and conflict resolution, they could enlist, rather than fight with, their own managers.

Successful communication could improve care processes, change the work environment, and possibly regain the doctors' (lost) leadership role in patient care.[10] Unfortunately, each side tends to see a we-they, adversarial relationship, and they communicate on that basis.

## REVIEW OF LITERATURE

### Prior Data

While much has been written about medicine-management relations, there is surprisingly little hard data. The lack of such evidence allows people to make definitive and unqualified statements about relations between physicians and hospital executives. Nonetheless, useful insights can be gained from perusal of previous writings.

Most agree that a fundamental disparity exists in the minds of many clinicians about how healthcare managers view the world of medicine and its practitioners.[12-16] Physicians intimately know and relate to the passages doctors endure on their way to becoming licensed practitioners. They intuitively understand, respect, and trust other physicians, even those in management positions, because of sharing a common professional background. Having these career paths in common usually leads to fruitful interactions and philosophical understanding about care delivery issues and problem-resolution methodologies.

In contrast, practicing physicians and hospital CEOs seldom share the same education, professional career path experiences, or organizational perspective.[17] The two can have great difficulty in reaching an agreement about how care should be delivered and resources apportioned. As a result, communication breaks down, suspicion germinates, and a cultural gulf forms that is extremely difficult to bridge.

### Recent Data

In an attempt to acquire accurate data about hospital management, we asked U.S. hospitals CEOs to describe: (1) the career path to CEO, (2) why they chose to become a hospital CEO, and (3) what were their concerns for the future of U.S. healthcare.[18] Six hundred and seventy U.S. hospital CEOs responded to our survey, representing 16 percent of those to whom letters were sent. Eighty-eight percent of the respondents were men, which slightly underrepresented women.[17] The median number of in-patient hospital beds was 229 (mean = 147).

*Career Path for CEOs*

The educational background of hospital CEOs was highly varied. Ninety percent of the CEOs had advanced degrees (Figure 2.1) beyond bachelors. Seventy-nine percent ($n = 529$) held masters degrees in public health or health administration; business administration; the arts, the sciences or some other field. Nine percent had a second degree such as RN (registered nurse); a different additional masters degree; CPA (certified public accountant); and others. Nine percent ($n = 63$) had doctorates in medicine, philosophy, law, and others. Contrast this diversity to the highly structured, lock-step requirements to obtain an MD (doctor of medicine) degree, specialty, or subspecialty certification. Furthermore, though women are ascending the ladders of both medical and managerial senior positions,[19] still only 12 percent of hospital CEOs were women.

Work positions held by the respondents prior to becoming CEO were categorized as follows (Figure 2.1): administration (or management)—starting at 37 percent, but the number goes up 60 percent before becoming CEO; finance—24 percent; operations—8 percent to 6 percent; 9 percent started in patient care (direct or support), enrolled in formal training, and held other positions (e.g., marketing, human resources, development, consulting, legal, or information technology). Administration or management was the leading career path according to the respondents. Sixty percent of the respondents indicated they moved from an administrative or managerial position to the CEO position. In comparison, 24 percent of the respondents indicated moving from a finance position to CEO. The vast majority of prior jobs held by the respondents (regardless of activity) were in healthcare delivery rather than other occupations.[20] In contrast to many other industries, job crossover is uncommon in healthcare. This may be due to the highly specialized nature of healthcare administration, the contentious environment, the lesser income compared with other industries, or a self-selection process as people enter the workforce.

Tenure as CEO is also displayed in Figure 2.1. Forty percent had been CEO less than five years ($n = 268$) and 25 percent had been in the position 5 to 10 years. In contrast to corporations such as General Electric, only 67 hospital CEOs (10 percent) had been in place for 20 or more years.

*CEO Concerns for the Future*

The constant expansion of unfunded mandates was by far the most frequent concern voiced by CEOs. Their institutions are required by law to provide services for which they do not have the resources—financial, physical, and human. Seventy-seven percent specifically expressed concern about reimbursement and cost issues (financing), while 66 percent indicated that personnel shortages were their greatest concern. These results are highly comparable to prior survey results.[21,22] The consistency of CEO concerns clearly documents the determinants of stress that CEOs experience trying to meet expectations of their boards of trustees, medical staff members, accreditation bodies, and patients.

**Figure 2.1 Ascending the Corporate Ladder to Hospital CEO**

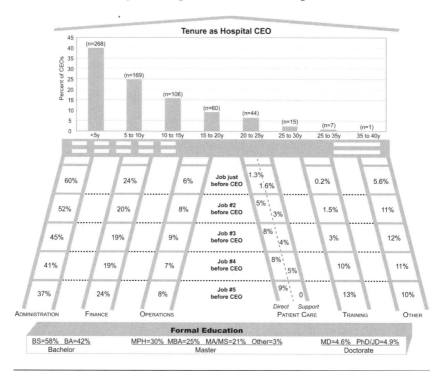

Results are displayed from a survey of 670 U.S. hospital CEOs. College and postgraduate education are the foundation, followed by ladders representing work experience leading to the CEO
position. Nine percent started as doctors or nurses. Increasing concentration is noted toward
administration. The length of time the 670 CEOs had been CEO is shown in the bar graph.

One-third of the CEO respondents protested the lack of national health policies
and inherent contradictions in the present system and similar large percentages crit-
icized the ubiquitous unfunded government mandates, the plight of the uninsured
or underinsured, and issues surrounding patient safety.[23,24] Other concerns voiced
by the CEOs included loss of public confidence, insufficient capital to provide
mandated services, keeping up with technological imperatives such as electronic
records, the impact of malpractice insurance, and the need for tort reform. Eleven
percent directly expressed concern over internecine competition between their
hospital and its own attending doctors.

A striking feature of the CEO responses was that their concerns mirror the
concerns of vocal clinicians.[10]

### CEO Values

As part of our research, we asked CEOs of U.S. hospitals why they chose to
become CEO. From the 670 responses, some very lengthy and passionate, we

could deduce a number of primary values. In Table 2.1, we offer a number of representative quotations made by the CEOs.

Thirty-one percent of the CEOs reported a primary focus on their own careers. Most then emphasized their desires to combine what they were good at with what would benefit society: in essence, a combination of a personal skill set and altruism. A separate group (26 percent) directly indicated altruism as their purpose in choosing a healthcare career. Thirteen percent stressed their desire to be in the healthcare field in contrast to the for-profit business world. Combining these three groups, one sees that altruism in various forms was a driving force in seventy percent of U.S. hospital CEOs.

Nineteen percent of the respondent CEOs indicated that the love of a challenge was the primary reason for their career choice; they liked the difficulty of combining good business with good medicine. As several wrote, their work was never boring. These people might be likened to the adrenalin junkies of medicine, such as heart or trauma surgeons and interventional cardiologists.

An interesting subgroup (6 percent) reported that hospital administration was a family tradition, crossing several generations, similar to the oft-touted, multi-generational physician families.

## Table 2.1
### Reasons for Becoming a Hospital CEO

Legend: *Gender; State; Number of hospital beds.* Quote follows beneath.

*Male; Pennsylvania; 95*
"It was a way to combine meeting the healthcare needs of people and my interest in business. On any given day, my busiest physicians might care for 10 inpatients—I care for all of them. I've been able to make a difference in the community by bringing technology, manpower, and a philosophy of care together to enhance a community resource."

*Male; Indiana; 70*
"There is simply no other job that gives you the challenge to run things fiscally sound, while doing our best to provide quality healthcare to our patients with a diverse and wonderful workforce dedicated to caring for patients."

*Male; Indiana; 108*
"I'm driven to succeed. I wanted to make greater contributions to society than being a clinician allowed."

*Female; Washington, D.C.; 130*
"Wanted to use financial and managerial skills in an environment that was socially responsible."

*Female; Georgia; 78*
"Because I wanted to influence decision making for patient care and maintain a patient advocacy role in the board room and at the bedside."

*Male; Illinois; 163*
"Father and older brother were physicians. Sister, a nurse. Thus had an interest in the medical field but did not desire to be a physician. Older brother recommended that I look into hospital administration. His words to me 41 years ago, 'Why don't you check out hospital administration, I think it's a good racket.'"

**Table 2.1**
**Reasons for Becoming a Hospital CEO** *(continued)*

*Male; Virginia; 153*

"My mother was an RN working at the Medical College of Virginia and my father was a practicing attorney. I intended to be an attorney like my dad, but my mom helped me get a part-time job at the hospital after high school in medical records. The administrator overseeing medical records who also taught in the graduate program took an interest in me and encouraged me to pursue a masters in hospital administration and forget law school. It was good advice and I have never regretted that decision."

*Male; South Dakota; 86*

"I had worked in a hospital as an orderly during early college, liked the field—helping people, and so forth—but was not suited to be a physician as I was more skilled in numbers, statistics, and working with groups rather than being autocratic, and not being a team member. Now some of that has changed for physicians coming out of school as they hopefully see the need to be team players, but in the 50s and 60s that was not the case."

*Male; Ohio; 453*

"This is one of the greatest jobs in this century. The opportunity to make a difference in the lives of individuals and the greater community occurs every day! Ninety-nine days out of 100, I can't wait to get to work. Many of my colleagues share this view."

*Male; Tennessee; 219*

"Didn't so much 'choose' what I'm doing as much as my passions led me here. I am a clinician at heart, and I approach administration the same way I would treat a client/patient through systems theory. This health system is like a great big (potentially) dysfunctional client/patient/family system. Strategic planning is nothing more than creating, with the patient/family involved, a detailed treatment plan with short-term, measurable objectives and long term goals. Then you work with your client/patient within the context of all the overlapping systems, including financial to achieve these goals. Concerns about money and the cost of care, as well as reimbursement (or benefits), is as relevant for an individual who is seeking treatment as it is for a large health system. I balance quality care/outcomes and fiscal responsibility every day."

*Female; Ohio; 651*

"I love healthcare. It is a sacred trust to care for others. I also enjoy people and serving their efforts to provide care. Finally, I feel that I am able to make a difference in the lives of those we serve in the community."

*Female; South Carolina; 106*

"My background is in Nursing and operations of clinical areas. I progressed in my positions above the staff nurse level to increase the voice of the caregiver. I accepted the CEO position for the same reason—to see if a hospital could be successful with the priorities and point of view of the physicians, nurses, and patients. Creating an environment to support the professionals caring for the patients instead of catering to the ego of an executive."

*Male; North Carolina; 50*

"I felt there were far too many MBAs running hospitals who have no understanding or appreciation what occurs at the patient's bedside. Financial decisions often have serious clinical consequences, and these folks either do not care or do not know how to adequately or successfully manage the consequences to minimize negative patient care impact. I feel more clinicians need to take the reins of the healthcare facilities to ensure that patients are truly getting the care they seek and deserve."

*Male; West Virginia; 168*

"Healthcare is a ministry; simply look at the work of Jesus! I take pride at using my business skills to keep a hospital going strong as opposed to lining my own pockets. I am not a clinician—I am a businessman—and a hospital requires many different types of people to

**Table 2.1**
**Reasons for Becoming a Hospital CEO** *(continued)*

be strong. Some CEOs want to think they are clinicians, and some clinicians thinks they are CEOs. The real truth is you can't be both, but both have equal merit and deserving of respect."

*Male; Minnesota; 215*

"Having begun life as a practicing pediatrician, then moving into academic medicine, I gradually became more interested in participating at a broader level in decisions and policy making. Never intended to go into hospital management, and was persuaded to take a VP position by a previous CEO/mentor who had never had physician on his executive team. Over the next decade, I handled most of the different portfolios, always learning on the job. Ended up COO, and one day was recruited as CEO at a different hospital. I never left any previous position because of dissatisfaction, only because of a new and exciting opportunity. Each phase of my life has been valuable and rewarding, and each new phase has built on skills acquired in the previous one. Being CEO of a large children's hospital system is, in my view, entirely consistent with the initial direction of my career as a pediatrician. However, now my decisions have the potential to have a much broader impact than when I was dealing with one patient at a time. (Probably more than you wanted to hear!)"

## COMPARISON OF ATTRIBUTES

For physicians, educational background and licensure/accreditation require-ments are highly structured and provide common rites of passage for all doctors, nurses, and therapists. This creates bonds of cohesion among clinicians. Socialization during postgraduate training, particularly the role models of teachers, emphasizes personal responsibility, individual goal setting, and autonomous decision making. Physicians have little knowledge and less interest in rule-following bureaucracy, organizational structure, accounting, personnel management, or strategic planning (Table 2.2).[16,17,25]

Those in management have a very wide diversity of educational backgrounds and no set job accreditation or licensure process. Not only is this markedly different from doctors, but during socialization, managers learn to make group decisions and to delegate responsibility. In strategic planning, managers generally try to forecast and anticipate, while physicians are typically in reactive mode, responding to the acutely ill patient.

In theory, the two sides of the gap have different time horizons: short- or moderate-term for doctors and long-term for healthcare executives. However, most healthcare managers are now judged on the variance from their monthly or annual budget. Because of the incentive structures and the constantly changing mandates, as well as regulations, healthcare executives are forced to focus on im-mediate concerns and ad hoc crisis management.

Changes in healthcare over the past 50 years have had profound effects on the power relationships within medicine. The power and influence of healthcare executives has increased with corresponding fall in power and prestige of physicians. Nevertheless, each side sees itself as on the top of the power pyramid, that is, most important in the system. Doctors reason that, as the patient comes first and the phy-sician or nurse are the only people legally allowed to touch the patient, they must be

Table 2.2
Contrasting Medical and Management Attributes

| | Attribute | Providers of direct care (Medicine) | | Organizational decision-makers (Management) |
|---|---|---|---|---|
| 1 | Responsibility | Personally held | | Oganizational; often delegated |
| 2 | Education | Structured. Uniform. | T | Unspecified. Highly varied. |
| 3 | How handle expertise? | Individually possess & use | H | Orchestrate. Facilitate. |
| 4 | Place in hierarchy? | On top [clinical] | | On top [CEO] |
| 5 | Focus | Individual patient survival | E | Organizational survival |
| 6 | Focus of work | Individual patient | | Patients in aggregate (market) |
| 7 | Time horizon | Short term | | Long term |
| 8 | Gratification | Immediate and specific | | Delayed or absent; diffuse. |
| 9 | Decision-making | Independent. Rapid | G | Group process. Deliberate |
| 10 | Strategic approach | Reactive | | Anticipatory |
| 11 | Mgmt approach | Authoritative; act alone. | A | Collaborative, communal |
| 12 | Professionally accountable to: | Professional standards & peers, external to hospital | | Hospital Board |
| 13 | Decisions impact: | Medical quality & resource use | P | Resource use & medical quality |
| 14 | Job defined by: | Accreditation, licensure | | Job description |
| 15 | Healthcare changes caused a | Loss of power | | Gain in power |
| 16 | Core Values | Altruism; Service; The Challenge | | Altruism; Service; The Challenge |

Mgmt=management.

on the top of the power hierarchy. In any situation involving strategic decisions and money issues, the healthcare executive is responsible. Since the ultimate decision maker is the hospital CEO, he or she must be at the top of the power hierarchy.

A real important, but subliminal, cognitive difference is the value of business. Academic physicians are socialized to disdain or at best ignore money, as everything should be done for the patient without regard to expense. Physicians in private practice have a similar problem to hospital executives: trying to balance escalating expenses with fixed revenues, while they have control over neither. The physicians' ethos places patient survival first, while for those in healthcare administration, the institution must survive by having the budget balance.

Despite the host of divergences between doctors and healthcare executives, we find that common core values—altruism, service, and the challenge—motivate both.[18]

## RELATIONS BETWEEN PHYSICIANS AND HEALTHCARE EXECUTIVES DIRECTLY IMPACT OUTCOMES

Today's medical center is a complex, matrix-structured organization. The results of modern medicine are summation effects of the activities of large numbers of people in multiple teams. The "'one-ill, one-pill, one-bill doctor' is a thing of the past," wrote Wittkower and Stauble over 30 years ago. [26]

When my (JDW) 93-year-old mother goes for her semiannual checkup, her care involves a general physician, several office staffs, at least five computer programs, central supply, patient transport, three separate laboratories, cardiology, radiology, and pulmonology, and she speaks perfect English. These diverse elements encompass function and expertise of both white coats and blue suits.

To the extent that medicine and management relate well, the patient gets what he or she needs. If physicians and hospital executives function independently (silo systems; minimal interaction), the care will be disjointed, less effective, and inefficient. If the providers and managers think and behave as adversaries, it is a wonder that anyone gets care at all.

Forces external to the medical center further complicate relations between doctors and healthcare executives. These elements include accreditation and licensure entities, insurers, advocacy groups, for-profit medical companies such as the pharmaceuticals, and of course, governments at state and federal levels, sometimes even other national governments. The rules, regulations, and laws must be interpreted and to variable extents implemented by both physicians and healthcare executives. If they are adversaries, each side will seek to game the system to individual advantage. The patient in many U.S. hospitals finds himself or herself in the middle of an internecine war.

## STRUCTURAL ASPECTS OF PHYSICIAN-HOSPITAL CONFLICT

### The Real Enemy Is the (Non) System

Reasons for physician-manager conflict can be viewed as structural, cultural, and perceptual. The cultural and perceptual reasons—how the two sides view and relate to each other—have been covered already. There are at least six structural reasons.

First, each stakeholder group—patients, providers, and payers—has expectations that are often unattainable or in conflict. Patients want all the care they want or need, when they want it and believe they are entitled. Providers behave as though there is no issue with resources, and payers want not to spend the country into bankruptcy. In a fixed reimbursement structure, for-profit entities, whether hospitals or insurance companies, generate profits by avoiding or delaying payment for healthcare. Furthermore, the outcomes we track are the opposite of what we want. We measure death, complications and costs when we desire longevity, good health, and resource responsibility.

Second, the whole system of medical payments is bizarre. It pits the physician (the cost driver) against the hospital manager, and the consumer (patient) against the payer(s). In a previous article, we called this "Billing Schadenfreude,"[27] where medical payment structures subvert the *fiduciary relationship* (position of trust) that is supposed to exist between doctor and patient.

Third, as all behavior is strongly influenced by incentives, what is the incentive system under which the physician and the healthcare executive must operate? Based on the confused, ill-defined, and contradictory expectations, both doctors and managers work in a world of conflicting carrots and sticks that has made them "accidental adversaries," as described in systems thinking.[28,29] George Bernard

Shaw, directly addressing the issue of financial incentives and profit-generating self-referral, wrote in his own inimitable way: "As to the honor and conscience of doctors, they have as much as any other class of men, no more and no less. But what other men dare pretend to be impartial where they have a strong pecuniary interest on one side?" and "That any sane nation, having observed that you could provide for the supply of bread by giving bakers a pecuniary interest in baking for you, should go on to give a surgeon a pecuniary interest in cutting off your leg, is enough to make one despair of political humanity."[30]

Fourth, healthcare organizational structures and management philosophies are holdovers from the nineteenth century—but healthcare workers care for patients in the twenty-first century. The power shifts that have occurred are in conflict with the desired outcomes as decision makers are given multiple, dichotomous mandates and are expected to achieve the impossible.

Fifth, while the external environment expects definitive answers to medical problems, it provides punishment for bad outcomes without corresponding positive incentives for improvement. Therefore, healthcare has become highly risk averse, which translates to defensive and dedicated to the status quo. If every incentive punishes risk taking and rewards stability, learning will be suppressed.[31] The environment—in theory, the marketplace—seeks to reward efficiency, but places a huge regulatory and bureaucratic, uncompensated burden on the healthcare industry.

Sixth and final, there is the unique nature of healthcare. It is a people-processing activity performed by people. A lug nut doesn't complain if you overtighten it. An overstuffed chair does not expect you to reduce its puffiness with a pill.

The primary cause of physician-healthcare executive conflict—the real enemy—is the healthcare system, which is not systematic and offers stakeholder contradictions, perverse incentives, microeconomic disconnection, punitive medico-legal environment, and overregulation.[32,33]

### Collaboration Is the Beginning

Russell Ackoff[34] makes an important distinction when he contrasts *resolving* a problem (making the best possible result) with *dissolving* a problem (changing the system so that the problem can never recur). We believe that collaboration between medical schools and management schools can begin to dissolve healthcare woes.

Management knowledge and expertise, and business experience and tools have much to offer healthcare. We and others have demonstrated the potential utility of proven management principles in the healthcare arena.[35–37] In collaboration, a medical school and a management school can begin to achieve high-quality, reduced-error, resource-sensitive healthcare. However, we also have noted with concern that most universities lack any bridge—physical, philosophical, cognitive—across what we call the chasm (Figure 2.2) separating medical schools from their university-affiliated management schools.

We believe that an analogous and equally unhealthy separation exists *within* most medical centers between the providers and the managers. We call this schism the Gap (Figure 2.3).

**Figure 2.2 The Chasm**

## What Is the Gap?

The gap represents a gulf, both substantive and perceived, between managers and care providers. The gap includes differences in thinking and approach, priorities and incentives, and responsibilities as well as roles. Most of the substantive distinctions are due to divergent educational backgrounds, temperament and self-selection, radically different professional socialization, alternate worldviews, and specific expertise.

**Figure 2.3 The Gap**

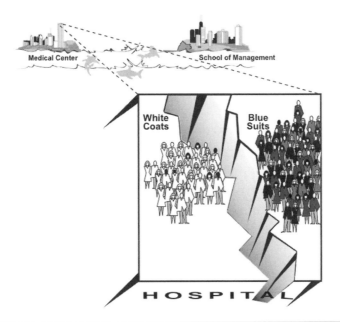

Most hospitals have a cultural and functional separation between direct care providers (white coats) and hospital administrators or executives (blue suits). The Gap prevents effective interactions.

The two sides also tend to have stereotypical and negative perceptions of each other. The manager sees a doctor who has no understanding of or interest in resource constraints or proper organizational behavior, even if the doctor has an MBA and manages a successful multimillion dollar division. The doctor sees a heartless bean counter who cares nothing for patients, despite the CEO spending seven hours before a state oversight committee aggressively seeking support for the doctors' medical programs. For example, scotoma is common in healthcare. It is the Italian word meaning that we see what we expect, and not necessarily what is there. This is true for both doctor and manager, and clouds what could become a fruitful collaboration.

Table 2.2 offers both the reasons for the gap and, based on recent data, what can be used to mend it. Physicians and CEOs (representing healthcare executives) share common core values. We suspect this similarity may surprise both sides of the gap. Such basic, gut-level commonality can provide the structural supports to bridge the gap.

## MENDING (ACTUALLY, BRIDGING) THE GAP

In trying to understand physician hospital relations, we begin by explicating who they are, what their attributes are, and end suggesting that we mend or actually bridge the gap (Figure 2.4). The differences between physicians and healthcare executives can be used to great advantage. We need to embrace this diversity rather than eliminate it. Combining the diverse talents of physicians and healthcare executives could dissolve (per Ackoff[32]) many of the problems healthcare faces every day.

Conflict is inevitable in times of rapid change.[4] Physicians and hospital leaders can no longer pass on cost increases at will to patients and third-party payers. Effective dialogue and collaboration are in all parties' interests to optimize patient

**Figure 2.4 Mending (Bridging) the Gap**

care and to develop innovative services. To improve the practice environment for physicians and patients and to keep hospitals financially solvent so that they can continue to serve the public good, physicians and hospital management must learn to work more interdependently.

At the local level, improved physician-management interaction may not immediately improve pricing power, but it could enhance efficiency and thus improve competitive position. Perhaps the greatest long-term value of improving physician-management communication lies in developing shared perspectives that enhance mutual respect and build trust. Because physicians collectively influence hospital revenue, clinical costs, quality, and safety issues, having practicing physicians involved in a meaningful way in a hospital priority setting may provide competitive advantage and improve quality.[38]

## Systems Thinking and Thinking Systems

General systems theory, complexity science, systems thinking, systems analysis or dynamics are names given to a school of thought initiated by Ludwig Bertanalanffy in the mid twentieth century, subsequently expanded and modified by others.[39-46] Its essence is the concept that all systems—biologic, mechanical, chemical, social—produce outcomes by the interactions of the parts, not by the parts in isolation, and that all systems are functionally subsystems of larger systems. Thus, the heart is part of the body; the body is a person that is part of a social group such as a hospital staff; the hospital functions within and for a community; healthcare is merely one of the systems within the community in addition to education, commerce, emergency services, and so on; the community is part of a nation state; the nations share a planet; the planet is part of the solar system. Thus, the heart is a tiny sub-sub-subsystem of the solar system.

Practical consequences flow from the general concept of interaction and causal loop relationships.[28] For example, study of and optimization of the function of a part of a system in isolation often does not improve overall system results and may actually degrade the system's output.[34,43] Consider a healthcare example. Improving the efficiency of the OR and balancing its budget may reduce patient throughput and cost more for the hospital than the savings in the OR.[46]

Systems dynamics describes what are called complex adaptive systems, which have three distinct characteristics. They *self-organize*, meaning that whatever organization may be imposed from the outside (or not), complex adaptive systems develop their own internal organizational structures and means of interaction. Such systems *coevolve*, so that they are changed by their own interactions. The results from systems that self-organize and coevolve *emerge*; they cannot be precisely predicted in advance.[42]

Thinking systems exhibit the three characteristics of complex adaptive systems—self-organization, coevolution, and emergence—but have two additional unique features: the ability to structure their own learning and goals different from and sometimes inconsistent with personal survival.[46] Healthcare is a paradigm of a thinking system.

Several authors have recommended the use of systems thinking and complexity science to healthcare.[10,45,47] The Pittsburgh Regional Healthcare Initiative is actively applying systems thinking to various medical centers.[48] We concur strongly, but add that the unique nature of thinking systems must be incorporated into any application to healthcare. With physicians and healthcare executives working together rather than at cross-purposes, healthcare institutions can improve their outcomes based on their own initiatives by applying systems thinking. The exact results cannot be predicted in advance, nor should they be. In order to achieve such a to-be-desired collegial relationship, doctors and executives need to communicate more effectively.

### Skills in Communication and Confrontation

Clinical training alone is insufficient to ensure quality patient care. Communication is a critical element in providing care, and physicians are not trained to communicate well. Their authoritarian style and limited listening skills hamper clear exchange of information. Healthcare professionals can improve their communication by utilizing the skills summarized below.[49]

### Communication

*Active Listening*. Like so many everyday, every minute activities, listening is considered a skill that everyone has. After all, we listen all the time—to the radio, to our children, to the people in the next office, and to the passing air stream as we drive the car. Listening is not something we all automatically do well, but is particularly important because it makes people feel that their concerns matter.[10] A mnemonic for improving listening skills is CLOSE:

- *C*oncentrate on the speaker, maintaining comfortable eye contact for 6 to 10 seconds at a time without staring, giving the person the feeling that nothing else matters but what the speaker is saying.
- *L*isten with multiple senses, paying attention to the speaker's body language, facial expression, and tone of voice, in addition to the content of the message.
- *O*pen one's stance to convey receptivity to the speaker's message; avoid crossing one's arms over one's chest, which imposes a barrier between the speaker and listener.
- *S*uspend judgment to maintain objectivity.
- *E*mpathize, trying to put oneself in the speaker's frame of reference with summary comments such as, "Do I understand you to say . . ." to build trust and credibility.

*Checklists*. A formal written checklist is highly useful to surface assumptions and discuss expectations proactively. At the beginning of a group project, a checklist helps people to adopt a common wavelength, to learn to welcome diversity of opinion, and to minimize feelings of disappointment, betrayal, and anger. Checklists will vary based on the nature of the project and the backgrounds of the participants, but common features include:

- punctual attendance and starting on time;
- active participation;
- building on others' ideas;
- avoiding personal attacks;
- developing win-win solutions;
- respecting members' confidentiality;
- monitoring progress at regular intervals; and
- sharing ownership of results.

*Sensitivity and Empathy.* As discussed in the previous case report and the physician-administrator exchanges, highly charged words can contribute to an us versus them, adversarial atmosphere and thereby interfere with successful communication. Listening with sensitivity and avoiding hot button words or phrases improves our listening and others' hearing. Saying, "Maybe there is another way to view this," is better than, "I disagree," because the latter creates a you versus me construct. Focusing on costs rather than benefits immediately after someone makes a suggestion often narrows the discussion focus and impedes collaboration.

## Confrontation Skills

Differences in strategy and responses to the environment are inevitable in times of rapid change.[49] Therefore, to communicate well and collaborate, professionals need confrontational and conflict resolution skills. As Grenny wrote, "We can either talk out or act out our differences; the choice is ours."[50] Having the same frustrating conversation repeatedly may reflect the lack of confrontation skills, in which the focus is on content the first time, on the pattern of events the second time, and on issues of competence, respect, trust, and loss of confidence in a relationship the third time. Patterson et al.[51] wrote that to avoid the fundamental attribution error, people need to ask questions and obtain information rather than assuming hidden and evil motives. Other causes for failure to meet expectations involve ability, training, and social and structural incentives. To influence others' behavior, we must start from a position of safety and security, maintaining respect, establishing mutual purpose, and ending with a question rather than a threat. In the process of discovery, skeptics can become believers and act more like long-term partners and owners rather than short-term renters, as illustrated in the following.

*Structured Dialogue.* Structured dialogue is a process that helps a group of practicing physicians articulate their collective, patient-centered self-interest. For example, structured dialogue can help physicians improve physician-physician communication, understand more fully the complexity of hospital operations, and articulate clinical priorities for their communities.[52] Structured dialogue can improve both physician-physician communication and physician-administrator communication.[38]

Unlike hospital-centric change efforts, the structured dialogue process is led by a medical advisory panel of high-performing, well-respected clinicians, who review and recommend clinical priorities based on presentations by the major clinical sections and departments. Contrary to the apprehensions of some hospital executives, the recommendations generally include performance improvements and minor expenditures that support these improvements, rather than a list of capital-intensive budget items. In return for giving physicians a say in clinical priority setting, the hospital is able to enlist physicians to attend meetings and outline their priorities.

Over 30 hospitals of varying sizes and locations in the United States have successfully undertaken a structured dialogue process, which has improved the practice environment, reenergized physician-physician and physician-hospital communication and collaboration, and has served as an effective training environment for new physician leaders. What has surprised one author (KHC) is the extent to which a process that improves hospital executives' standing with their physicians and board engenders suspicion and mistrust on the part of administrators. A Western CEO, considering using the structured dialogue approach at his hospital, when asked by his board chair if losing control to physicians upset him, replied, "Heck no. I never had control in the first place!" (A surprising commonality found in our 2006 study[18] was the sense of powerlessness felt by many U.S. hospital CEOs.) The Western CEO decided to use the structured dialogue approach and has since been a speaker at national seminars about the value of physician engagement. Healthcare professionals need to understand that control is illusory[53] and the only control we have is over our own response to our helplessness in the face of rapid change.

We can also build on what is going well. Rather than complaining and blaming, we can focus on what is going right and build on success, as described below.

*Appreciative Inquiry.* Appreciative inquiry (AI) is a technique that focuses on building on success. Practical applications of AI in healthcare settings include[54]:

- Making rounds with front-line workers, asking:

  - "What is going particularly well for you?"
  - "Do you have the tools and resources that you need?"
  - "What can I do to help you?"

- Asking affirming questions during performance appraisals and following up with thank-you notes in response to the question:

  - "Do you have colleagues or coworkers who have been particularly helpful?"

AI is based on the premises that people respond favorably to positive reinforcement and that sharing stories of past successes generates more energy and less defensiveness than analyzing problems and attributing blame. Storytelling, which is an integral part of AI, decreases the inhibiting effects of hierarchy on sharing knowledge, uses metaphors to summarize important points and make them vivid, and provides vignettes that are remembered more readily than facts.[55] Healthcare professionals may not feel comfortable using AI, incorrectly perceiving it to condone poor performance rather than as an alternative to consider when problem solving hits a wall because of defensiveness. Work at the Baptist Hospital has made AI easier to operationalize, such as rounding on wards, rewarding positive behavior, and being more proactive and receptive to improvement opportunities.[56,57] Another important development involves bottom-up efforts that change the culture, as described below.

*Positive Deviance.* Positive deviance (PD) is an approach to organizational change based on the premise that solutions to problems already exist within the community. It encompasses intentional behaviors that depart from the norms of a group in honorable ways.[58] PD seeks to identify and optimize existing resources to solve problems rather than using the more conventional identification of needs and obtaining of external resources to meet those needs.

For example, healthcare workers at Waterbury Hospital used the PD method to analyze and resolve problems in communication at discharge. Miscommunications over discharge medications were responsible for an average of two readmissions per month. By observing the steps physicians and nurses used in discharging patients, a process was created that prevented the miscues. To follow up, a nurse called the patient within 48 hours of discharge to review discharge medications.[49]

Keys to the PD method include[59]:

- Self-identification as a community by members of the community; people see themselves as alike rather than conflicting
- Mutual designation of a problem by the community members, that is, a bottom-up rather than a top-down approach
- A search for community members on the leading edge who have managed to surmount a problem
- Analysis of meritorious behaviors that enable outliers (positive deviants) to achieve success
- Introduction and adoption of new behaviors into group practice

PD appears to work by unfreezing commonly held perceptions without threatening people. It hastens the transition from early adopter to early majority by creating a safe environment for learning that does not make anyone feel stupid. It is based on adult-learning principles of learning by doing and mentoring. Finally, it avoids the transplant rejection approach to best practices adopted from other institutions because it celebrates the accomplishments of local heroes with whom insiders can relate.[60]

## Financial Confrontation or Collaboration

Berenson et al.[61] recently wrote that economic pressures have greatly exacerbated the potential for physician-hospital conflict in many areas of the country. According to their survey of 1,008 healthcare leaders, relations were under greater strain in 2005 compared with 2000 to 2001. They cited selective employment and financial collaboration as two strategies that have been used in response to an ever-changing economic environment.

Several U.S. states prohibit physician employment by hospitals based on the fear of conflicts of interest or, worse, collusion. Other states allow such employment. All jurisdictions accept a variety of medical school–hospital financial arrangements. Berenson and colleagues report on the increasing fears of private practice physicians that *their* hospitals are competing with them by selective employment or, worse, exclusionary methods such as economic credentialing to prevent physicians who compete with the hospital-employed physicians from practicing within the hospital. We will focus below on opportunities for collaboration.

The goal of physician-hospital financial collaboration should be to create value for patients, physicians, and hospital. Collaboration implies win-win-win scenarios that enlarge the economic pie rather than divide a predetermined, insufficient, and contracting pot of money. Both parties gain if physicians act as owners rather than clients, increasing revenue and collaborating on ways to improve processes and outcomes.

Regardless of how deals are structured,[62] successful financial collaboration between physicians and hospitals requires[63]:

- mutual understanding of each party's interests and needs;
- sharing information widely;
- distinguishing negotiating from thinking aloud;
- stepwise building of transparency and trust; and
- both sides acting as a team of active owners rather than as individual, passive investors, jointly improving care processes in an ongoing fashion.

### Dealing with Physician-Hospital Competition[64]

We doubt that physicians and hospital leaders were ever in alignment. A difference now, however, is that neither party can pass on increases in costs independently of the other as was the case in the era of cost-based reimbursement.

Like it or not, they are bound together in a complex web of interdependence. We offer a three-part strategy of proactivity, collaborative conflict (not an oxymoron), and containment as a guide for dealing with physician-hospital competition. With the difficulty of predicting how events will unfold, we empathize that both sides must begin to respect and trust the other or healthcare will never break out of the current cycle of conflict. Both parties can actually become stronger by loosening individual control.

> *Proactivity*. It may seem counterintuitive for hospital leaders to take the lead in partnering with their highest revenue generating physicians, but a proactive approach minimizes the opportunity for turnkey operators to create unrealistic expectations among physicians looking for greater efficiency and reimbursement. In turn, a more content medical staff can help the hospital and the community by increasing revenues, decreasing the costs of clinical care, and improving outcomes.
>
> *Collaborative Conflict*. In collaborative conflict, people attack problems rather than one another. They solve problems in a way that satisfies both parties and builds long-term relationships. Success depends on each party's preparation and their understanding of what each wants and needs to accomplish, what each is willing to concede, and what hot buttons might cause an angry response.
>
> *Containment*. When negotiations break down, the prior effort that went into them was not wasted. Both parties have learned more about each other and about areas of mutual interest. It is important to depersonalize potential conflicts by agreeing to revisit the issues in the next two to three months rather than assigning blame and walking away. Discussions may be more favorable after each side learns more about the costs and possible consequences of continuing physician-hospital competition.

## RECOMMENDATIONS

In computer terms, both physicians and healthcare executives should delete their files containing stereotypical images of each other. They need to learn who the other really is and accept the fact that they have similar core values: altruism, service, and love of a challenge. As suggested before, this can provide the foundation for a bridge across the Gap.

Malcolm and colleagues[65] use the same term—gap—to describe the separation between clinical culture and governance or managerial culture. They believe that New Zealand is seeking a convergence of cultures, meaning two fundamental changes are in store: (1) "A shift from preoccupation with resource management to health outcomes as the 'bottom line' of the organization"; and (2) "Acceptance by clinicians of a key role in managing resources and in achieving the organization's goals." Malcolm et al. then foreshadow what we advocate here by writing that the converging cultures need a "more trusting relationship based on . . . shared values." As our data show, physicians and healthcare executives *have* shared values and core ideals in common. They act, however, as though they have irreconcilable differences.

We would prefer avoiding military analogies in healthcare. However, we must recognize that there is a mindless, unintended but real and *very* powerful enemy of what we all want: high quality, compassionate, and efficient healthcare. It is a system that does not work. Hospital management and doctors must become allies, brothers-in-arms. The patients are noncombatants and insurance companies are the accidental adversaries of both patients and hospitals.[28] If goals were clearly defined and outcomes tracked by appropriate measures, incentives could be aligned with desired results. The relationships between patients and providers or hospitals and payers would not be win-lose scenarios and the so-called enemy would cease to exist. One phrase mentioned in Malcolm's opinion piece[65] was crossing over to the "other side." When the cultures converge and a trusting relationship of colleagues develops, there will not be two sides, just one team with members having different talents and responsibilities. Continuing the military analogy, an effective army does not have the infantry and artillery think of each other as being on opposite sides.

Physicians and managers need to learn about and learn from each other. If they do so, their differences can become strengths. Physicians need to educate executives about research and rigorous science so that managerial decisions can be based on proof rather than just logic. Healthcare executives need to educate doctors about proper management, from financial planning to proven error-reduction techniques and application of queuing theory, namely, in the ER. There are dozens of powerful and applicable business-proven management tools and approaches that can be adapted to healthcare. While we mention (above) some useful techniques such as structured dialogue and positive deviance, others with great potential include continuous quality improvement,[66] learning curve theory,[31,37] total quality management,[67] the theory of constraints,[68] failure mode and effect analysis,[69] the internal customer concept,[70,71] generative relationships,[72] lean systems,[73] and possibly most important, systems thinking.[28,34,39-47,74]

Together, physicians and healthcare executives can accomplish most of their goals-in-common. If they continue the present adversarial relationship, nothing will improve. What Benjamin Franklin said about revolutionary politics is equally true for the revolution needed in healthcare: "We must hang together, gentlemen...else we shall most assuredly hang separately."[75]

Key Concepts

- Over the past 50 years, the functions of healthcare institutions and the people within them have changed dramatically. The system for healthcare delivery has not experienced corresponding changes or adjustments.
- Both physicians and healthcare executives are frustrated by the confusion, systemic contradictions, perverse incentives, and opposing priorities of the stakeholders in healthcare. They tend to behave like adversaries, competitors, and even combatants.

- An adversarial relationship between physicians and healthcare executives negatively impacts both clinical as well as financial outcomes.
- Numerous differences exist between physicians and hospital executives in education, background, socialization, and work experiences. However, they share striking similarities in core values and future concerns. Neither side behaves as though it is aware of the commonalities.
- Physicians and hospitals executives have a common enemy: the system, or really, the absence of a functional system.
- The core values that physicians and hospital executives share could provide a foundation for developing a collegial relationship. Each has important skills and knowledge that the other needs. Working in collaboration, together they could solve many of the challenging problems in modern healthcare.

## REFERENCES

1. Pathman, D. E., T. R. Konrad, E. S. Williams, W. E. Scheckler, M. Linzer, and J. Douglas. 2002. "Physician Job Satisfaction, Dissatisfaction, and Turnover." *Journal of Family Practice* 51: 593.

2. Zuger, A. 2004. "Dissatisfaction with Medical Practice." *New England Journal of Medicine* 350 (1): 69–76.

3. Waldman, J. D., J. N. Hood, H. L. Smith, and S. Arora. 2004. "Changing the Approach to Workforce Movements: Application of Net Retention Rate in Healthcare." *Journal of Applied Business and Economics* 24 (2): 38–60.

4. Cohn, K. H. 2005. "Embracing Complexity." In *Better Communication for Better Care: Mastering Physician-Administrator Collaboration*, ed. K. H. Cohn, 30–38. Chicago: Health Administration Press.

5. Waldman, J. D, H. L. Smith, and J. N. Hood. 2006. "Improving Medical Practice Outcomes by Retaining Clinicians." *Journal of Medical Practice Management* (March/April): 1–7.

6. Landon, B. E., J. Reschovsky, and D. Blumenthal. 2003. "Changes in Career Satisfaction among Primary Care and Specialist Physicians, 1997–2001." *Journal of the American Medical Association* 289 (4): 442–449.

7. Barnard, A., and K. Tong. 2000. "The Doctor is Out." *Boston Globe* (July 9): A18.

8. Weil, T. P. 1987. "The Changing Relationship between Physicians and the Hospital CEO." *Trustee* 40 (2): 15–18.

9. Feldstein, P. J. 2005. *Health Care Economics*. 6th ed. Clifton, NY: Thomson Delmar Learning, 207–208.

10. Cohn, K. H., and M. E. Peetz. 2003. "Surgeon Frustration: Contemporary Problems, Practical Solutions." *Contemporary Surgery* 59 (2): 76–85.

11. Weick, K. E. 1993. "The Collapse of Sense-Making in Organizations: The Mann Gulch Disaster." *Administrative Sciences Quarterly* 38: 628–652.

12. Cohn, K. H., C. Scott-Conner, K. Lewis, and E. Ullian. 2006. "Collaborative Leadership at Academic Medical Centers." In *Collaborate for Success! Breakthrough Strategies for Engaging Physicians, Nurses, and Hospital Executives*, ed. K. H. Cohn, 143–153. Chicago: Health Administration Press.

13. Ashmos, D. P., J. W. Huonker, and R. R. McDaniel. 1998. "The Effect of Clinical Professional and Middle Manager Participation on Hospital Performance." *Health Care Management Review* 23 (4): 7–20.

14. Loop, F. D. 2001. "On Medical Management." *Journal of Thoracic Cardiovascular Surgery* 121 (4): S25–S28.

15. Shortell, S., T. Waters, P. Budetti, and K. Clarke. 1998. "Physicians as Double Agents: Maintaining Trust in an Era of Multiple Accountabilities." *Journal of the American Medical Association* 23: 1102–1108.

16. Wood, K. M., and G. E. Matthews. 1997. "Overcoming the Physician Group-Hospital Cultural Gap." *Healthcare Financial Management* 51: 69–70.

17. Engstrom, P. 1995. "Cultural Differences Can Fray the Knot after Physicians, Hospitals Exchange Vows." *Medical Network Strategy Report* 4: 1–5.

18. Waldman, J. D., J. N. Hood, and H. L. Smith. 2006. "Hospital CEOs and Physicians—Reaching Common Ground." *Journal of Healthcare Management* 51 (3): 171–187.

19. Phillips, K. 2005. *Hospitals Increasingly Tapping Female Executives.* Available at: http://www.nursezone.com/stories/SpotlightOnNurse.asp?articleID=12529. Accessed August 19, 2005.

20. Ocasio, W., and H. Kim. 1999. "The Circulation of Corporate Control: Selection of Functional Backgrounds of New CEOs in Large U.S. Manufacturing Firms." *Administrative Science Quarterly* 44 (3): 532–563.

21. Anonymous. 2003. "Research Notes." *Healthcare Executive* 18 (2): 42.

22. Bolster, C. J., G. Hawthorne, and P. Schubert. 2002. "Executive Compensation Survey: Can Money Buy Happiness?" *Trustee* 55 (10): 8–12.

23. Jones, W. J. 2000. "The 'Business'—or 'Public Service'—of Healthcare." *Journal of Healthcare Management* 45 (5): 290–293.

24. Schyve, P. M. 2004. "What Feigenbaum Says; One of Four Essays on 'Can the Gurus' Concepts Cure Healthcare?'" *Quality Progress* (September): 30–33.

25. Kissick, W. L. 1995. "Medicine and Management—Bridging the Cultural Gaps." *Physician Executive* 21: 3–6.

26. Wittkower, E. D., and W. J. Stauble. 1972. "Psychiatry and the Role of the General Practitioner." *Psychiatry in Medicine* 3: 287–301.

27. Waldman, J. D. 2006. "Billing Schadenfreude." *Congenital Cardiology Today* 4 (1): 1–5.

28. Aronson, D. 1996–8. Systems thinking Web site and specific pages as: www.systems-thinking.org. Accessed April 2004.

29. Atwater, J. B., and P. H. Pittman. 2006. "Facilitating Systemic Thinking in Business Classes." *Decision Sciences Journal of Innovative Education* 4 (2): 273–292.

30. Shaw, G. B. 1913. *Preface to The Doctor's Dilemma.* Baltimore: Penguin, 1954.

31. Waldman, J. D., S. A. Yourstone, and H. L. Smith. 2003. "Learning Curves in Healthcare." *Health Care Management Review* 28 (1): 43–56.

32. Waldman, J. D., and F. Schargel. 2003. "Twins in Trouble: The Need for System-wide Reform of Both Healthcare and Education." *Total Quality Management and Business Excellence* 14 (8): 895–901.

33. Waldman, J. D., and F. Schargel. 2006. "Twins in Trouble (II): Systems Thinking in Healthcare and Education." *Total Quality Management and Business Excellence* 17 (1): 117–130.

34. Ackoff, R. L. 1999. *Ackoff's Best-His Classic Writings on Management*. New York: John Wiley & Sons.

35. Arndt, M., and B. Bigelow. 2000. "The Transfer of Business Practices into Hospitals: History and Implications." *Advances in Health Care Management* 1: 339–368.

36. Waldman, J. D., and R. A. Spector. 2003. "Malpractice Claims Analysis Yields Widely Applicable Principles." *Pediatric Cardiology* 24 (2): 109–117.

37. Waldman, J. D., S. A. Yourstone, and H. L. Smith. 2005. "Learning-The Means to Improve Medical Outcomes." *Proceedings of the Decision Sciences Institute 2005*: 12041–12046.

38. Cohn, K. H., S. Gill, and R. Schwartz. 2005. "Gaining Hospital Administrators' Attention: Ways to Improve Physician-Hospital Management Dialogue." *Surgery* 137: 132–140.

39. Bertalanffy, L. 1975. *Perspectives on General Systems Theory: Scientific-Philosophical Studies*. New York: George Braziller.

40. Beinhocker, E. D. 1997. "Strategy at the Edge of Chaos." *The McKinsey Quarterly* (Winter) 1: 24–40.

41. Davidson, M. 1983. *Uncommon Sense—The Life and Thought of Ludwig von Bertalanffy (1901–1972), Father of General Systems Theory*. Los Angeles: Tarcher, Inc.

42. Johnson, S. 2001. *Emergence—The Connected Lives of Ants, Brains, Cities and Software*. New York: Scribner.

43. Kauffman, S. A. 1995. *At Home in the Universe*. New York: Oxford University Press.

44. Lazlo, E. 1972. *The Systems View of the World*. New York: George Braziller.

45. McDaniel, R. R., and D. J. Driebe. 2001. "Complexity Science and Health Care Management." *Advances in Health Care Management* 2: 11–36.

46. Waldman, J. D. 2007. "Thinking Systems Need Systems Thinking." *Systems Research and Behavioral Science* 24: 1–15.

47. Ashmos, D. P., D. Duchon, and R. R. McDaniel. 2000. "Organizational Response to Complexity: The Effect on Organizational Performance." *Journal of Organizational Change* 13 (6): 577–594.

48. Dobyns, L. 2006. *How Hospitals Heal Themselves*. Available at: http://www.managementwisdom.com/goodnews.html. Accessed September 16, 2006.

49. Cohn, K. H. 2006. *Collaborate for Success!: Breakthrough Strategies for Engaging Physicians, Nurses, and Hospital Executives*. Chicago: Health Administration Press.

50. Grenny, J. 2006. "Knowing No Boundaries: Five Crucial Conversations for Influencing Administration." *Physician Executive* 32 (4): 12–15.

51. Patterson, K., J. Grenny, R. McMillan, and A. Switzler. 2005. *Crucial Confrontations*. New York: McGraw Hill.

52. Cohn, K. H., A. H. Nighswander, J. L Dorsey, and R. B. Harrington. 2006. "The Benefits of a Structured Dialogue Process in Fostering Collaboration." In *Collaborate for Success!: Breakthrough Strategies for Engaging Physicians, Nurses, and Hospital Executives*, ed. K. H. Cohn, 1–9. Chicago: Health Administration Press.

53. Waldman, J. D., R. M. Ratzan, and S. J. Pappelbaum. 1998. "Physicians Must Abandon the *Illusion* of Autonomy...." *Pediatric Cardiology* 19: 9–17.

54. Ludema, J. D., D. Whitney, J. Bernard, and J. Thomas. 2003. *The Appreciative Inquiry Summit: A Practitioner's Guide for Leading Large-Group Change*. San Francisco: Berrett-Koehler.

55. Cohn, K. H., P. H. Araujo, and S. Gill. 2005. "Appreciative Inquiry." In *Better Communication for Better Care: Mastering Physician-Administrator Collaboration,* ed. K. H. Cohn, 24–29. Chicago: Health Administration Press.

56. Stubblefield, A. 2005. *The Baptist Health Care Journey to Excellence: Creating A Culture That WOWs!* Hoboken, NJ: John Wiley & Sons.

57. Studer, Q. 2003. *Hardwiring Excellence.* Gulf Breeze, FL: Fire Starter Publishing.

58. Weber, D. O. 2005. "Positive Deviance, Part 1." *Hospital and Health Networks.* Available at: http://www.hhnmag.com. Accessed October 9, 2005.

59. Weber, D. O. 2005. "Positive Deviance, Part 2." [Online article; retrieved 10/9/05.] *Hospital and Health Networks.* Available at: http://www.hhnmag.com. Accessed October 9, 2005.

60. Pascale, R. T., and J. Sternin. 2005. "Your Company's Secret Change Agents." *Harvard Business Review* 83 (5): 73–81.

61. Berenson, R. A., P. B. Ginsburg, and J. H. May. "Hospital-Physician Relations: Cooperation, Competition, or Separation." *Health Affairs.* Available at: http://content/healthaffairs.org/cgi/content/full/hlthaff.26.1.w31./DC1. Accessed December 6, 2006.

62. Cohn, K. H., T. R. Allyn, R. Rosenfield, and R. Schwartz. 2005. "Overview of Physician Ventures." *American Journal of Surgery* 189 (1): 4–10.

63. Cohn, K. H., and T. R. Allyn. 2005. "The Spectrum of Physician-Hospital Financial Collaboration." In *Better Communication for Better Care: Mastering Physician-Administrator Collaboration*, ed. K. H. Cohn, 12–16. Chicago: Health Administration Press.

64. Cohn, K. H., and T. R. Allyn. 2005. "When Physicians Compete with the Hospital." In *Better Communication for Better Care: Mastering Physician-Administrator Collaboration*, ed. K. H. Cohn, 17–23. Chicago: Health Administration Press.

65. Malcolm, L., L. Wright, P. Barnett, and C. Hendry. 2003. "Building a Successful Partnership between Management and Clinical Leadership: Experience from New Zealand." *BMJ* 326 (7390): 653–654. Available at: http://www.bmj.com/cgi/content/full/326/7390/653. Accessed August 31, 2006.

66. Center for Advance Palliative Care. n.d. *Continuous Quality Improvement.* Available at: http://64.85.16.230/educate/content/development/cqi.html. Accessed September 10, 2006.

67. Cohn, K., P. Batalden, E. Nelson, T. Farrell, D. Walsh, R. Dow, J. Mohr, J. Barthold, and R. Crichlow. 1997. "The Odyssey of Residency Education in Surgery: Experience with a Total Quality Management Approach." *Current Surgery* 54: 218–224.

68. Goldratt, E. M., and J. Cox. 1984. *The Goal.* Great Barrington, MA: North River Press.

69. Grout, J. R. 2003. "Preventing Medical Errors by Designing Benign Failures." *Joint Commission Journal on Quality and Safety* 29 (7): 354–362.

70. Heskett, J. L., W. E. Sasser, and L. A. Schlesinger. 1997. *The Service Profit Chain.* New York: Free Press.

71. Rucci, A. J., S. P. Kirn, and R. T. Quinn. 1998. "The Employee-Customer-Profit Chain at Sears." *Harvard Business Review* 76 (1): 83–97.

72. Zimmerman, B., C. Lindberg, and P. Plsek. 1998. Edgeware: *Insights from Complexity Science for Health Care Leaders.* Irving, TX.: VHA Inc.

73. Eagle Group. n.d. *Description of Lean Systems*. Available at: www.eaglegroup usa.com/Lean percent20MFG.htm. Accessed November 10, 2006.

74. Sterman, J. D. 2002. "Systems Dynamics Modeling: Tools for Learning in a Complex World." *IEEE Engineering Management Review* (First Quarter): 42–52.

75. Franklin, B. n.d. *Quote World*. Available at: http://www.quoteworld.org/ quotes/4954. Accessed September 24, 2006.

# CHAPTER 3

# A Seat at the Power Table: The Physician's Role on the Hospital Board

Jayne Oliva and Mary Totten

The boards of today's healthcare organizations face unprecedented challenges in the areas of quality, care delivery, financing, physician relations, and information technology. More often than not, trustees seek counsel from members who are successful corporate and civic leaders, philanthropists, and activists who draw on their personal and professional achievements to help guide and define healthcare services in communities across America. Indeed, it is predominantly the board's business dealers—and not its patient healers—who are reshaping the delivery of healthcare today.

But as guardians of patient and community health, physicians in boardrooms across America may be in the best position, if not the driver's seat, to articulate and advance clinical excellence. They bring to the table their unique vantage point, skill set, and understanding of process and protocols to help ensure that hospitals embrace and facilitate a mission of health, healing, and access for all.

To be truly effective, physicians on boards must connect their message to the organization's mission and strategic goals, as well as the legal and governance responsibilities for which the board is accountable. Understanding the nuts and bolts of governance can help physicians to more effectively translate their vision of clinical excellence into organizational imperatives and enlist fellow board members as partners to lead the charge toward accomplishing them.

This chapter provides the information and tools physicians need to ensure they are involved, informed, and engaged members of the governance team, specifically:

- Insights and Strategies to Support the Physician Trustee
- Boardroom Basics: A Primer for Physicians Who Serve

**Figure 3.1 Today's Challenges for Hospital Board of Trustees**

- Growing consumer demand for information and accountability fueled by the Internet, consumer-driven healthcare, and the publication of quality and pricing information by payers
- Growing demands from patients and payers for improved quality and safety
- The effect of the baby boomer age wave on healthcare financing and delivery
- Growth of complementary and alternative medicine
- Technologic innovation in care and delivery such as telemedicine and robotic surgery
- Treatment advances resulting from genomics and new drug treatment therapies
- Increasing demand for inpatient and outpatient services that strain capacity and resources
- Increasing costs to build needed infrastructure
- Ever-declining reimbursement
- A continued nursing shortage and predicted physician shortage
- Shifting relationships with physicians – from one of seeking cordial relations to one of market-based collaboration
- Unfunded federal mandates, such as HIPAA compliance
- Cultural competence and sensitivities in delivering care to diverse populations
- Proactively managing patients with chronic medical conditions

- How Physicians Can Maximize Their Impact on Boards
- Advancing the Clinical Agenda

## INSIGHTS AND STRATEGIES TO SUPPORT THE PHYSICIAN TRUSTEE

Physicians typically arrive in the boardroom with different skills, background, experience, and expectations than their fellow board members, who frequently hail from business or corporate environments. As William Fulkerson Jr., MD, chief executive officer (CEO) of Duke University Hospital, and Deedra L. Hartung, MA, vice president and practice leader of Cejka Search, explain, "Most non-physician executives are trained in thought leadership and are process driven, team oriented, consensus builders, and facilitative. Physicians, on the other hand, are trained to be decisive, data driven, action oriented, and more individual focused and values driven."[1] Understanding these differences, and the board's fiduciary duties and governance responsibilities, can help physicians maximize what they give to and get out of their board service.

## Who's on Board

Generally, two types of physicians serve on boards. Traditionally, most hospital boards include the chief of the medical staff, who serves in an ex officio capacity, that is, because he or she holds the chief of staff position. Some boards also appoint other physicians to represent the medical staff or key physician groups. Boards may also ask retired physicians who live in the community or physicians from outside of the hospital's service and geographical area to serve. The board's expectation for these "outsiders" is the same as those for all board members—to govern on behalf of the organization's stakeholders and in support of its mission.

## Allegiance to Mission or Practice?

Physician board members nominated by key practice groups or from within the medical staff may feel pressured to represent and advance group concerns ahead of the organizational agenda. Governance experts contend that because these physicians come from specific physician groups or organizations that often expect them to advance the group or organization's interests, they do not always vote like the rest of the board—on behalf of stakeholders and in support of the hospital's mission. A duality of interest emerges that can polarize the board and contribute to ineffective governance. In order to govern most effectively, it is important that boards clarify expectations, roles, and responsibilities for all members.

Physicians on boards face other challenges in the way of scrutiny and accountability. The Internal Revenue Service allows so-called interested persons to comprise up to 49 percent of the membership of not-for-profit, tax-exempt boards. Interested persons include employees of the organization, such as the CEO, and physicians who treat the hospital's patients or who do business with or receive financial benefit from the hospital. This "49 percent rule" only applies if the organization meets specific other requirements that show it operates for the community's benefit and not for the benefit of board members. These requirements include enforcement of a strict conflict of interest policy—a key issue for physician trustees as hospitals and physicians increasingly compete and collaborate in the marketplace—and periodic reviews of hospital activities to make sure that the organization operates according to its tax-exempt purpose. Further, if the Sarbanes-Oxley legislation that raised the bar on performance and accountability for publicly traded for-profit company boards were to be applied to healthcare, physician group representatives who serve on the board would be considered non-independent board members and would be prohibited from serving on important board committees, including the audit, CEO compensation, and governance/nominating committees.[2]

## Maximize Physician Participation

Insights into what physicians bring to the table, as well as role and responsibility clarification, can better position boards for success. To make the most of physician participation in hospital governance, Orlikoff and Totten suggest[2]:

- Clearly and explicitly distinguish the role and function of the medical staff (or other physician group) representative ("insider") on the board from that of the "outsider" physician trustee. Develop written job descriptions for each board position and use them as part of the recruitment process.
- Educate all new trustees—especially physicians—about the distinction between the roles of the insider physician trustee and the outsider physician trustee. Use the written job descriptions for both insider and outsider positions as the foundation for this part of the orientation.
- Routinely review this physician role and responsibility distinction with all board members during annual retreats and continuing education sessions.
- Educate the entire medical staff about the distinction between the two types of physician governing board members.
- Recruit physicians from outside the community or physicians who are not members of the medical staff to serve on the board. Retired physicians who are truly independent minded and removed from current medical staff politics and physician practice pressures may also be appropriate.
- Develop concrete conflict of interest policies and procedures for physicians on the board. These policies should clearly define those situations where specific physicians are in conflicted situations, as well as outline the procedures to follow when there is a tug of loyalties. Such procedures might stipulate abstaining from voting on an issue in which the physician board member has a conflict, recusing the conflicted physician during board discussions, and removing any information from the board agenda book relating to the situation or decision involving the conflict.
- Ensure that all board members clearly understand the roles and responsibilities physician members play on the board. During the full board and individual board member self-evaluation processes, include an assessment of how physician trustees are fulfilling their roles and determine if the roles are properly discharged. Use the individual assessment process and the resulting personal development plans as an opportunity to identify and address specific board needs and concerns.
- Consider developing a physician leadership academy or providing other education and support to help physicians maximize their effectiveness as board members and organizational leaders.

## BOARDROOM BASICS: A PRIMER FOR PHYSICIANS WHO SERVE

Arguably the most important strategy for empowering physicians in the boardroom and ensuring their success as valued members is to be certain that they recognize what it takes to govern effectively. The first step is to understand the organization's corporate purpose as well as the legal duties and accountabilities that flow from it.

A majority of the nation's hospitals are nonprofit organizations. According to Fredric Entin, Janice Anderson, and Katherine O'Brien, healthcare attorneys with Foley & Lardner LLP:

> Nonprofit healthcare organizations have a charitable purpose that focuses on preserving the health status of the community the hospital serves. . . . Charitable trust law in many states considers the assets of nonprofit organizations to be held "in trust" for the benefit of the communities they serve. Taken together, these laws require that the nonprofit corporation's purpose focus on the interests of the community and not on the individual self-interest of any person or group.[3]

### Varied Stakeholders

In this context, unlike for-profit boards who are accountable to shareholders, nonprofit healthcare organization boards answer to a variety of stakeholders and constituencies. Each healthcare organization must define its stakeholders, and these may differ among organizations. But, typically in healthcare, key stakeholders include patients, employees, physicians, strategic partners, and legislative and regulatory bodies. In governing on behalf of these parties, boards safeguard the corporation's best interest as legally accountable fiduciaries, making certain that the organization reasonably and appropriately deploys its assets and resources.

### Three Primary Duties

As fiduciaries of nonprofit organizations, boards must act in accordance with key legal duties that, crisply defined, encompass care, loyalty, and obedience.

- *Duty of Care*. According to Entin et al., "The Duty of Care requires board members to act in good faith and to use the same degree of diligence, care and skill that a prudent person would use in similar situations or circumstances."[3] In essence, board members must:

  - make informed decisions;
  - ask questions and request additional information if facts come to light that raise issues about the validity and thoroughness of the information the board has received; and
  - follow the business judgment rule, which releases board members from personal liability if they make an informed decision in

good faith, without self-interest, and in the best interest of the corporation.

- *Duty of Loyalty.* This duty obligates nonprofit board members to protect the corporation's business interests and decline personal gain to the corporation's detriment. Making decisions on the corporation's behalf demands that trustees act in good faith and without self-interest. The duty of loyalty requires board members to:

  - avoid prohibited conflicts of interest;
  - avoid pursuing an opportunity for personal gain that would be of interest to the corporation; and
  - uphold the confidentiality of the organization's affairs.

- *Duty of Obedience.* At times, this duty can supersede the others, calling on board members to:

  - comply with applicable laws, rules, and regulations;
  - follow the organization's mission, bylaws, policies, and procedures; and
  - act within the authority granted to the board by the corporation's articles, bylaws, and applicable laws.

## Oversight Responsibilities: From Planning to Performance

Duties of care, loyalty, and obedience provide a framework in which the governing board discharges its primary oversight responsibilities, which include:

- mission and strategic planning;
- financial health;
- quality of care and patient safety;
- CEO and executive management performance; and
- board development and effectiveness.

## First and Foremost: Mission and Strategic Planning

According to Orlikoff and Totten,[4] a strong mission forms the bedrock for effective governance. The mission defines the organization's belief system, values, philosophies, and, ultimately, its culture. It is the basis for the board's decision making, strategy formation, and policies. As stewards of the organization, the trustees' most fundamental responsibility is the mission, from which all other board responsibilities emanate.

A good mission statement guides the board through difficult decisions. The values, philosophies, and beliefs expressed in the mission serve as a touchstone for the board and help the organization realize and express its identity and purpose. The board can apply these noble and sound standards in each situation it confronts, to uphold consistent and predictable board policies that serve to integrate and align the organization's disparate stakeholders.

A clear mission also becomes the basis for a focused strategic plan. The mission establishes the parameters of the strategy, providing direction for the organization's actions. In other words, considered in the context of current market conditions, the mission should inform the strategy, and the strategy should reflect the mission.

Unfortunately, the mission statements of many hospitals are generic, bland, and not useful in determining strategic directions. Too many hospitals simply claim to be the leading provider of high-quality, cost-effective care. Physicians can take a leading role in ensuring that the hospital's mission statement is distinctive and connected to its daily activities. In addition, physicians can advocate that the process of forming and reevaluating the mission statement includes people involved in the provision of care.

Through overseeing the strategic planning process, a board can frame and address the tension between the often-conflicting demands of mission and market. Some boards may pursue a strategy that is incompatible with the mission, which leads to a jarring disconnect between the board's formal belief system and the direction of the organization's actions (the strategic plan). This inconsistency then alienates key organizational stakeholders, such as physicians, employees, patients, and payers. A pattern of erratic decisions based on circumstance rather than principle will condemn a board to profound ineffectiveness.

The strategic plan is the springboard for specific annual goals and objectives, which are tactical in nature. They detail the game plan for accomplishing, and incrementally measuring, the strategy. Both the CEO and the board operationalize these goals and requirements through annual performance objectives.

### Financial Responsibilities

Trustees are responsible for their organization's financial health and well-being. In order to discharge these duties on behalf of stakeholders, they must:

- specify financial objectives;
- make sure that management's plans and budgets align with and promote achievement of financial objectives, key goals, and the board's vision;
- monitor and assess financial performance and ensure that management undertakes corrective action to address any problems; and
- confirm that necessary financial controls are in place.

Financial objectives are the parameters for overseeing financial planning and budgeting, for assessing financial performance, and for developing needed financial controls. Financial objectives, say Dennis D. Pointer and James E. Orlikoff,[5] should answer three questions:

- What is the board's definition of financial health?
- What must the organization achieve financially to accomplish key goals and fulfill the vision?
- How should the organization assess financial performance?

Every year, the board, with help from the chief executive officer and chief financial officer, should draft quantifiable, comprehensive financial objectives that are tied to the organization's key goals and focused on achieving the vision.

Budgets are the end result of an organization's financial planning process. The board uses revenue and spending estimates as guideposts to monitor the organization's operations, cash flow, and capital expenditures. Effective trustees view budgets as management's blueprint for resource allocation to accomplish the board's financial objectives. Therefore, good boards forgo meddling in budget details and focus their activities instead on how well the dollars support organizational achievement of financial objectives.

Boards must also see to it that appropriate controls are in place to discharge the organization's and the board's financial accountabilities and responsibilities:

- Do existing accounting and information systems generate accurate and timely information for review and evaluation?
- Are financial transactions handled appropriately?
- Do financial statements accurately portray the organization's current financial status?

Boards also appoint the organization's external auditor and review the auditor's opinion and findings regarding the organization's financial condition. Determining that the internal audit function is alive and well is yet another board responsibility.

Boards use a variety of tools and processes to monitor the organization's financial well-being. Generally, indicators of financial health are selected and standards specified for each. Then the board's finance committee, along with the entire board, routinely reviews each indicator's measurements against previously established standards. If performance is unacceptable, the board asks management for an improvement plan.[5]

A financial dashboard indicator report is one tool a board can use to monitor ongoing performance. Dashboard reports measure performance over time against an established target. Typically presented in concise, at-a-glance formats, dashboards focus attention on critical performance measures linked to strategic priorities. Often explanatory notes accompany the dashboard report to help managers and trustees interpret the information.

The financial dashboard in Figure 3.2 depicts an organization's operating margin over five quarters against an annual target, and includes a revised target for the upcoming year. As shown, performance has generally exceeded the existing target, except for the most recent quarter. Questions board members might ask based on this report include:

1. Why did the operating margin so significantly exceed the established target in the fourth quarter of 2005 and the third quarter of 2006?
2. Why did the operating margin fall below target in the fourth quarter of 2006?
3. What does management anticipate the organization's operating margin to be in the next quarter?

**Figure 3.2 Sample Financial Dashboard Report**

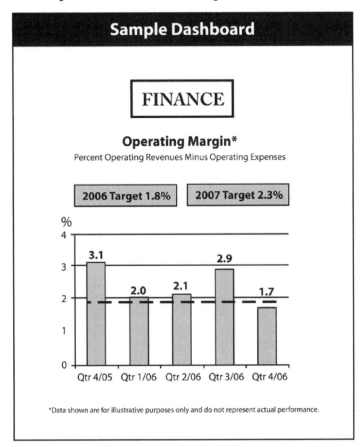

*Source:* Adapted from Kumar, S., and Carson-Martin, C. 2005. *Patient Safety and Quality Reporting for Governance: Data Reporting Guide for Hospital Staff.* Chicago: Center for Healthcare Governance.

4. If management anticipates that performance will remain below target for the next quarter, what are management's plans for improving performance?

5. What impact might current and projected operating margin performance have on the organization's ability to meet the more aggressive target established for 2007?

## Quality of Care and Patient Safety

In order to effectively discharge their responsibility for watching over quality and patient safety, governing boards need to first participate in and understand how their organizations define quality. Healthcare organizations might consider many different perspectives of quality when approaching this task, including clinician, patient, payer, hospital employee, regulatory, and public and consumer groups. However the organization chooses to define quality, the board should make certain that the needs and views of significant stakeholders take priority.

Armed with a clear definition of quality, the board can then participate more effectively in key quality oversight activities. These include credentialing of the medical staff and other licensed practitioners, monitoring the organization's quality and safety efforts, and evaluating overall performance.

Medical staff credentialing involves the appointment, reappointment, and delineation of clinical privileges for physicians on the hospital's medical staff. While the medical staff itself does the heavy lifting in terms of gathering the necessary data and information about a physician's background and performance—and formulating a recommendation for the board—it is the board's responsibility to make the final credentialing decision about each medical staff candidate. To carry out this responsibility, the board ensures that a fair and effective credentialing process exists and is based on objective criteria associated with appointing, reappointing, and delineating clinical privileges. The board can then compare the medical staff's recommendation against the criteria, and either approve the recommendation if it meets guidelines, ask for additional information, or reject the recommendation if it falls short of meeting the criteria. Because physicians play such a central role in allocating hospital resources and delivering care and service, ensuring that the hospital has a competent and effective medical staff is one of the board's most important oversight responsibilities. Physician trustees can play an important role in helping the full board better understand the credentialing process and how the medical staff makes its recommendations to the board so that board members have the knowledge and the information they need to make sound decisions.

Beyond credentialing, the board participates in upholding quality care and patient safety by deeming that systems are in place and functioning to provide performance data. Trustees must also review and analyze the effectiveness of care processes, outcomes, and use of resources against established quality, patient safety, and compliance indicators. Figure 3.3 includes examples of these indicators.

It is the board's job to assess performance against the targets set for each indicator and determine whether achievements meet, exceed, or fall short of expectations. When performance is below established standards, trustees ask managers to implement a performance improvement plan and share results with the board.

The sample radar chart in Figure 3.4, sometimes referred to as a spider diagram, is one type of report that boards can use to evaluate the hospital's quality and patient safety outcomes. This report shows a snapshot of performance at a given time across a number of different indicators. It allows board members to compare outcomes against established targets and note possible relationships among performance measures.

The outside circle of the radar chart shows the highest anticipated level of performance, the next circular line shows the performance thresholds for each indicator, and the center or bull's-eye of the chart shows the poorest performance level. The boxes depict actual performance data for each indicator.

Questions board members might ask based on this radar chart include:

1. What factors contribute to low performance in the customer satisfaction category?
2. Is it time to set new goals for areas such as staff injury, percent of registered nurses, or patient falls since performance in these areas has exceeded the benchmark?

**Figure 3.3 Sample Quality, Patient Safety, and Compliance Indicators**

---

**Quality Indicators**
- Acute Inpatient Mortality Rate

**Failure to Rescue Rate**
- Ventilator Pneumonia Rate
- Surgical Infection Rate

**Patient Safety Indicators**
- Patient Falls
- Medication Errors
- Nosocomial Infection Rate
- Birth Trauma Rate

**Compliance Indicators**
- Joint Commission Standards Compliance
- National Patient Safety Goal Compliance
- Leapfrog Group Compliance

---

*Source:* S. Kumar and C. Carson-Martin. 2005. *Hospital Patient Safety and Quality Monitoring: A Resource for Governing Boards and Trustees.* Chicago: Center for Healthcare Governance.

**Figure 3.4 Sample Radar Chart**

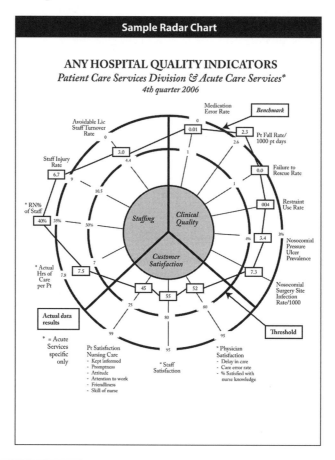

*Source:* S. Kumar and C. Carson-Martin. 2005. *Hospital Patient Safety and Quality Monitoring: A Resource for Governing Boards and Trustees.* Chicago: Center for Healthcare Governance.

3. What benchmarks do managers use to establish performance targets?
4. Is there any relationship between our nurse staffing ratio and safety metrics such as patient falls or medication errors?

## CEO and Executive Management Performance

The board fulfills most of its responsibilities through the CEO. Therefore, the board's most important relationship is with the CEO—its only direct report. David A. Bjork and Dan Fairley of Clark Consulting-Healthcare Group describe[6] the board and CEO relationship as follows:

The board's role is to develop policy, set goals, and provide overall guidance to the CEO on strategy, plans, financial management, and investments; keep the organization focused on its mission and the community's needs; promote improvement in clinical quality, patient safety, and customer service; and help the CEO maintain an effective, supportive medical staff.

The CEO's role, in relation to the board, is to identify issues needing the board's attention, set them in context, and provide information that will help the board make good decisions. The CEO should recommend or at least suggest ways to address these issues, too, especially if they require research or knowledge of financial, clinical, or technical issues.

Bjork and Fairley go on to describe the boundary between governance and management that both parties should recognize and respect:

> The board's role is more about providing sage advice than about making decisions. The decisions it makes, outside of those related to supervision of the CEO, should be limited to setting policies, goals, and performance expectations. The board should steer clear of operational and management decisions, if it wants to hold the CEO accountable for the results of these decisions. It should recognize and respect the boundary between governance and management.
> The CEO's role includes advising the board on policies, goals, and expectations, and helping the board make good decisions. But once the board has made its decisions, the CEO's role is to implement the board's policies and manage the organization as well as possible to meet the board's goals and expectations. The CEO should respect the board's primacy in defining the organization's mission, prioritizing its goals, and deciding how to best use the organization's resources to meet the community's needs.[6]

Even though this relationship is critical to board effectiveness, many boards have not given it adequate care or attention. Boards and CEOs that work well together not only understand each other's responsibilities, but set expectations for one another and participate in managing and evaluating each other's performance. Trustees must cultivate and sustain this alliance, understanding that they are responsible for:

- hiring, retaining, and, if necessary, firing the CEO;
- motivating, managing, and developing the CEO;
- evaluating CEO performance;
- setting CEO and executive compensation; and
- overseeing and participating in succession and leadership transition planning.

As Bjork and Fairley suggest, "[I]f the board accepts and acts on its responsibility to nurture this relationship, it will make the CEO's job easier, the board's job easier, and the organization more successful."[6]

## Board Development and Effectiveness

An old adage suggests that self-regulation is a hallmark of effective leadership. The only way for boards to stay ahead of the curve, especially in the current climate of heightened legislative and regulatory scrutiny of board performance and accountability, is to take responsibility for their own effectiveness.

Strong and self-sufficient boards establish and participate in a number of activities to ensure that the right people with the right skills come on board and continue to grow and develop throughout their service. Effective governance requires that boards put into place and execute sound processes for trustee selection, orientation, continuing education, and ongoing performance evaluation.

A good board is not a chance occurrence, but rather a carefully orchestrated and thoughtfully composed mix of individuals with complementary skills and competencies necessary to advance organizational goals. While some board seats are held by individuals who serve by virtue of their position in the organization, such as the CEO or chief of the medical staff, most boards select members to serve on behalf of the community and the organization's stakeholders. Productive boards develop a current profile of board membership and compare it against the organization's strategic priorities to identify gaps in skills, experience, or competencies that should be filled if the board is to further organizational success. Wise boards understand that regardless of how they select individual members, every trustee serves to meet stakeholder needs and to help the organization achieve its mission and goals on their behalf.

Boards use a variety of techniques to orient new members to the organization and their governance roles. Typically, new trustees will participate in a board orientation program that reviews healthcare issues and trends; national and local markets and competitive issues; the healthcare organization's structure and function; and the board's key roles, responsibilities, and relationships. An orientation manual can provide more depth on orientation topics and serve as a reference for board members. Some boards also pair new trustees with seasoned board and executive-staff colleagues, who act as mentors during the first year or so of service. Mentors help new trustees acclimate to the board and their governance role.

Responsible boards provide a variety of ongoing education for their members. Opportunities range from reviewing an in-depth topic at each meeting; conducting annual off-site board or leadership retreats where trustees can learn from, and network with, each other and with executive and physician leaders; and attending conferences focused on healthcare and governance issues of importance to the board. Some healthcare organizations also offer leadership development academies or similar opportunities, especially for physicians interested in assuming broader organizational leadership roles.

One of the most important ways boards can continuously improve their performance is to participate routinely in individual and full-board performance evaluation. These processes are typically survey based, to assess and discuss overall performance and to develop action plans for improvement. Most boards conduct annual full-board evaluation and action planning, often as part of a board retreat, and review individual trustee performance at least once before the member's term of service expires.

## HOW PHYSICIANS CAN MAXIMIZE THEIR IMPACT
## AS BOARD MEMBERS

While physicians are no strangers to boardrooms across America, it is true that many have traditionally and comfortably confined their roles to serving as ombudsmen to the medical staff. They survey medical colleagues and report on the need for new technology, novel equipment, and/or expanded services. When in the boardroom, they are a resource for fellow trustees, fielding questions about care quality and patient safety, and serving up a medical-staff perspective on issues of the day.

Physicians on boards, however, can play more pivotal governance roles by recognizing the benefits of board service and becoming more active, engaged members. For physicians, the opportunity to sit on the hospital's board allows them to:

- Set policy that guides the organization in care delivery on behalf of stakeholders, including physicians, patients, and the community.
- Help the board identify, clarify, and focus on the wants and needs of key stakeholders on whose behalf the board governs. Physician board members often have better insight than their board colleagues about the needs of key stakeholders, such as patients and physicians.
- Share physician and patient needs and concerns and ensure that these stakeholders have a voice at the table as the board makes decisions. Board service affords physicians a unique opportunity to leverage their expertise and make an impact that extends beyond any individual patient to meet the needs of a broader population. The board, therefore, becomes a platform for expanding the physician's capacity to do good and help others, which is why many doctors wanted to practice medicine in the first place.
- Influence resource allocation decisions in ways that maximize benefits across all key stakeholders.
- Help align physician and hospital interests by acting as an opinion leader and influence broker with both the medical staff and the board.
- Learn valuable skills about leading in a group setting that could translate to their own group practice or participation in medical society or other professional organization activities.
- Better understand the broader healthcare environment and where the advantage points and opportunities are for all providers going forward.

### Making a Contribution

Physician trustees can take full advantage of these opportunities to sway colleagues by moving out of the comfort zone and into the power seat. In this way, they can do more to rally clinical and administrative troops, direct the discussion, mediate consensus, and chart the hospital's course, which ultimately will lead toward improved community health. Indeed, there are those who argue that if physicians fail to embrace a more commanding role in the boardroom, it could prove hazardous to not only patient and community health, but in today's climate, the very well-being of the organization itself.

Fortunately, the lay members serving in today's medical boardrooms generally support a changing and more pivotal role for their physician colleagues. Board members want physician peers to weigh in and to contribute to setting the agenda on quality, retention, reimbursement, cooperation, and innovation, representing the perspective of the entire medical staff, and guiding the way toward productive change and collaboration. They understand that accomplishing the hospital's goals is dependent upon dynamic, mutually beneficial hospital-physician partnerships. And they want the physician trustee to lead the way.

### Stepping Up to the Plate

Physician trustees have the wherewithal, clout, and respect—from both boardroom and clinical colleagues—to advocate for the health needs of their communities and transform the delivery of services. Their unique perspective counts, maybe more than any other, in devising strategies to safeguard quality, foster access to care, and ensure appropriate utilization of services and technology.

Still, for all their collective insight and expertise, physician board members are sometimes guilty of falling short in a few key areas:

- Not putting aside personal views to focus on a broader organizational picture
- Not representing the needs of younger physicians or those outside their own specialty
- Not understanding the operational complexity of the organization and its facility, labor, and information technology challenges
- Not being sensitive to the burden of regulation and accreditation
- Not grasping the full picture as it relates to the needs of the community served

In fact, to help address these shortcomings, some experts advocate for more formal ways (such as developing written position descriptions) to achieve greater clarity between the roles of those physician trustees who serve in the same capacity as any other board member and those who are typically selected by the medical staff and serve ex officio (usually because they are either the hospital's chief of staff or medical staff president).

## ADVANCING THE CLINICAL AGENDA

Just as passengers would not want an airline's chief financial officer to fly the airplane, hospital trustees want the care-delivery agenda piloted by those who understand it best. Trustees appreciate that physicians are:

- orchestrators of quality and clinical performance;
- advocates for easy access and productive partnerships;
- overseers of reimbursement trends and sound finances;

- catalysts for collaboration; and
- champions for information technology applications.

By capitalizing on these strengths, physician trustees can take the lead in developing, spearheading, and nurturing a vision of clinical excellence.

Successfully advocating for the clinical agenda requires that physician trustees stay abreast of industry trends, the actions of peer institutions, and the needs of the medical staff and patient community. Because of their unique skills and perspective, physician trustees should not shrink from asking penetrating questions, clarifying the outcome that is expected, and charting the organizational course more closely, speaking out if hospitals and administrators appear to veer off track. However, no trustee, physicians included, should dictate the course of action to get back on track and/or meet organizational goals; that challenge is management's job.

There are five critical areas where physician trustees can marshal forces to make a significant difference for their hospital and community.[7]

### Orchestrators of Quality and Clinical Performance

First and foremost, the physician trustee should be the prime advocate for quality, improved patient care outcomes, patient safety, and clinical care excellence. Physician trustees and their fellow board peers should thoroughly understand, and tenaciously address, several key questions:

- What is the impact of transparency on our organization? Specifically, how will we respond to public reporting on our quality and outcome measures, what will we implement in the way of clinical improvements to stay ahead of public data releases, and where do we stand vis-à-vis payers (who need our data) and competitors (who look to capitalize on their own outcome achievements)?
- How do our patients use publicly reported data to make healthcare decisions?
- Do we participate in, or measure our performance against, national benchmark initiatives such as Leapfrog or Bridges to Excellence?
- Have we assessed, for example, if our patient volume—from routine to complex cases—meets the six Bridges to Excellence primary quality attributes: safe, effective, efficient, patient centered, timely, and equitable care delivery?
- Do quality measures include patient mortality, nurse patient index, nurse Magnet status, and patient care coordination, as appropriate?
- Does the hospital use CareMaps, best practice protocols, and clinical guidelines?

### Advocates for Easy Access and Productive Partnerships

The physician trustee is a proponent for community, patients, and providers alike. Together with fellow board members, trustee physicians must set the tone, positioning the organization as consumer-friendly, responsive to patient and community needs, supportive and efficient for employees and providers, and accessible for all. The following questions can stimulate discussion and spark action:

- Are our constituents—patients, physicians, employees—satisfied with our organization? How do we measure their satisfaction? Are our scores where we want them to be? How do we communicate, celebrate, and reward performance and leadership?
- How quickly can our patients get appointments, book surgeries/procedures, or access ancillary services?

**Figure 3.5 Orchestrators of Quality and Clinical Performance**

There are many national organizations developing guidelines to improve quality of care and outcomes. Physician board members should be aware of these groups and their guidelines and understand the impact on both the institutions they represent as board members, and on the constituencies served. Below are some thoughts to get the ball rolling:

- Is the organization up to speed on major quality initiatives (such as those from The Leapfrog Group) that include technology (Computerized Physician Order Entry), staffing ratios, demonstrated proficiency in high risk treatments, and implementation of National Quality Forum (NQF) safe practices?

- In each specialty or service area, whether for care of routine or the complex cases, is there sufficient volume to ensure staff competencies?

- Does each specialty or service have in place its own quality indicators that are benchmarked and monitored consistently, with immediate action taken for remedial interventions as indicated?

- Depending on the institution or patient venue, quality indicators may also include patient mortality, nurse/patient ratios, Magnet status, patient care coordination and patient/family communication. Where is the institution on these measures?

- Physicians should be the conscience of the board on quality care, reporting at least quarterly but preferably at each meeting on quality initiatives, outcomes, areas of strength and weakness, organizational needs to provide quality care. Do our organization's physician board members play this role?

- Physicians should be the Board's 'trainers' on quality – keeping all members up to date on initiatives by national organizations such as Leapfrog, AHRQ, CMS, IHI, and NQF. How well-prepared are our physician trustees to act as such a board resource?

- Do our non-physician board members participate in institutional quality initiatives, especially in response to a specific community need? If so, what have been the outcomes?

- Are surgeries and diagnostic testing procedures scheduled and coordinated for our patients, or must patients navigate a maze of services and offerings independently?
- Are we the provider of choice for all referral sources in our community? Do we actively and swiftly facilitate physician-to-hospital and physician-to-physician referrals?
- Do we have minimal errors and complaints? Do we take prompt action on patient, family, and referrer incidences and complaints when they occur?
- Should we adopt innovative customer service programs such as same-day appointment scheduling, patient care coordination, online history and physicals, medical record access by patients, and provider/patient email?
- Are we prepared for the increasing demands for service excellence that aging baby boomers will make?
- Is there a better way to manage chronic care by reexamining ambulatory strategies and tactics? Can we develop and implement disease management systems to screen for, and prevent, chronic disease and illness?
- What will be the direction and pace of change in our organization?

### Overseers of Reimbursement Trends and Sound Finances

Hospital management is responsible for, and usually quite savvy about, reimbursement, billing and financing. However, physician trustees must be well versed in the two major environmental trends affecting patients, providers, and hospitals alike: pay-for-performance initiatives and consumer-driven health plans and health savings accounts.

Insurers drive pay-for-performance criteria in order to tie reimbursement to quality improvement. Physician trustees can guide their board colleagues through these tough questions:

- Are we knowledgeable about initiatives among our payers?
- Against what criteria are our physicians measured, and are there additional performance measures we should anticipate?
- How can we help our providers and clinicians improve their performance?
- Are there unintended consequences of pay-for-performance plans for which we need to prepare?

Employers are leading the charge to empower employees to comparison shop and make healthcare choices based on costs and customer satisfaction. It's a fact: consumer driven health plans and health savings accounts are shifting control of purchasing decisions and dollars from insurers to patients. Physician trustees should be certain their board colleagues and the organization itself are positioned for success by asking:

- Are we ready to respond to increased consumer expectations?
- Are we set up, as an organization, to help consumers easily compare and choose our services over competitors?

- Have we ensured that expense management strategies are sound from both a quality and cost standpoint to bolster our cost-effective position?

## Catalysts for Collaboration

While the physician trustees *contribute* to the board's agenda—as orchestrators of clinical performance, advocates for access and partnerships, and overseers of finance—they should *lead* in the development of strategies to strengthen hospital/physician collaboration. Today's hospital/physician collaboration agenda has two components. The first is to redefine the rules of engagement. The changing medical landscape is forcing trustees and management to reexamine the traditional relationship between hospital and physician. Orlikoff and Totten[8] suggest that board members and physician leaders jointly consider these questions:

- What terms would we use to describe the current relationship between the hospital and physicians, and how can we achieve the relationship we want?
- How would we characterize the traditional social contract that has existed between the hospital and physicians?
- What is changing, what should we preserve in this contract, and what should we rewrite?

The second agenda is an economic and business one:

- Will our hospital partner with physicians to deliver branded services and/or facility joint ventures?
- Will the hospital offer special incentives and support for physician practices including:

  - Recruiting primary care and specialty physicians into our community?
  - Employing physicians?
  - Offering practice management services—from basics such as billing and malpractice insurance procurement, to more sophisticated offerings such as quality management/reporting and electronic medical record acquisition/support?

## Champions for Information Technology Applications

It's a wild Wi-Fi and Web-based world today, where doctors can provide care and consults off-site, from remote locations, and patients can tap into portals and pages that offer health advice and diagnostics. If trustees, physicians, administrators, managers, and, indeed, anyone connected with the healthcare organization don't speak the language or use the tools or haven't mastered the technology, it's time for a crash course. Otherwise physician trustees—as practitioners and as stewards of the organization—risk falling behind with a new plugged-in generation that will soon receive all the information it needs via cell phones.

The Partners Health Care System in Boston is one forward-thinking organization that has jumped on board the technology bandwagon. Partners has adopted five signature initiatives, each supported with information technology (IT) tools:

- Investing in quality and utilization infrastructure
- Enhancing patient safety by reducing medication errors
- Advancing uniformly high quality by comparing performance to benchmarks for select inpatient and outpatient conditions
- Expanding disease management programs by supporting activities for patients with chronic illnesses
- Improving cost effectiveness by tracking and managing utilization trends and variances

Physician trustees can make an invaluable impact as power brokers to vet their own hospital's IT initiatives from the provider perspective. These questions can help boards assess and address current capabilities:

- Where are we in introducing, implementing, and/or expanding our electronic medical record capabilities?
- Is the clinical information supporting our IT tools accurate, and up to date?
- How will our IT tools allow for improved care coordination between the hospital and its physicians?
- How will we use our IT tools to manage our costs? What is the role of our physician community?
- How will our IT tools help involve our patients in proactively managing their care and in strengthening the patient/physician relationship?
- How will we use IT to develop our own quality reporting systems to provide our stakeholders with a more robust and accurate picture of our performance than external source reporting?
- Have we adequately funded the venture to ensure that our physician community can acquire, install, integrate, and optimally utilize the IT tools?
- Have we seeded the transition from paper to electronic tools with enough capital to train physicians and staff and to provide transition support?

## COMING OF AGE

Physician trustees, as guardians, stewards, and orchestrators, are in a unique position to shepherd healthcare systems and organizations through some of their toughest medical, operational, and financial challenges to date. It's a time for setting bigger goals with broader horizons, for expecting much of self and peers, and for motivating all to make the best choices for improved patient and community health. By understanding basic board duties and responsibilities, asking the right questions, and investing in the right resources, physicians on boards can help shape a preeminent position for their organizations. The physician trustee perspective will help ensure that, community by community, American citizens will receive the best healthcare in the world.

## NOTES

1. Fulkerson, Jr., W., and D. L. Hartung. 2006. "Creating a Healthy Hospital—The Demand for Physician Executives." *Group Practice Journal* 55 (9): 41–47.

2. Orlikoff, J. E., and M. K. Totten. 2005. "Physicians in Governance: The Board's New Challenge." Trustee Workbook 3. *Trustee* 58 (7): n.p.

3. Entin, F., J. Anderson, and K. O'Brien. 2006. *The Board's Fiduciary Role: Legal Responsibilities of Health Care Governing Boards*. Chicago: Center for Healthcare Governance.

4. Orlikoff, J. E., and M. K. Totten. 2001. "The Pyramid: A Model for Effective Governance." Trustee Workbook 3. *Trustee* 54 (10): n.p.

5. Pointer, D. D., and J. E. Orlikoff. 1999. *Board Work*. San Francisco: Jossey-Bass.

6. Bjork, D. A., and D. Fairley. 2006. *Creating a Culture of Collaborative Leadership Between Boards and CEOs: A Practical Guide for Trustees*. Chicago: Center for Healthcare Governance.

7. Oliva, J. 2006. "A Seat at the Power Table: The Physician's Role on the Hospital Board." *Physician Executive* 32 (4): 62–66.

8. Orlikoff, J. E., and M. K. Totten. 2005. "The Hospital-Physician Relationship: Redefining the Rules of Engagement." Trustee Workbook 3. *Trustee* 58 (2): n.p.

# CHAPTER 4

# The Impact of Biotechnology Advances on the Healthcare System

Neil J. Campbell

Biotechnology has existed for thousands of years. When the first humans realized that they could plant and crossbreed their own crops and breed their own animals, they learned to use agricultural biotechnology. The discoveries that fruit fermented into wine or that milk could be converted into cheese or yogurt or that beer could be made by fermenting solutions of malt and hops were momentous—and practical applications of biotechnology. When the first bakers found that by adding leavening they could make a soft, spongy bread rather than a firm, thin cracker, they were developing biotechnology for useful purposes to improve their lives.[1]

The age-old adage, "Necessity is the mother of invention," has driven many advances by humankind. Nearly 10,000 years ago, our ancestors were producing wine, beer, and bread by using fermentation, a natural process in which the biological activity of one-celled organisms played a critical role in everyday life. This discovery had a profound effect on those civilizations and improved health and life when applied in positive ways. Let's take a closer look.

## PRACTICAL BIOTECHNOLOGY

In the fermentation process, microorganisms such as bacteria, yeasts, and molds are mixed with ingredients that provide them with food. As they digest this food, the organisms produce two critical by-products: carbon dioxide gas and alcohol.

In beer making, yeast cells break down starch and sugar (present in cereal grains) to form alcohol. The froth, or head, of the beer results from the carbon dioxide gas that the cells produce. In practical terms, the living cells rearrange chemical elements to form new products that they need to live and reproduce.

Bread baking is also dependent on the action of yeast cells. The bread dough contains nutrients that these cells digest for their own sustenance. The digestion process generates alcohol (which contributes to that wonderful aroma of baking bread) and carbon dioxide gas (which makes the dough rise and forms the honeycomb texture of the baked loaf).

Discovery of the fermentation process allowed early civilizations to produce foods by allowing live organisms to act on other ingredients. But our ancestors also found that by manipulating the conditions under which the fermentation took place, they could improve both the quality and the yield of the ingredients themselves.[1]

What are today's practical applications of biotechnology? Some think of developing new types of animals. Others dream of almost unlimited sources of human therapeutic drugs that one day will be tailored or personalized to an individual's genetic makeup. Still others envision the possibility of growing crops that are more nutritious, require less environmental inputs, and are naturally pest-resistant to feed a rapidly growing world population.

## THE PREMODERN PHASE OF BIOTECHNOLOGY

The term *biotechnology* was coined in 1919 by Karl Ereky, a Hungarian engineer. At that time, the term meant all the lines of work by which products are produced from raw materials with the aid of living organisms. Ereky envisioned a biochemical age similar to the Stone and Iron Ages.[2]

The premodern phase of biotechnology started in the late eighteenth century and continued into the nineteenth century. This period saw the advent of vaccinations, crop rotation involving leguminous crops, and animal-drawn machinery. The latter half of the nineteenth century was a turning point for human and animal biology and our understanding of life, death, and the nature of disease. New microorganisms were discovered, Gregor Mendel's work on plant genetics opened our eyes to the passing of inherited traits, and institutes for investigating fermentation and other microbial processes were established by Robert Koch, Louis Pasteur, Joseph Lister, and others to further this new field of science.[2] The goal was to expand this knowledge into useful, everyday applications for society.

As we neared the end of the premodern phase, we began to see more rapid development of knowledge into uses in the everyday world. This new age of biotechnology began to expand at the beginning of the twentieth century, as the convergence of industry and agriculture came together in very useful ways. This period was instrumental in setting up many of the great discoveries that would later enable the advancements of the latter half of the twentieth century. During World War I, fermentation processes were developed that produced acetone from starch and paint solvents for the rapidly growing automobile industry and for the war production effort. Industrial applications of the biological and chemical sciences were greatly studied and applied in many varied ways.

One notable discovery was the work by Alexander Fleming in 1928.[3] Dr. Fleming was working with yeast cultures at St. Mary's Hospital, now part of Imperial College in London, when he had inadvertently left the petri dishes in his lab unattended. When he returned, he found this new growth among the cultures. This growth was penicillin, which yielded an antibiotic derived from the mold. Large-scale production and distribution of penicillin was achieved in the 1940s and proved instrumental in treating infections during World War II. Penicillin became one of the most important tools in the fight against bacterial infections for many decades there after.

One other notable discovery, among many others, was the work of Oswald Avery, Colin MacLeod, and Maclyn McCarty who, in 1944,[3] demonstrated that deoxyribonucleic acid (DNA)—not proteins—was the hereditary material in most living organisms. However, the revolution in understanding the chemical basis of cell function and eventual engineering that stemmed from the postwar emergence of molecular biology was still to come. It was this phase of biotechnology that led to its recent explosive development and ushered in the modern phase of biotechnology.

## THE MODERN PHASE OF BIOTECHNOLOGY

The discovery of the double helix as the structure of DNA by James D. Watson and Francis Crick in 1953 started the revolution of what we now call the modern phase of biotechnology.[4] That work eventually led to the Nobel Prize for both men in 1962. With that seminal discovery came an amazing amount of research in the 1960s and 1970s that led to the current understanding of molecular biology and its many applications today. This notion of the double helix structure of DNA and the power of genes to control many aspects of human, animal, and plant function and health is the basis today of all pharmaceutical, diagnostic, and animal and plant research.

It is this search for understanding the genetic code and its direct implications in disease and wellness that drive biotechnology research and development and will directly impact the way healthcare will be managed and delivered for many decades to come. It is this simple-looking, but complex, genetic code system that forms the infrastructure from which all life originates and operates.

What we must remember is that biotechnology is not new. But how this technological shift is moving will be important in how we apply new logic and technology to further our understanding of life. The resulting success will be greatly determined by the applicability of the technology and its uses to the needs of society.

In the context of today's world, the term *biotechnology* refers to the modification and engineering of living organisms or their products to address human health and the human environment. Biotechnology has also evolved into many industries and converged with other nonmedical ones as well. From a modern day viewpoint, biotechnology encompasses the fields of pharmaceuticals, medical devices, and laboratory diagnostic technologies, as well as products used in basic research within companies and universities, agriculture, cosmetics/cosmaceuticals, nutrition/nutriceuticals, and nonbiologic fields like high-performance computing and information technologies.

The ability to shape and transform the genetic code or DNA started with the work conducted by Herb Boyer, Stan Cohen, and Paul Berg in the late 1960s, continuing into the 1970s.[3] These scientists discovered novel enzymes that were located in the body that would normally repair and organize DNA in a daily process. By isolating these enzymes and using them outside the body, scientists can cut the DNA like molecular scissors and piece them back together into various new structures. This process has now become known as genetic engineering, and allows us to study various forms of our genetic makeup and perform studies that can help our understanding of disease.

In the 1970s, researcher Kerry Mullis[3] was working on various ways to manipulate DNA while working as a researcher at a small biotech company called Cetus. While daydreaming during a now famous drive on California Highway 128 from San Francisco, he conceptualized and, later, invented a method whereby one could multiply the amount of DNA one started with for experiments. This process, called the polymerase chain reaction (PCR), revolutionized the ability of scientists to work with and conduct in-depth studies of processes involving DNA. Because of this seminal work, Dr. Mullis won the Nobel Prize in 1993, and the PCR process has continued to be used in every academic and industrial laboratory around the world as the gold standard for DNA amplification.

With this advancement in the biological sciences has come a responsibility to the proper use of these technologies, and the field of bioethics has grown to establish a balanced viewpoint on the use of them. All enabling technologies can have a common good when applied appropriately to society. They can also have a dark side if not properly managed and developed within ethical guidelines. The manipulation of living organisms to cause harm or death, currently known as bioterrorism, can cause widespread, horrific outcomes similar to the advent of nuclear technologies during World War II. With the international community engaged in controlling this negative use of biotechnology, hopefully we can avert any large-scale disasters. The potential of biotechnology to advance life spans, human and animal health, and our environment looms large. Many governmental and international organizations have stated that the two most life-changing industries of the twenty-first century will be the fields of biotechnology and computer sciences, and these two have and will continue to advance and converge when necessary to create many far-reaching applications for everyday life.[5]

## THE CHALLENGES OF TODAY'S HEALTHCARE LANDSCAPE

The world is becoming a much more divided place of the haves and have-nots. We see this deepening divide in real wealth of nations and the economic impact this has on every facet of daily life. The world's wealth is distributed in a very small number of countries, but these countries—where the work of biotechnology is being performed—have the potential to bring more equity to the rest of the world by making medicines cheaper and more effective and by creating better disease-management tools and better agriculture products that can thrive in the underdeveloped countries of the world. It is this aspect of biotechnology that makes the field so valuable.

Many healthcare systems of the world are nationalized and/or socialistic in nature and are stressed under the burdens of escalating costs, aging populations, and fragmented delivery of services. Providing social programs comes at a great cost to society, and the economic health of that society is directly tied to its ability to provide for itself. The "health" of a nation is both an economic advantage as well as an important piece in the national security strategy of any country.

The healthcare system of the United States is not socialistic and does not provide for universal care, but is a system of private, market-driven organizations that choose the parameters in which to deliver healthcare. We also have government-sponsored systems, like Medicare or Medicaid, that help to provide healthcare coverage to specific populations, but large cracks remain. When you have busloads of the elderly crossing into Canada to buy prescription drugs that they can't afford in the United States, something is arguably wrong.

The cost of healthcare has skyrocketed in the United States due to many factors, but two things are sure in the medium term: (1) that the system will continue to be very inefficient and fragmented with outdated processes and technologies and (2) that due to these inefficiencies and fragmentation, the system will continue to increase in costs and burden on companies and society.

Many hope that biotechnology can play a vital role in decreasing the cost of healthcare and increasing the quality of life. At the moment, biotech products have greatly improved the management of some diseases, but the cost reductions expected have not followed. For example, the biotechnology industry has developed and introduced human-engineered insulin for diabetics and human growth hormone for dwarfism. The development and use of personally tailored medicines for genetic predisposition such as Herceptin for a Her-2/Neu particular type of breast cancer or Gleevec for specific use in leukemia has made personalized treatment for particular diseases a reality, although a limited one at the moment.

Some say that the industry is just exiting its adolescence and has not been able to take advantage of economies of scale in the way products are developed. The process of development is improving, and the financial markets that provide the funding are becoming more mature and larger to support the growing industry. One thing is certain—that in order for biotechnology-derived products and services to make a substantial impact long term, they will have to be able to decrease costs and provide for more efficacious treatments that are not possible today.

One area that has seen justifiable applications is the field of agricultural biotechnology, or AgBio. Examples of more effective crop technology management include pest-resistant crops, crops that can survive the trip to market and shelf life, and crops that require less water in arid climates. However, not all AgBio advances have survived the market test. For instance, the Flavr-Savr Tomato of the 1990s was engineered to be juicy, meatier, and able to survive longer during the shipment to market. The tomatoes lasted on the store shelves longer, but people were not used to the look or consistency of the tomato and sales eventually declined until the product was withdrawn. It was a "product in search of a market"; marketers should have done customer research and then developed a product to meet those tastes. More successful have been initiatives in providing food such as rice, corn, and other staples to underdeveloped regions or regions where food crops are difficult to grow. AgBio is now a multibillion-dollar industry in sales.

Nevertheless, genetically modified foods still generate a lot of controversy regarding their long-term health impact. The Food and Drug Administration has declared that genetically modified crops are safe to eat. However, there are no long-term studies to support the overall safety of the crops. Most genetic modifications are fairly straightforward and the risk is probably very low, but in order for society to accept these products, the industry will have to be more mindful of the concerns. Society, especially in less fortunate areas of the world, needs these crops. A large amount of the criticism of genetically modified foods comes from the developed countries at the expense of the more underdeveloped ones. The debate, it should also be noted, is also as much about national economics as potential safety. The issue of American corn or rice being planted in Europe is a very economic one and can change the economic picture versus indigenous crops and revenues to indigenous companies.

## OUR CHANGING LIFESTYLES AND ATTITUDES

The other element of our present-day society is the rapid pace and multitasking nature of how we live. We are a service and information technology driven society, and with that our lifestyles have changed greatly. With technology all around us, our lives have sped up, resulting in changing diets, less exercising, more stress, and a blending of work and personal lives into one with the advent of Blackberries, computers, e-mails, and text messaging. The negative consequence is a society that is pressed to its limits and rapidly becoming less healthy and more clinically obese. It is estimated that up to two-thirds of adults in the United States are clinically obese and subject to downstream ailments like diabetes, heart disease, cancer, and physical ailments that threaten to impact the quality of life of those who will have a longer life span. These trends are seen in the majority of developed nations of the world and could be prevented to a large degree by changing our lifestyles, our diets, and with exercise.

Biotechnology can have a positive or negative effect on this issue. There are drugs in development that will turn off or inhibit the production of certain chemicals that can cause several problems that diabetics endure such as kidney, liver, heart, or eye damage. However, one disturbing trend is that many adults in the United States have stated in several independent studies that they would opt for taking a pill to prevent a certain condition or disease versus changing their behavior or diet to effect the same outcome.[4] Taking a once-daily pill for weight loss or to increase longevity are just two of the holy grails in maintaining good health that people seek. And products such as Botox (which is bioengineered botulism, or—better stated—a toxin) continue to be popular.

Not all is lost if we apply technology and, of course, some logic to the current dilemma that we face. Although the deliverables that will come from biotechnology and computational medicine will probably not slow down, we can improve how we manage these processes and provide products and services that improve our lifestyles. Many times in the development of biotechnology products, the intellectual stimulation that comes from working in a leading-edge field blinds the scientists to a point at which they do not look realistically at the consequences of the product being developed. As organizations become more professional and objective in their commercialization of research, we will see more market acceptable products reach the market, and the impact on healthcare, of course, will greatly improve. This prediction is based on observations of applied research strategies that are being adopted by both universities and commercial research organizations.

## WHAT DOES THE FUTURE HOLD FOR HEALTHCARE AND THE IMPACT OF BIOTECHNOLOGY?

Tomorrow's healthcare solutions start with today's research and development. The understanding of the mechanisms of disease and how to quantify and organize them will be one of the greatest impacts of biotechnology. This process will require the applications of computer technology along with medical technology to handle the vast amounts of data in the decision-making process needed to treat patients and their diseases.

## THE ROLE OF PERSONALIZED MEDICINE

Personalized medicine is the cataloging of various diseases and their differences in the human population from a genetic or DNA sense and applying that knowledge to predict, diagnose, or monitor the course of disease in each individual. For example, by understanding the genetic differences of two women, both with breast cancer, individualized courses of treatment can be developed, each with the same positive outcome of eradicating the disease. The question we ask now is why do two seemingly similar patients react differently to the same treatments? Some progress rapidly towards death, and others go into remission and are "cured."

We are gaining weapons in our arsenal to aid in the fight to understand disease. There are diagnostic laboratory tests that can be performed that highlight differences among women who are at risk for breast cancer and help develop distinct courses of treatment for them. Two such genetic tests—BRCA1/BRCA2 and Her-2/Neu—can identify the possible type of breast cancer and possible courses of treatment options and predict eventual outcomes for the patients. Based upon this genetic understanding, we now have a few pharmaceutical products that can treat these forms of breast cancer. Herceptin, a drug researched and developed by Genentech (one of the first biotech companies), is available to treat women with the Her-2/Neu type of breast cancer.

The notion of personalized medicine is active today in many areas, although the larger understanding and implementation is nascent. The current numbers of products are growing and are starting to take hold and should greatly impact the delivery of healthcare in terms of patient outcomes, but the jury is still out on how personalized medicine will really change medical economics for the future.

## THE INDUSTRIAL REVOLUTION OF BIOTECHNOLOGY

The large scale and automation of biotechnology research and manufacturing are becoming more factory-like; the scale of costs will decrease and the output of knowledge and value-added products will increase. These factory-like processes should speed up the understanding and commercialization of technologies by taking a systemic approach to the understanding of disease or to understanding the completeness of an organism, such as the avian flu virus or the retrovirus that causes AIDS (acquired immunodeficiency syndrome). As the costs of these applications are reduced, it will allow large-scale sequencing and testing of our genetic makeup. This will provide a profile of who we are and our possible risks for various diseases.

New approaches have begun to look at epidemiological studies of disease and their carryover of genetic traits. These new testing technologies will become more affordable in the near future and allow for us to have our profiles compared to knowledge databases of disease and potential treatment options. With new pharmaceutical drugs that are tailored to our genetic makeup, we will forego taking drugs that will not help us, or drugs that could have terrible side effects for us, or that may counteract with other drugs we already take. This approach should, over time, decrease the cost of treatment and improve long-term health.

One area that is crucial to making personalized medicine work, other than the continued research and development of the biotechnologies, is the computerization of medical records, sharing those records among healthcare organizations, and the protection of that information. Without the seamless and dynamic updating of electronic medical records, caregivers will not be able to provide the most efficient, cost-effective, and optimal choices of products and services. This knowledge and convergence with computer technologies will allow us to be proactive and manage the treatment of lifestyles and health. This proactive approach will be furthered by the Internet and its associated technologies and by a deeper understanding from biotechnology of the cause and effect of our environment and health.

## THE CONVERGENCE OF BIOTECH AND COMPUTERS

This convergence of computer technologies and biotechnology has been occurring since the early 1990s and has provided us with many current applications of designing and experimenting on an "in silico," or computer modeling, basis. Creating synthetic organisms or disease models that are generated by mathematics, supercomputers, and digital technologies have allowed researchers to model potential products with indications of disease, both in humans as well as in plants and animals. The applications range from providing expertise of specialist physicians to remote villages to assessing and monitoring current treatments for patients in remote locations like assisted living or home-based care programs. CAT (computerized axial tomography) and PET (positron-emission tomography) scans that can provide high-density imaging to find small differences over the less specific X-ray technologies have provided caregivers more tools to assess and diagnose potential diseases. Physicians and surgeons can perform practice procedures or perform specialist surgical procedures remotely via a virtual environment in geographical areas that may not be able to sustain physicians with this knowledge. The application of nonbiotechnology technologies can greatly equalize the disparities in healthcare quality and access between developed and underdeveloped countries.

The use of computer technologies have, in the end, allowed biotechnologists to experiment in a larger context than would be possible with the human body alone. The exponential growth of computing power will continue to drive the pace of biotechnology research capabilities by providing both a computational as well as laboratory approach to understanding the processes of life.

An interesting trend is the convergence of engineering technologies with biomedical applications. Biomedical applications utilizing engineering principles have spawned a whole new industry around biotechnology product materials. The development of compatible bio products that can coexist with our body is becoming commonplace. Tissue regeneration in conjunction with bionic prosthetics for arms and legs, for example, can harness the mind and electrical impulses to make these devices move. Replacement materials that allow us to grow skin and collagen for birth defects and burn victims are a very important part of biotechnology. Utilization of genes delivered as drugs (gene therapy) and the potential use of stem cells to program the body's existing cells will require both the use of biotechnology and computer technology to study the possible outcomes.

## THE WORLD OF NANOTECHNOLOGY AND ITS BIOTECHNOLOGY COMPONENT

The science is moving towards creating even smaller environments in which to operate. This need to understand how things work in real time in vivo is driving researchers to create synthetic worlds for genes, proteins, cells, and models for disease. To create synthetic, virtual bio worlds, researchers have moved to utilize the realm of nanotechnology in their biotechnology approaches. Nanotechnology is the science and resulting applications of creating and working with materials and organisms on the scale of a billionth of a meter or 1/80,000th the size of a strand of human hair.[6] The technology is being used, for instance, to formulate more efficacious and cost-effective drugs by using nanotechnology scale materials as scaffolds or delivery vehicles for drugs, to make laboratory tests more specific to the type of disease, and to ultimately create a synthetic cell for research study. These biomedical computer models that simulate a human body and its functions are called avatars, and they will allow us to model and study the course of lifestyles, environments, and progression of disease, and to conduct virtual human studies before actual clinical studies in humans. These technologies could change the nature of preclinical research and reduce or eliminate the need to use animals for prehuman testing of biotechnology products. The end goal, yet to be realized, is to make research practical, useful, and affordable.

## A PARTING THOUGHT ON THE FUTURE OF HEALTHCARE

Although there are many stakeholders that have an economic need to maintain the status quo, the current healthcare system is extremely inefficient, escalating costs to disproportionate levels that will eventually stress the system and force change. A more optimistic, but probably unrealistic, approach is to believe that the forces of this current state will naturally change how healthcare is being managed before these healthcare systems are forced to change. The more pragmatic and most probable forces of change will be these computer and biotechnology technological shifts that push the current practice of medicine towards a more personalized approach to understanding and treating human diseases. With a deeper understanding of how our biology works, we can tailor the development of products to match this targeted and specific understanding and deliver customized products for agriculture, animal, and human health.

As with any enabling technology, the long-term use of the products will come with an economically driven proposition. Only those technologies that result in cost-effective advantages for better patient care, reduced healthcare costs, and an improved ability to manage our lifestyle and health will stay the course.

A famous quote in the high technology world is attributed to the Nobel Laureate physicist, Dr. Richard Feynman: "The best way to predict the future is to invent it." This approach has yielded societal-changing technological shifts such as the automobile, electricity, powered flight, portable communications, computers, and the Internet. In all instances, the ultimate success of these inventions was the ability for society to understand their usefulness and to apply them in constructive ways. The long-term sustainability of these inventions was their cost effectiveness relative to the alternative choices.

The needs of the healthcare system of the twenty-first century will require us to realize Dr. Feynman's vision. We must develop the ability to tailor or personalize our approach to medicine and healthcare in general, which will allow future generations of healthcare providers to offer solutions to problems that could not be solved in generations past.

## REFERENCES

1. Biotechnology Industry Organization. 1989. *Biotechnology at Work*. Washington, D.C.: Biotechnology Industry Organization; Biotechnology Industry Organization. 1990. *Biotechnology in Perspective*. Washington, D.C.: Biotechnology Industry Organization.

2. Peters, P. 1993. *Biotechnology: A Guide to Genetic Engineering*. Dubuque, IA: Wm. C. Brown Publishers.

3. BayBio: The Northern California Biotechnology Association. 2004. *The History and Timelines of Biotechnology*. San Francisco: The Biotech Communications Group.

4. Watson, J. D. [1968] 1996. *The Double Helix: A Personal Account of the Discovery of the Structure of DNA*. New York: Simon and Schuster.

5. Robbins-Roth, C. [2000] 2001. *From IPO to Alchemy*. Cambridge, MA: Perseus Publishing.

6. Murphy, A., and J. Perrella. 1993. *A Further Look at Biotechnology*. Princeton, NJ: The Woodrow Wilson National Fellowship Foundation.

# CHAPTER 5

# Healthcare Informatics: The Intersection of Information Technology and Care Delivery

## Edwin E. Lewis, Jr.

Informatics is the application and use of computing technologies that assist an organization in meeting its business objectives. As with anything that involves computing, those technologies are never dormant, and the only constant is change. Whether the technology is found in the computer hardware or the software that runs on it, it will change. This chapter addresses some of the key premises associated with deploying and using information technology (IT) systems to improve the quality of healthcare. This chapter is not meant to be a comprehensive treatise of the topic, but instead focuses on some concepts and pitfalls that IT professionals in the area of healthcare often face. Along the way, it will also address cost and design drivers that if not identified as a project begins, will almost certainly result in a cost overrun. The intent of this chapter is to help the IT professional be successful in a difficult and challenging market segment.

Healthcare C-level executives must maintain their roles and responsibilities to identify and implement strategy, as with any organization. In healthcare, those C-level executives must also work closely with their physicians and medical staff to assist in the identification of those strategies. This chapter also provides guidance and insight into some of the areas in which strategic implementation of healthcare services can be enhanced through the implementation of IT.

## DEFINING MEDICAL INFORMATICS

The business objectives of most healthcare organizations are focused on both patient care and operations management across all aspects of their operations. From a care delivery perspective, these objectives may cover issues ranging from the reduction of mortality rates in an intensive care unit (ICU) to effective decision support and drug-interaction management. From an operational management perspective, goals would include items such as capturing billable costs at the conclusion of each patient encounter to minimizing the administrative work required of nurses to reduce turnover and recruiting costs. The application of IT in healthcare and the management of the data contained therein, or medical informatics, is an area in which exceptional benefits are possible.

Medical informatics is defined as "the application of computer technology to all fields of medicine—medical care, medical teaching, and medical research."[1] This definition is broad and implicitly addresses related topics that include the use of the applications by healthcare and the management of the information created, collected, or processed. A broader definition is "the intersection of information science, medicine, and healthcare. It deals with the resources, devices and methods required to optimize the acquisition, storage, retrieval and use of information in health and biomedicine. Health informatics tools include not only computers but also clinical guidelines, formal medical terminologies, and information and communication systems."[2] There are many aspects of this definition that have significant implications to the application of IT to medicine.

### Improving the Quality of Care

A primary goal, if not the ultimate goal, of most healthcare practitioners is the delivery of quality patient care that expedites healing, lessens pain, and promotes the general health and well-being of their patients. To achieve this objective, technology has a major role to play. In the current areas of medical research and development, the profession of medicine is changing at a rate greater than any time in its history. Changes resulting from research in genetics, medicine, and environmental research all are leading to a vast improvement in treatments and protocols available for use. The need for systems that effectively provide decision support, drug-interaction alerting, or simply speed the delivery of lab reports to the requesting physician are subsets of problems that could be solved with the application of technology. They are needed to improve patient care.

### Managing Healthcare as a Business

A major element of management in healthcare is the confluence of the methods and processes to use the underlying information systems. For many healthcare organizations, the management of IT across departments and care provider organizational specialties has been restricted by artificial silos of bureaucracy, whose boundaries are defined by the business objectives of each department. Although many organizations have had some successes in collaboration and integration between departments, for the most part, these efforts have been limited in scope and proved difficult to achieve due to financial and regulatory constraints.

### The Progression of Technology

In medicine, the application of IT as a means to improve patient care and organizational performance has become recognized as an achievable objective for most healthcare organizations. Though intuitive, the economic realities of healthcare organizations—in terms of income to invest in these new technologies, the price of those technologies, and the related issues with deploying and then using them all—have resulted in a slower deployment of technology as compared with deployment occurring in other industries. At present, the price of the hardware continues to drop; applications and the systems that run on those platforms are becoming more capable, and, most importantly, early adopters of the technologies are beginning to realize true gains in efficiency, which are being communicated across the industry.

Organizations have seen the reported benefits, so there are compelling reasons to examine the use of the technology to meet each organization's objectives. With quantitative proof, most organizations are now examining solutions and planning to deploy pilot projects to take advantage of the more recent advances in IT within the medical field.

## HEALTHCARE INFORMATICS PROJECTS AND REQUIREMENTS

A successful project is defined as one in which the end solution or product performs as required, is delivered at estimated cost, and meets the agreed upon schedule. Unfortunately, IT project success rates, those meeting all three criteria, are only as high as 49 percent, as reported by *Software* magazine.[3] It should be noted that this statistic represents a 15 percent increase in performance over the preceding 10 years. By any standard, this is an abysmal success rate. In healthcare informatics projects, though the types of stakeholders may be different from those in other organizations, the issues that are faced by the project teams are the same.

In this section, we begin to address some of the more fundamental issues of IT management and introduce some concepts that a typical manager in a healthcare IT environment would expect to encounter in establishing project priorities, based on alignment with organizational objectives and identifying all aspects of the requirements of a project. Though not exhaustive, it should provide the reader with a basis of reference in moving forward with a project.

### Project Alignment and Requirements Identification

Aligning a project with an organization's strategic goals and objects is usually key for it to survive through implementation. Alignment with those goals can help achieve long-term commitment by the sponsors through their continued funding. In addition to alignment, correct and complete requirements need to be identified to ensure that the expected benefits from that project are fully realized. Each of these elements is a key starting point for any successful project. The field of healthcare is no different.

In the general area of planning IT implementations, it is critically important to fully understand, define, and then document the problems that need to be solved prior to the initiation of any project. This includes understanding each problem's interdependencies with different influencing elements, both within and external to the organization. An effective problem analysis cannot be done successfully without considering contributing factors to the problem. As an example, a high nursing staff turnover rate in an ICU may not rest solely with the stress of caring for patients in that unit. Contributing factors may include patient density (bed count), physical layout of the floor (distance between room and the nurses station), support resources, patient-related paperwork, outside competition, or simply a bad supervisor.

To solve a problem, you have to understand it and all of its contributing elements. The risk of not doing this in the field of medical informatics is not just getting the solution wrong and realizing it after the project has begun (along with all of the career damage). In doing so, you will also most likely incur significant costs for the technology and its implementation in the process.

Unfortunately, many organizations, regardless of industry, fail to address these criteria before moving forward with a project to solve a problem or to take advantage of an opportunity. As often happens, unstructured analysis of either a problem or opportunity may lead to less than desirable outcomes. As such, several approaches have been identified within the consulting industry and in project management organizations that can assist a manager in meeting these objectives. These approaches build frameworks that can support the needed analysis.

In the current areas of IT project management, two general approaches are usually suggested by consultants and industry experts. These approaches are the Balanced Scorecard (BSC) and Information Technology Integrated Library (ITIL). In the BSC approach, IT organizations focus on strategic alignment with organizational goals and objectives. The second of these, ITIL, usually focuses on a micro analysis of the IT environment and the comparison of the specific industry's best practices with those practices currently in place and used by the organization. The effectiveness of each methodology usually depends on the goals being sought and, perhaps of greater importance, the skill of the individual(s) performing the data collection and assessment. Therefore, it is important to recognize this need to engage skilled, and where possible, experienced resources in either analytical undertaking.

### Balanced Scorecard

A BSC framework is designed to bring focus and clarity to measure an organization's success in moving towards and reaching its strategic objectives. Robert Kaplan and David Norton (of the Harvard Business School) created the BSC in the early 1990s as a measurement approach to facilitate strategic management.[4] The BSC has gained recognition because it approaches an organization's operations from a holistic (balanced) and strategic manner. This approach contrasts with the more common reality of an organization being run through vertical silos of operational management.

In healthcare, physician practices or hospital departments tend to work as individual operational units. As an example, the chief radiologist seeks an additional modality to perform advanced magnetic resonance imaging system that operates at 3 Tesla. The argument supporting this acquisition is that the technology will enhance imaging resolution associated with studies that seek to identify small malignancies such as those found in the brain. Medically, this is a sound capability that could benefit the organization in diagnosing those conditions. Strategically, this may or may not align with the goals of the facility. Questions of alignment could be as simple as, "Does the facility perform services that could fully utilize this type of system as opposed to the two less powerful systems purchased last year?" or, "How does this proposal coincide with the goals of the chief of surgery or the chair of the oncology department? Will they use it, and if so, at what rate?" The answers to these types of questions can determine if there is an alignment with the acquisition of this modality and with the overall goals and objectives of the facility. This may address the medical aspects of the acquisition, but there are other elements that should be addressed as well. These would range from financial commitment and return on investment (ROI) analysis to questions regarding the structural soundness of the flooring where the new system would be installed.

Within an organization, multiple activities affect the ability of an organization to operate effectively. The BSC approach looks at the overall management objectives, as defined by their vision and strategy, and how the organization is moving to achieve each one. It segments the management of the organization into four general areas or perspectives: Learning and Growth, Internal Business Process, Customer, and Financial perspectives.

1. Learning and Growth—This perspective addresses the need for continuous education in the staff of the organization to enhance corporate objectives. This would include changing cultural norms such as moving away from a silo-based knowledge structure and replacing it with integrated objectives and jointly developed solutions across departments.
2. Internal Business Process—This area is designed to determine how well businesses are running using metrics and objective data analysis. The goal is to monitor strategic-based processes and ultimately ensure that those processes that are in place are repeatable so that consistent results can be achieved. Strategic processes are difficult to monitor quantitatively due to the nature of the activities surrounding them. As an example, a strategic budget development process may be arduous and difficult, yet still generate excellent results. The outcome is more qualitative than quantitative. Repetitive processes, such as posting accounts and system reconciliation, may be more conducive to quantitative measures, such as the number of errors in posting, or the duration of time to perform reconciliation.

3. Customer—This perspective focuses on meeting the needs of the customer, both internal and external. Items such as patient satisfaction with meal service may have more visible metrics than those associated with mortality rates, yet both certainly are concerns of external patients. Internal customer satisfaction is of equal importance. Items such as the timeliness of lab reports, decision support, patient access, or any number of other issues could fall into this category, making the need for sharing data more important.

4. Financial—This perspective is based upon the conventional use of timely and accurate financial reporting. As such, objectives in this area would include the distribution of information in a timely manner. Monthly financial reporting may be acceptable in some areas, while in others, such as IT project management, they would not meet the needs for short-duration projects with tight budgets. In such cases, daily cost reporting may be required.[5]

As with any organization, the existing segmentation of each perspective may be difficult to fully identify and manage, because each perspective will cross multiple departments within the organization. This requires significant coordination between departments and the integration of like objectives. All departmental management must be in agreement with the approach that will be used to meet the organizational objectives. Within each of these perspectives, departments would also be expected to develop metrics, collect data, and analyze their ongoing operational results both within their department and in their support of other departments in meeting those objectives. From a manager's perspective, it becomes incumbent upon them to understand all aspects of each measurement, in that each manager's organization's performance will be rated by those measures. In areas where objectives are not being met and gaps exist, each department would participate in the development of projects that would either close or at least narrow those gaps.

Objective analysis may be difficult to obtain using existing resources, because those resources may accept what they currently do as optimal and changes to processes that they own could create problems for them. These problems may range from physicians and staff simply being uncomfortable with the changes being proposed to optimizing a care delivery process that would eliminate their own job or the jobs of their friends and coworkers. Care should be taken when selecting resources for this activity.

### IT Integrated Library

In the second framework, establishing the efficiency of an organization's IT department is key. Collecting data and then performing a comparative analysis establishes both an organization's current IT posture and, perhaps of more importance, it identifies where the organization needs to be. Once the gaps are identified—and the organization's industry best practices are reviewed and validated as acceptable to the organization—an implementation plan can be developed and an estimate proposed, approved, and funded. To move forward with a project that has a high probability of success, the organization should know where it is and where it needs to be, what it has to do, when the project needs to be done, and/or what the project manager has to do to complete the project. Most successful program managers will recommend that this final point be aggressively addressed in any IT effort. This approach is the most efficient way to minimize scope creep (growth of additional requirements that must be met and that are usually not funded).

The ITIL was developed by the Office of Government Commerce and the IT Service Management Forum in the United Kingdom. It was designed to promote the best practices developed within an industry (or industry segment). It consists of formal papers prepared by industry experts that document those best practices.[6] ITIL has emerged as one of the leading techniques to drive IT projects from concept to postdelivery operations and support. It addresses five major elements within the scope of IT services: Business Perspective, Service Delivery, Service Support, Information Communications Technology (ICT) Infrastructure Management, and Applications Management.[7] These service elements, whether under an ITIL structure or other similar monikers, such as COBIT[8] or ISO/IEC 20000,[9] are required for the department or, at a minimum, the service offering to be successful.

1. The Business Perspective of IT services—This is the functional requirement to maintain a liaison role between the business needs and the translation of those needs into formal requirements that can be met. (The difference between a requirement and a need may be confusing. As an analogy, an individual purchases a three-eighths inch drill bit because he needs it to drill a three-eighths inch hole. The hole is the requirement.) Establishing a clear dialogue and documenting what is really needed and what is required to meet that need are key objectives of this role. Assigning individuals with the technical and communication skills is very important to complete this function. In healthcare, this usually requires people who can discuss both the medical requirements for information flow and access as well as the ability of the IT community to deliver those needs.

2. Service Delivery—The service delivery element identifies the services required to provide adequate support to the business concern. In a hospital, the service delivery element is usually a jointly managed functional element requiring the support of the medical staff, administration, and the IT departments. It cannot be emphasized enough that the participation of these three groups is critical in the successful delivery of IT services.

3. Service Support—Interconnected with service delivery, service support seeks to ensure that the services needed by the business elements of the organization are being met. This is also a joint function across all elements within the organization. The separation of service delivery and support becomes more important as the organization becomes more

reliant on IT to conduct operations. As organizations become larger, it becomes incumbent on management to ensure that both the requirements for services are understood and that the delivery of those services are meeting those requirements. Since the requirements often change with medical technology, these elements are never fully complete.

4. ICT Infrastructure Management—This element refers to the management of the IT resources associated with the operation of the IT department. This specifically addresses the management of the network services aspects of the firm (e.g., wireless network management), the operations of the IT systems (e.g., ICD9 claims processing), the management of those systems (e.g., both operating system and application patch management), and the local processes needed to efficiently execute those management services so that consistency and repeatability are achieved.

5. Applications Management—The element addresses the applications used by the organization and matches the changes associated with them and the business process changes that are implemented to facilitate their use. As an example, the use of a computerized provider order entry (CPOE) solution with charge capture and decision support should change the way physicians and caregivers conduct patient encounters. The changes in business operations as a result of the use of that application must be addressed to optimize its benefits.

The ITIL framework provides a clear and concise structure that requires each element to be addressed on an ongoing basis. To optimize competitiveness within an industry, ITIL requires that *specific* practices need to be obtained and used for comparison purposes. The ITIL solution base is significant, but may not have readily available solutions that match the specific or unique needs of an organization. To gain that knowledge, an organization may need to bring in outside resources.

When reviewing framework processes for use in a healthcare environment, it is important to remember that three decision makers need to be won over before making a final decision. First, the physician or caregiver needs to provide support to the methodology. Healthcare professionals are experts in what they do and are often disinclined to depart from their own operational doctrine. A nonstandard treatment may open them to professional liability should it fail. Therefore, care providers tend to be cautious in adapting new methods or processes. It is important to gain their commitment on these types of efforts.

Second, administrators, who usually control the funding, may need to be persuaded that the cross-organizational commitments of time and money are worth the investment. Additionally, they will also be able to direct the various department heads to support the initiative.

Finally, there is the IT department. It is at the end of the approval chain and is usually responsible for some aspects of the deployment or at least operational support of the end solution. IT can seldom say no to a project and must find technical solutions to meet operational requirements. In many cases, resources are thin, so those needed to support a framework implementation should be recognized.

A healthcare-based BSC or ITIL solution is a disruptive influence to an organization and should be managed accordingly. One must recognize that these methodologies for alignment and requirements analysis help facilitate the development of a medical informatics project. However, the proper alignment and understanding of a project's relationship with the strategic objectives of a firm and the full understanding of the requirements that need to be met are required for any project to be successful.

### Meeting Healthcare Delivery and Business Needs

The delivery of healthcare services combines two elements. First, it requires that the caregiver have preexisting knowledge of healthcare and its delivery. The second element is the ability to obtain patient data. Patient data is usually obtained in two general ways. The first is for the caregiver to access historical data on the current patient. Historical data, or a patient's medical history, is key to optimizing effective treatments in the current encounter. A caregiver needs to have an understanding of any preexisting conditions, the patient's current care being delivered by other providers, current medications being taken, drug allergies, care preferences, family history, and other historical data.

The caregiver must be able to access that data rapidly. In an average primary care practice, most physicians will spend between 8 and 12 minutes during an in-office patient encounter. In such an encounter, the physician may spend up to two minutes reviewing the paper chart (which was updated by the patient in the waiting room and the nursing staff just prior to the patient being led into an examination room). After a brief greeting, the patient is asked about medications that he or she is taking, other doctors he or she is seeing, and so forth, and the physician spends one to three minutes discussing with the patient why he or she is there. Next, the physician will spend two to five minutes performing the actual exam and either diagnosing the problem or calling for additional tests to collect additional information. At the conclusion of the visit, the physician discusses the recommended treatment with the patient, writes prescriptions, schedules a follow-up, or otherwise concludes the encounter. Prior to the next encounter, the physician will also write any final notes and provide billing instructions. This process allows a physician to see approximately five to seven patients an hour.

In this scenario, there are multiple areas for problems to occur during the early stages of the encounter and at the end of the encounter where applied technology can help. Both cases involve accessing data and updating data. Early in the encounter, a patient may fail to disclose all other doctors that he or she is seeing, medications that he or she is taking, or any other number of things. The physician may also have failed to thoroughly review all the pertinent information contained within the patient's record. (Consider that some older patients may have paper records roughly the size of a small town phone book.) Should either the patient or the physician miss any aspect of the initial data disclosure/collection process, problems can occur with the delivery of healthcare services. Automated drug interaction and alerting systems, electronic medical or health record systems, and decision support may minimize some of these issues.

At the conclusion of the encounter, the physician must document a diagnosis, update the chart, and prepare the billing information. It is during this period that the physician answers questions, returns phone calls, and tries to coordinate the next series of encounter activities. During this phase, significant losses of revenue frequently occur as a result of the physician not recording all billable activities during the encounter. Studies indicate that applying charge capture technology to address missed billings may generate additional revenue generation exceeding $100,000 per physician.[10] As a caveat to such statistics, revenue generation can depend on many factors, ranging from the diligence of the physician to the extent of his or her workload. A busy physician may first focus on care delivery, updating patient diagnostic and treatment data before addressing billing information. In a busy office, billing may be the last element that is addressed, and as such, details relating to charge capture may be missed.

Similar problems exist throughout healthcare. The use of technology can improve the synchronization of objectives between the clinical and the business goals.

### Availability and Reliability

In healthcare informatics, system availability has to remain a primary concern. A key requirement of any solution is to provide information when it is needed and in a consistently reliable manner. This is true if the system is collecting data, such as in a patient monitoring system, or if it is accessing data, such as an electronic medical records (EMR) system. To achieve reliability, both technological and system-use conditions must be met. Fortunately, the technology to do this has matured beyond the mainframe realm and is now readily available across most network and server products at an affordable cost.

Many current servers are designed to run multiple hard drives that can be configured in redundant arrays to provide internal data availability through redundancy. Servers commonly have dual power supplies with automatic failover, controllers, and cooling fans. Multiple network devices, such as switches and routers, can usually be configured to run in redundant fashions. The software to manage many of these configurations is available, at no additional cost, with the operating systems. Though such software is not necessarily the best, these no-cost applications are available and have driven down the cost of the higher end applications.

Of equal importance is the daily operation and management of these systems. IT staffs with the skills needed to maintain healthcare systems are often difficult to obtain or retain. Due to the wide variety of skills that are often needed, multiple individuals are usually required to support a complex environment. When considering the overall scope of a project, staffing requirements to support reliability and availability need to be considered as part of the overall project plan.

As a caveat, some aspects of some systems can only be maintained either by, or under, the supervision of the original equipment manufacturer (OEM). In some cases, systems have Food and Drug Administration (FDA) approval, which is contingent upon a set configuration being maintained when the system is in use for care delivery. The installation of an unapproved patch may cause serious problems or introduce failure points into the system. As an example, several electronic medical record system manufacturers use highly customized Microsoft Windows operating systems as the base operating system. Using a standard patch or upgrade directly from Microsoft will most likely cause problems, or in a worse case scenario, a system failure. In such circumstances, the maintenance and support costs from those OEMs can be significant, and as a manager, these requirements should be considered as well.

## Confidentiality of Data

In healthcare, a primary regulatory requirement is to ensure the privacy of health records. Specifically this regulation requires the protection of personally identifiable (protected) health information (PHI)—codified within 45 CFR (Code of Federal Regulations) Parts 160 and 164 and commonly referred to as the Health Insurance Portability and Accountability Act (HIPAA). To clarify that statute and some of the earlier rulings in this area, the Office of Civil Rights within the Department of Health and Human Services (HHS OCR), which is responsible for the enforcement of HIPAA, has issued numerous guidelines, most recently in December of 2006, for controlling access to and the use of PHI in electronic form (EPHI). The protection of this data remains problematic. In late 2006, a Veterans Administration employee had his laptop stolen, which contained 1.8 million patient records. In early 2007, a leading medical institution on the east coast had 80,000 records possibly misplaced when backup tapes were mishandled by a subcontractor. The Medicare contractor for the state of Georgia reported a similar loss of the names, addresses, and social security numbers of 2.6 million beneficiaries. There are numerous other examples of these types of loss of data, each creating liabilities to the institution or organization.

In terms of HIPAA, the dissemination of PHI in any form is managed by three guiding principles: treatment, payment, and operations (TPO). Treatment refers to the delivery of care. Payment refers to exchanging information in sufficient detail to facilitate payment or related accounting activities. The term *operations* refers to all aspects of an organization's operational environment (excluding direct patient care), ranging from room assignments to quality assurance work.

Under these conditions, PHI may be shared. If TPO is not present, then the PHI data must be kept confidential and protected from access by all unauthorized individuals. This would include those individuals with similar roles and responsibilities. The bottom line to this regulation is that if it is not a specific physician's patient, then that physician cannot have access to that patient's information.

### Segregating Duties

In the area of business operations, it is good business practice to separate the responsibility of entering invoices into the system from the responsibility of writing checks to pay those invoices, in order to prevent embezzlement. This same separation of responsibility should be extended into the IT department. In IT security, there is a similar principle used as a basis for granting access to a system, referred to as least-privileged access. This means that only the absolute minimum rights needed for that user to do their job and only their job are granted. To illustrate this concept, there is no need for an administrative file clerk to have database administrator (DBA) privileges to process ICD9 claims. A DBA would normally have the ability to make significant changes to a database, whereas a file clerk would not normally have the skills to perform that level of activity nor ever need to in their capacity. The file clerk's user account should have fewer privileges that the DBA's user account.

To implement this concept, IT administrators manage most large systems using what is referred to as role-based access, which controls who may use their systems and when.[11] Role based access has some distinct advantages over granting access to individual users. With this type of approach and continuing the previous example, all file clerks with similar job assignments would be granted user accounts with the same rights because their job role is the same. Therefore, all clerks would be able to access the same data entry screens, get the same reports, and access the system in the same manner. They would have the least amount of access needed to allow them to perform their jobs. This system ensures that access is consistent by job role and avoids having to apply the same individual or group of rights to each individual's account, one at a time (which would increase the probability of errors). Role-based access control is a cost-effective and efficient approach to applying access rights to a system.

Unfortunately, the regulations associated with HIPAA do not easily allow for all physicians within the same role to have the same access to all records. If PHI access were configured this way, it would violate the TPO rule previously discussed. Older electronic health or medical record system designs may not have the capability to segregate access based on assignment; those systems were usually designed to work on a general role-based access model. Newer systems provide such access control granularity, but may require more manual activity to assign a physician to each patient or will need to integrate into the staff scheduling on-call systems or patient check-in systems.

There are three approaches to addressing the problem of access control. First, some aftermarket solutions are available that provide more capable access control; these may be implemented and installed external to the data management systems (i.e., electronic medical records, radiological information system). The integration of these systems may be complex and expensive. The second alternative is the introduction of newer data management systems, which can be installed either through conversion or upgrades that provide these capabilities. These systems will often meet the confidentiality and segregation requirements, but can be disruptive during the implementation and ramp up periods. The third alternative that many organizations implement is to set policy and procedures prohibiting the unauthorized access to patient records and rely on manual spot-checking for enforcement. Though not efficient, many organizations consider this approach adequate in view of the lack of aggressive enforcement by HHS OCR. However, there are risks to the organization if strict access controls on key systems are not applied.

### Integrity of Data

Integrity of data specifically addresses the unaltered quality of the data that is both at rest (that is, written to a file or hard drive) and used by end users and other systems. Data that is to be used for any reason must be accurate and not altered from its originally accepted format. Data is collected from various sources and may be entered into a system either manually or automatically by the collecting sensors or probes.

Clinical systems, such as electrocardiogram monitors, have the ability to connect to a central repository for posting patient information. Additionally, record-creation work associated with a new patient is usually entered manually into EMR systems. In other cases, the raw data, such as that derived from a blood test, may be processed to some degree prior to its being posted for use by the caregiver. There are multiple data samples taken from a specimen prior to a specific result being calculated or determined, to ensure that the results are consistent prior to using a single determination as a basis for treatment. The caregiver is most interested in the postprocessing data and not necessarily how those results were determined, so long as an approved protocol was followed to develop them.

Once the data is collected and loaded into a record system, controls and safeguards must be implemented to ensure that the posted data is not altered without authorization and that any alterations be documented. Authorization is usually accomplished through the use of aggressive controls on data and system access, turning on system and application audit logs (which are default capabilities found on most database applications), and establishing procedures to ensure that the logs and configurations are aggressively and consistently monitored. Additionally, both incident management and sanction policies are developed and used in support of the monitoring activity.

## INFORMATICS APPLICATIONS FOR HEALTHCARE

Informatics in healthcare is focused on improving patient health and quality of care and achieving operational efficiency across the organization. As with many industries, there are unique requirements and challenges in implementing technologies to solve the specific problem areas within healthcare. In this section, some of the basic solution areas will be identified and their uses discussed.

It is important that the reader understand that there are certain parameters that constrain the use of these products, both within a department and across an organization. First and foremost, these products are available from a wide range of vendors and vary from a single application to a suite of integrated applications. More often than not, healthcare organizations will select and implement solutions from different vendors. Since these solutions are different and may not be built using compatible standards, they may not readily work with other existing products currently in place, even from the same vendor. Additionally, any specific solution should not be expected to solve all of the problems faced within that department or across the entire organization.

The core challenge is that the use of a specific application, without its customization, will almost certainly require the department or organization to adapt its processes to accommodate the functionality provided by the application. Conversely, the customization of any application can usually be achieved by incurring development costs as well as some level of compromise in terms of performance, heuristics, and/or functionality. This problem is not unique to healthcare.

In the late 1980s, SAP introduced some of the first enterprise resource management and enterprise resource planning (ERM/ERP) solutions available. This industry has grown significantly, with other software manufacturers entering this space (such as Oracle and Microsoft), and in doing so, the products have significantly matured. With that maturation, the benefits of a fully integrated ERP/ERM solution are generally recognized, but the problems of integration and customization remain. This, in turn, has driven an entire consulting industry to develop skills in this area. Firms such as IBM, CSC, EDS, and Accenture, as well as some others, all have mature and capable practices in ERP/ERM consulting.

In the healthcare market, the potential customer base is estimated to be less than 20,000 for large deployments. Unfortunately, part of that base is barely financially viable and therefore cannot make the investments needed for a fully integrated system. The common alternative for these organizations is to procure stand-alone systems and worry about integration later. Additionally, the overall healthcare product market is less mature, comparatively speaking, to the nonhealthcare market, which means that many of the existing applications do not integrate well with others. Additionally, the integration tools and solutions themselves are not always as mature as they are in other industries. As a result, healthcare applications tend to be less than fully integrated with other applications. This situation has created a market for upgrades and many software developments, and consulting firms are aggressively moving into this space.

In this section, the basics of each general class of healthcare applications are presented. In terms of basic functional requirements, each system must be easy and intuitive to use, be capable of supporting high availability with reliability, and be secure in its design, deployment, and use. It should also be noted that as technologies evolve and newer products reach the market, the functionality described will evolve as well.

## Clinical Systems and Monitoring

Clinical systems are specifically designed for collecting and monitoring patient data and then presenting it in a cohesive manner. The collection of the base data, that which is populated in the system for a specific patient, may originate from a wide range of sources. These sources would include patient clinical history (previous lab work, etc.) and current data such as pulmonary and cardiac data that is collected and recorded in real time or close to real time. The focus of these systems is to provide the caregiver with accurate and timely data on the patient's conditions based on the assumption that timely data improves the quality of care. In most healthcare organizations, patient care and patient status are monitored during rounds performed by the various physicians and nurses assigned to the patient. Charts are updated when an encounter occurs. If the patient load for the floor is properly sized for the staff available and on duty, rounds occur regularly and the data collected should be accurate as of the time of the encounter. In many cases, comprehensive patient data collected during and between encounters could yield beneficial information that would facilitate treatment regimes. In such a situation, a clinical system that records information from the patient's various monitoring systems and identifies anomalous readings within a database or alerting system in real time would be very advantageous to the delivery of care. Unfortunately, in most organizations providing in-patient care, there are ongoing problems with this scenario that result in interruptions of regular rounds.

The actual source of the data will vary depending on the clinical applications and the type of care being delivered. As an example, an ICU clinical system may need to collect data from real-time monitors as opposed to historical data used in an outpatient wellness center.

### Decision Support Systems

The concept behind the development of a decision support system is based upon the presumption that a tremendous amount of information is available to caregivers when treating a patient. The key premise is that there is potentially so much information available that options may be overlooked, or simple mistakes in the delivery of care could be made as the result of incomplete information. Patient information drives the selection and delivery of specific treatment protocols. Therefore, details of the success or failure of previous treatments for a specific patient, ranging from effectiveness to side effects, should be examined and understood prior to delivery of specific care. For referential purposes and from an IT perspective, this information may require both data collection on treatment results as well as detailed analysis of that data for care protocol reviews and enhancements.

The second challenge is the delivery of what is considered the optimum care for a patient's specific condition(s) at a specific point in time. As medicine progresses, the recommended treatment protocols evolve. The problem for caregivers is attempting to stay current with newer protocols and technologies. The amount of information being introduced into medicine is significant. Large amounts of research results are being published by many leading institutions directly to their Web sites. Some are very reputable, while other research may not have been subjected to rigorous verification. This creates the need for the caregiver to apply diligence to both the source and content of the information being considered for use.

In addition to the challenges of information overload (or the lack of easily accessible information on a patient) and the need of the caregivers to stay current, there is also the simpler problem that caregivers make mistakes even when they have the needed information and are current with their profession. Dr. Charles Vincent et al. wrote in the *British Medical Journal* that medical errors originate in three general categories.[12] The first category is errors of actions. These would be categorized as a caregiver attempting to deliver the proper care in accordance with the correct protocol and therapy, but making a mistake in its delivery, such as picking up the wrong syringe. The second class of error is a deviation from the approved or optimal care delivery protocol. This can be a conscious decision, such as deciding that a particular protocol and associated therapy were not appropriate for a specific patient and then altering care based on what is thought to be sound medical practice. Should the resulting outcome be negative, then this action would be considered a deviation error. The third category is the cognitive error, such as a memory lapse. A common example of this error occurs when a long-standing protocol or therapy is updated to improve results, yet the practitioner forgets about those changes and delivers the previous version to a patient. There are several subcategories for each cognitive error that are associated with many factors that affect caregiver performance. These may range from fatigue to lack of training or education.

Decision support systems are designed to solve or at least reduce the occurrence of one or more of these problem areas while providing the caregiver with the most current information, a partial analysis of that information, and verification of the viability of decisions. Decision support systems do not replace the decisions made by the caregiver. They are designed to be able to provide or even suggest treatment alternatives. Decision support systems, in their optimal form, not only host all of the information available, but also supplement care delivery decisions by suggesting possible improvements. These may include alternative drug therapies, warnings about protocol variances, or suggested supplemental information on a diagnosis. Some may go further and provide treatment checks and third-party alerting if certain problems or risk factor thresholds are reached. This type of support would be useful for supporting the learning process of a first-year resident, supplementing the decisions of a physician's assistant at a walk-in pediatric clinic, or helping an experienced physician work the eighteenth hour of a shift.

## Pharmacy and Medicine Management/Drug Interaction

Pharmacy informatics is an emerging field of study that combines the uses of IT with the practice of pharmacy.[13] Pharmaceutical informatics systems may provide a wide variety of functionality to support the operation of a pharmacy. Depending on the location and customer service base (retail stand-alone, in-store, hospital, clinic), these systems may be designed to provide for support functions ranging from business management, customer services and sales (filling prescriptions for patients), supply chain management, inventory management, billing (including formulary verification and validation by insurance carriers prior to preparing the prescription, product transfers and record keeping), basic security, HIPAA privacy functionality, and remote transactions. Some features or functions, such as automatic notification to patients of pending refills, enhance both revenue generation and improved patient care. If viewed in context of any business, these functions are key capabilities that provide levels of automation, management, and reporting that are found in most businesses today. In pharmacy operations and management, as with any other business, manual paper trail documentation work is no longer cost effective, functionally sufficient, or competitive.

Beyond the business functions, a major benefit and focus espoused by many pharmaceutical system OEMs are features that provide caregiver decision support capabilities. Functionality, such as drug interaction alerting, adverse reaction warning, and order validation address specific problems associated with pharmacy services. In a study conducted at Seattle's Children's Hospital, it was found that up to 6 percent of orders had common errors. The majority of these errors involved dosing, incorrect route of administration, and illegible handwriting. As such, most errors occurred at the physician ordering stage. More than 70 percent of those errors were considered preventable by the application of real-time decision support at the time the prescription was prepared.[14] To solve these specific problems, the automation of a prescription system that allows for remote access of prescription services, automatic drug interaction, and order verification to the physician as the prescription is being written has the potential to improve care and reduce costs. It should be noted that a pharmaceutical system and a decision-support system integration may eliminate duplicative functions such as drug interaction. Again, as previously discussed, successful integration has the potential to increase efficiency and reduce costs.

In filling a prescription, the pharmacist is subject to the same information overload that a physician faces. There are many new drugs, new research on existing drugs, and the optimization of drug delivery for specific conditions that are changing daily. A system that provides automated drug interaction alerting has the potential to significantly reduce the number of avoidable errors within a pharmacy. The key presumption in this statement is that for a system to identify interactions or adverse reactions for drugs being taken by a specific patient and do so with a high degree of accuracy, it must have access to information concerning all other drugs currently prescribed and being taken by the patient. For that to be accomplished, access to the patient's current medical records and their medical history from all other medical sources is needed. This would include the identification of all other prescriptions having been filled (including those by other pharmacies), as well as the identification of all over-the-counter drugs being taken. Information on the patient's use of each of these drugs would also be optimally needed to support a more thorough decision support process. With these data, there is a much higher probability that any drug interactions can readily be identified by the pharmaceutical system. The actual consumption of the drugs being taken still must be confirmed during the actual encounter with the patient. Although it is not practical to achieve that level of integration in most organizations or localities, the basic capabilities to achieve integration are beginning to appear across many healthcare organizations. The systems needed to collect this level of data are beginning to be deployed more universally. The next step will be the secure integration of these divergent systems while recognizing that privacy rights will need to be maintained.

### Radiologic Information Systems/Picture Archiving and Communications Systems

Radiologic information systems (RIS) and picture archiving and communications systems are the basis for managing modern radiology studies. An individual study is the collection of information obtained from an exam (e.g., X-ray) combined with the collection of information pertinent to that study. The technology that serves as the driver for these systems is the partial (or in some environments, the complete) replacement of films with digital images. Since the late 1990s, most devices used for medical imaging have begun to be built using digital imagers as a replacement for older analog-based systems. With digital data being generated by these modalities, the files generated can be transferred and managed along with any other digital solution. With digital data collection and processing as the basis for work, ancillary items, such as data management, patient processing, and overall work flow, can also be automated and combined into one integrated solution.

Typically, a picture archiving and communications systems (PACS) network consists of a central server that stores a database containing the images. For reference purposes, a large PACS environment running several hundred CT (computerized tomography) studies a week will generate between one and two terabytes (1 terabyte = 1,000 gigabytes) of data per week. To optimize the potential of this type of solution, a RIS may be deployed to facilitate the creation of a patient record, often automatically doing so when a study is scheduled in the hospital's information system. In this way, data is automatically input into the RIS by the hospital system, minimizing data entry errors. The images are fed directly into the database by the modalities. To manage the images themselves, records are created using the Digital Imaging and Communications in Medicine (DICOM) standard. Specifically, DICOM is the primary standard for managing, processing, storing, printing, and transmitting information generated by an imaging system. The details of this standard are extensive, but for compliant systems, the data embedded within each image greatly enhances the accuracy of the findings associated with each study.[15]

With the creation of a server that manages digital records and images, the benefits of an all-digital solution become available to the radiology community. The most current systems usually employ Web interfaces, thereby allowing studies to be forwarded and read by remote staff or contractors literally any place in the world. By enabling remote analysis of a study, the problem of having qualified radiologists on duty or on call at all times is lessened. Additionally, remotely reading a study when needed offers the potential for improved outcomes based on a quicker diagnosis. This can be a critical factor in critical or emergency care situations.

## Laboratory Information Systems (LIS)

A laboratory information system (LIS) is a class of applications that processes lab orders. Each order is processed based on workflow and priority scheduling. In general terms, the order is received, scheduled, and processed using the appropriate tests. Scheduling coincides with the collection or receipt of specimens, which are then processed. As data is collected, either through manual data entry or automatically with the test instruments, the data is recorded and stored. An LIS must be preconfigured to include data collection parameters and reporting configurations from all disciplines of laboratory science—hematology, chemistry, immunology, blood bank (donor and transfusion management), surgical pathology, anatomical pathology, flow cytometry, and microbiology[16]—based on the capabilities and resources used within the laboratory at the facility. Once data is collected, the results are then returned to the requesting caregiver. Within an integrated healthcare environment, the results are returned electronically as soon as they are confirmed. As with most other healthcare systems, the results are also recorded in the patient record and, depending on results, such as a contagious pathogen finding, to other units within the organization to facilitate disease control and containment. Such alerting would ideally be structured to be automatic.

## Charge Capture

In the majority of medical practices, patient encounters are scheduled for the caregiver to occur in rapid succession. Each encounter is driven by meeting the treatment needs of the patient. As described earlier, this rapid progression of encounters often results in some of the details of the encounter being missed. A caregiver's professional training is always patient centric so his or her focus is always placed on exercising diligence in delivering treatment. At the end of the encounter, prior to initiation of the next encounter, the caregiver is required to document all aspects of the treatment and, often, what supplies were used during that treatment. The result is that unless specific cost elements associated with the care delivery (supplies, tests performed, and specimens) are recorded in some manner, billable services are missed, and the organization's revenue stream suffers. The informatics solution associated with solving the problem of missed charges is referred to as charge capture.

Charge capture solutions are integrated with the delivery of service and are designed to be used by the caregiver during or immediately after each encounter. A key motivation for the use of charge capture systems is revenue generation. Estimates vary on their value in terms of increases in revenue, but are usually considered positive for successfully deployed systems. These revenue increases are usually reported as increases in billable charges over comparable periods using normalized data. Other ancillary benefits are reductions in billing errors and quicker invoice generation, improving cash flow. In one example, Mount Carmel St. Ann's Hospital in Franklin County, Ohio, reported gross revenue increases in excess of $3.6 million in their emergency department (approximately 69,000 patient visits annually) over a 12-month period using a charge capture system.[17]

The use of a charge capture system by the caregiver is a key feature to most systems. The benefit is that these systems assume responsibility for entering the services delivered or ordered into an invoicing model in close to real time. In doing so, this method reduces the reliance on administrative or nursing staff to transfer oral, dictated, or written instructions into a billing system, a patient record system, or some combination of systems. With the elimination of one or more manual data transfer points, the number of potential errors is reduced. This also greatly reduces labor costs associated with the documentation effort.

However, simply directing an already busy caregiver to perform data entry activity is not reasonable. This approach will generate little or no support with the end user communities, will not be used, and may very well reduce revenue generation further. A charge capture system becomes efficient when it is integrated into other informatics functionalities, such as patient scheduling, lab reporting, or with an EMR system. Ideally, when a lab result is entered into a system, costs would be generated behind the user interface from that action. A requirement for listing itemized supplies used to meet that diagnosis would be avoided. As an example, if lab findings are entered into a patient's record that streptococcal bacteria is present, then several cost elements could be presumed and be associated with that test. A swab was used to collect the specimen and, assuming that the rapid antigen test (RAT) system is available and is part of the normal protocol for that facility or office, the rapid antigen test is used. Then the costs for the use of the RAT (labor, time, cleaning, maintenance) and supplies associated with the delivery of that protocol are automatically recorded for billing. These cost elements would be preloaded into the charge capture system.

In addition to the capture of these costs, the system would also verify the reimbursable amounts associated with the performance of that protocol. This verification is conducted with data obtained from the patient's insurance carrier. With verification, those costs form the basis for the invoice. Differences between what the patient's insurance carrier considers to be an allowable cost and the actual cost incurred, as well as other reimbursement factors (such as patient co-pay), are not technology issues beyond the development and application of rules to the charge capture system for integration with the accounting and billing systems. Rather, processing these receivables and their associated costs properly are accounting issues.

From a technology perspective, providing the caregiver with the ability to capture costs either directly or indirectly in real time requires that the caregivers be able to use the system wherever the encounter occurs. To meet this requirement, patient encounter areas either need to be wired and workstations installed, or a mobile solution needs to be installed and deployed that uses wireless PDAs (personal digital assistants), laptops, or tablet PCs (personal computers). Once completed, these technologies will help ensure that encounters are documented and the associated billing costs captured.

The actual application logic of this functionality is based on a series of decision points which, in turn, are based on rules, similar to care delivery protocol decision points. Such decision tree rules are easily coded into any system and simply pull data from, or write data to, various tables within one or more databases. The challenge remains in initially developing the rules and integrating them into an existing (or legacy) system. Though stand-alone charge capture systems can be beneficial, optimal performance suggests that they obtain data from other systems within the organization or from remote data sources, such as a carrier's system. Recognizing this need, most OEMs have designed their solutions to be integrated with larger systems, which, if done correctly, improves both efficiency and functionality.

## Electronic Health and Medical Record Systems

Electronic health record (EHR) and EMR systems are software applications designed to replace a patient's paper records. The formal distinction between an EMR and an EHR remains somewhat blurred. Various healthcare organizations use these terms interchangeably in that most systems perform the same basic functionality. Some manufacturers may use these terms as product differentiators within their competitive sales literature. In reviewing some of that literature, it appears that *health* record systems designs focus on the integration of multiple data sources into each individual's record, striving to make it complete and portable, while *medical* record systems perform the exact same functions but their designs tend to focus on the efficient management of multiple records. In both cases, the functionality is limited only by system configuration and setup. In reality, most care providers want complete functionality that encompasses both of these descriptions. Both EMR and EHR can refer to an individual's health or medical record, or, as in the context of this section, to the IT systems that manage the health and medical records of multiple individuals.

In the simplest form, EMRs/EHRs are large-capacity databases that contain records stored in structured, relational tables. These relational tables allow thousands of pieces of information on a person's health condition to be collected into a single searchable resource. In front of the database are a series of forms and reports that allow the user to quickly see any aspect of a patient record, either in part or in whole. Many systems allow for data feeds to be exchanged with other systems, allowing data to be received, compiled, and sent to other systems as reports.

The healthcare data stored in these databases is generated by each of a patient's encounters with a caregiver and, ideally, in any care delivery setting. In general, these systems are designed to be progressive, that is, patient records are updated by adding new information derived from each subsequent encounter without overwriting or deleting previously written data. As an example, a patient with a bronchial infection who was treated with amoxicillin showed improvement but had an adverse reaction. This reaction is an important reference point for future encounters where treatments can be tailored to provide an alternative therapy. As such, this information would not be overwritten by a conclusion that "the patient has recovered." Historical data is key, including patient historical and updated demographics, progress notes, problems and reasons for encounters, medications, vital signs, past medical history, immunizations, laboratory data, and radiology reports.[18] Within an EMR/EHR, each of these elements should be searchable and cross-indexed.

With this information, the caregivers have the ability to implement efficiencies in their encounter processes to optimize workflow. In practice, an EHR or EMR will eliminate or at least minimize redundancies, thereby lowering costs. A fully populated EHR has the ability to generate and maintain a complete record of a clinical patient encounter. With this information, improvements in care associated with evidence-based decision support, quality management, and outcomes reporting are possible, as long as the collected data is regularly reviewed and analyzed to identify operational efficiencies.

From a functionality perspective, user interfaces supporting data input screens, reports, and related information access are designed to be intuitive. These systems are often Web-enabled, which reduces the reliance on custom installations on office computers or wireless systems. The better designed systems reflect great amounts of time spent by the design teams to optimize these interfaces to support the caregivers and simplify their workload.

There are several challenges with the implementation of these types of systems. First, they are complex systems to set up, install, and train staff to use. Even as difficult as these steps can become, the major problem many organizations and OEMs identify is the conversion of a patient's historical paper records into an electronic record. Paper records contain notes that are handwritten, lab reports in different formats, and hosts of other data, none of which can be imported into a database without special applications for conversion, reading, imaging, and processing. Services are available, but conversion is an involved and time-consuming process.

The next problem area arises when a patient visits multiple caregivers in different disciplines at different facilities. EHR manufacturers have developed their products as customized applications that focus on organizational services and do not always embrace standards that would allow data transfers between systems. Another potential problem is the lack of motivation by caregiver organizations to develop IT protocols to exchange data between their respective systems. Although the technology exists to exchange data, the economic reasons to develop the code or deploy the applications to accomplish it are not always present. As an example, it is highly unlikely that a cardiology practice would accrue a material financial benefit if it were to develop an EHR/EMR data exchange system with a podiatry practice.

Recognizing this problem as a barrier to EHR interoperability is one of the primary reasons many organizations, such as the Healthcare Information and Management Systems Society (HIMSS) and agencies within the federal government, are all advocating the adoption of application standards by EHR/EMR product manufacturers and vendors. This need for interoperability is also driving the adoption of open source healthcare applications, such as the Veterans Administration's Computerized Patient Record System (CPRS) component of the Veterans Health

Information Systems and Technology Architecture (VistA®) system, and the Armed Forces Health Longitudinal Technology Application (ALTHA), offered by the Department of Defense's medical services infrastructure.

The EHR is the basis for all integrated healthcare systems. If optimally deployed, connectivity with all other systems across the organizations is implemented, allowing for automatic updating of a patient's record regardless of the caregiver seen or service received. The problem of integration between care providers is significant, but the benefits of accomplishing this are undeniable. Several studies (including those published by HIMSS ANALYTICS, a vendor/product neutral healthcare technology organization) have documented statistical correlations between integrated EHRs and improvements in the quality of care delivered to patients, reduced acute and ambulatory cost, and positive patient outcomes.[19]

### Computerized Physician Order (Online) Entry Systems

Clinical, decision support, drug interaction alerting, and charge capture systems all bring significant benefits to a healthcare organization. As the benefits provided by these systems within the caregiver community are recognized, certain operational needs begin to be identified to facilitate their effective deployment. Architecturally, the different features of each of these systems need to be integrated to optimize performance. Ideally, this integration would provide users with the ability to access all systems through the same interface. The solution to these problems is the computerized physician order (online) entry (CPOE) system.

Organizations that operate within business networks of hospitals, physician offices, clinics, and/or pharmacies have the potential to share information on each encounter or order completed. An integrated CPOE solution is designed to access one or all of each of these different systems. In doing so, on order entry by the physician performing the encounter, the application cross-checks historical information, recommended protocols for therapies, and drug interactions, and provides other decision-support recommendations for the caregivers. Once a therapy is ordered, a CPOE system validates insurance for charge capture purposes and sends the appropriate orders to different systems. Error reduction is often greater than 50 percent, greatly improving outcomes and quality of care.[20] Studies indicate that areas that resulted in the greatest cumulative savings were renal dosing guidance, nursing time utilization, specific drug guidance, and adverse drug event prevention.[21]

### System Integration

In the field of healthcare, the application of information technologies can take advantage of the gains made in other industries. The maturity of open source technologies, the acceptance of standards, and other evolutionary changes have paved the way for the integration of systems. This is specifically true in the areas of integration between legacy systems and between legacy systems and newly deployed systems.

Many healthcare delivery organizations have evolved into organizations that are aggressively using IT. The evolutionary cycle for most organizations within and outside of healthcare begins with the incremental introduction of some information systems into different departments. As those initial systems show value, other departments recognize that value and begin to implement systems that add value to their own operations. This process usually continues until information systems are used in multiple departments at various levels. At some point in this evolutionary cycle, one or more members of the C-level executive team recognize, or are made to recognize by others, that integration between these systems will bring additional benefits to the organization. This is the evolutionary point that many healthcare organizations have reached. They recognize the value of technology and have legacy systems in place. They now need to move to the next level to begin to share information between departments and organizations; that is, integration. Unfortunately, old and new systems may not work together without developing or buying custom software.

There are two general approaches to achieving system integration. The first is the development of custom code connecting existing systems to new systems. The function and design of the custom code can vary greatly and is largely dependent on the configurations of the original systems. Common functionality would include pulling or pushing data from one system to another to allow the receiving system to perform some function. An example of this could be a lab system posting lab results to a specific medical record within an EMR solution.

The technology and methodology to achieve these types of conversions and linkages between systems is mature, and conversions can be accomplished by most skilled developers. Once developed, the conversion code and the configuration of both systems that were current then must be placed under stringent configuration control and management. If changes to either system are made, there is a possibility that the connectivity code will be broken, disrupting services. To avoid this, a more managed change process must be implemented. In this context, each change must be thoroughly reviewed by multiple parties, including developers, system administrators, network resources, and end users, before it is implemented. Building structured code is often favored when both applications are co-located or managed by the same team because the management of both systems can be more easily accomplished.

The second approach is to develop some form of middleware between applications. Many developers currently favor the use of extensible markup language (XML) as an approach to achieve middleware development goals for physically dispersed applications. XML is very similar to HTML (hypertext markup language), the language commonly used to develop Web pages. Most Web servers receive and send data in several different formats, including XML. The XML file can then be transmitted, usually via a Web server.

Without undertaking a lengthy description, data exchanges based on XML programs are straightforward and sequential so long as both applications meet two criteria in advance. First, the applications needing to exchange the data must be able to export or receive data in an XML format, either directly or through the use of a third party product. Most healthcare applications being offered today have this capability. Secondly, both applications that need to exchange the data must use the same data conversion dictionary. Data dictionaries using XML standards are easily portable between systems and can be based on one or more of many readily available healthcare templates.

The sequence for an XML file transmission begins as the result of a request (user or system), a scheduled event, or other trigger seeking information from a source application. The source application selects the data and marks it using the previously agreed to XML conversion data dictionary and places the data into an XML formatted file or document that is ready to transmit. It is then sent to the Web server for transmittal to the destination system. The destination system then receives the data through its own Web server and converts it from the XML format to a file format that it can use. With this approach, the data is converted to a neutral format that can be reconverted to any format that is usable by any system so long as data dictionaries match. Although it sounds complicated, it is often simpler than developing structured code between one or more systems.

An emerging solution that warrants some discussion is the use of services-oriented architecture (SOA) as an integration approach. An SOA is a design approach that creates middleware objects that perform similar conversions as XML, but can also perform simple, concise tasks. An SOA object will often go beyond moving data from one location to another; it may also compile the data and place it in a format that is usable by the requesting system or user.

As an example, the admissions coordinator for a large teaching hospital may need to know how many encounters occurred during the last 24 hours. His or her area of responsibility may include five hospitals and dozens of ambulatory care clinics located in the local metropolitan area and perhaps around the world, across multiple time zones. These facilities would likely use dozens of applications to register and record patient encounters and treatments. The coordinator's problem is how to get this information without setting up a complex system of fixed, structured connections or assigning staff to manually generate reports at each facility. To solve this problem using SOA, a single software object would be built that would automatically connect to each system and compile only the admissions or encounter data and send a report back to the admissions coordinator. A key element in this approach is that the object is designed to perform only limited functions. This constraint forces a concise development effort to achieve a very limited goal, but it also makes it more suitable for reuse in other SOA applications.

As the SOA object is completed, it is also registered on a universal description, discovery, and integration (UDDI) repository. The UDDI is basically a network/ systems directory that allows authorized users to connect to the SOA object. For a single report, creating one object would be a tremendous amount of work, both in terms of effort and the associated cost. However, if the concept of software object reuse were embraced (which is one underpinning of SOA), then parts of that object could be reused for other purposes since they already have the ability to connect to each system. Other similar reports (such as identifying types and quantities of drugs dispensed) could identify public health issues and use trends and possibly serve as a basis for negotiating better rates from the pharmaceutical firms.

An SOA has several key characteristics:

1. *Loosely coupled.* Services are designed to be autonomous and independent of implementation, which enables greater flexibility in introducing new services, aggregating existing services into composite solutions, and changing the deployment of services versus having to address inherited levels of dependence.
2. *Service encapsulation.* This involves the separation of the interface to the service from the detailed internal specification and implementation of the service.
3. *Interface standardization.* A standardized vocabulary to service interoperability ensures interservice communication.
4. *Shared semantic framework.* This is a method to ensure the comprehension of the content of messages communicated between services.
5. *Access services.* Reliable and secure system and people-based access to services and necessary system artifacts within the SOA.
6. *Development facilities.* Full life-cycle support and software versioning of services, messages, including modeling, coding, debugging, testing, deployment, and change control.
7. *Security and management services.* Service and process monitoring, management, security, and ID management.
8. *Application and data services.* Services built around the supporting data persistence and data semantics.

As other departments identify data that would facilitate their operations, they could build and deploy their own SOA objects, following the same process. Once tested, deployed, and registered on the UDDI, any user with the appropriate security permissions could access that SOA object and access the data that it was designed to obtain. Over time, the UDDI could host literally hundreds, if not thousands, of SOA objects. These objects would greatly enhance operational integration between legacy systems and simplify the exchange of data between those systems.

SOA has tremendous potential. However, that is not to say that it is a perfect fit for healthcare. First and foremost, the development costs of the SOA objects, as well as their testing and validation, can be prohibitive. Additionally, a robust UDDI repository may be difficult to set up and manage. If multiple groups within the parent organization have the ability to build and deploy SOA objects, there is a need for centralized management to avoid duplicative efforts.

Of greater concern to healthcare organizations is the small number of very large firms that have expertise in this technology. Fewer still have experience in building and deploying an SOA for healthcare organizations. This is changing, however, and as more organizations incorporate SOA, the availability of SOA objects suitable for reuse will also grow. As that happens, the startup costs and subsequent SOA management costs will go down, making SOA a very viable solution.

As a final word of caution, healthcare organizations commonly use applications that are FDA certified and are covered by warranties issued by the original equipment manufacturers (OEMs).[22] Many FDA-certified applications are problematic when originally sold, and as those problems are fixed by the OEMs, third-party structured code may break. Additionally, changes to those applications could violate both the FDA certification and the warranty. Alternatively, developing a data exchange methodology that transfers data used in delivering care to patients may very well create liability issues for the developers' organization should erroneous data be used as the result of incomplete or problematic coding from which some type of adverse reaction occurs.

## INFORMATICS TECHNOLOGY OVERVIEW

In the previous section, the software applications discussed are varied and are increasingly capable. However, applications unto themselves cannot meet the needs of the healthcare user community. An infrastructure must be able to support those user requirements. Application support consists of several general classifications of computing and network systems. For better or worse, as hardware and software evolve, technologies are being comingled and individual products and systems can be configured to perform functions that were not historically associated with their names. Examples include that desktops running most common operating systems (Windows, Linux, Solaris, etc.) can share or route connections, allowing those computers to become a router, and a router or switch (such as those provided by Cisco, Juniper, and others) can act as an authentication points, a function historically reserved for servers.

In this section, we provide a general discussion of systems and network devices commonly used in medical informatics. These definitions are accurate to industry standards as of this writing. As a subtext of these descriptions, the implementation of any healthcare system or solution should incorporate high availability and reliability features into its deployed design.

### Servers and Storage

The term *server* has two general meanings. From a software perspective, a server refers to an application that runs on a computer that responds to requests for information from client computers. It does so by "serving" those clients the requested information. Those responses are usually delivered via a continuous network connection, allowing for multiple simultaneous connections and transfers. Server applications range from simple, shared storage spaces, such as a mapped drive on the client computer logged into the network, to specific applications, such as e-mail, databases, or EMR systems.

A second, generally accepted (if not completely correct) definition of a server refers to a single computer that runs an operating system and other server software applications. In this context, the computer is designed and purchased with heavier duty hardware components installed over lighter duty systems such as desktops.

It is worth noting that hardware has continued to evolve so that even common desktops have a mean time between failures of at least five years. The difference is that a desktop computer seldom has redundant components within it, and its duty cycle elements, such as CPU (central processing unit) utilization, are significantly lighter than systems that have multiple users attached to them. From a healthcare perspective and considering the need for reliability and availability, redundancy of hardware is a highly recommended configuration.

There are several types of internal and external storage that are commonly found in healthcare IT centers. These range from internal drives to storage area networks requiring dedicated networks, security, and management systems. Each has its place, and storage should be examined very carefully. With the price of hardware continuing to fall and the capabilities of hardware continuing to increase, care should be taken in selecting the management software that will be used to manage these large amounts of storage and the data contained within it. The efficient use of indexing, searching, and related information retrieval systems should be considered in selecting any solution. Long-term storage of data should also be addressed, both in terms of accessibility as well as durability of the solution. It is important to exercise the appropriate amount of due diligence to facilitate a product selection that meets the requirements of the end user community.

### Server Availability

It is a common practice for important or mission critical systems supporting healthcare operations to use multiple computers to perform those roles. By using multiple computers, if a single computer fails, the applications or functions continue to be available for client use. For this to work effectively, the data received by each computer must be shared among all of the computers, and multiple servers supporting the same function must appear as a single server to the client computers. To achieve this, a software application called clustering is installed. This application allows multiple computers to perform the server functions while synchronizing data across the different systems, allowing those multiple physical systems to appear as one single system to the end user. Clustering is an effective solution to improve system availability, but it does have some limitations. Clustering software requires that additional application licenses and specific server clustering licenses be purchased, increasing base costs. To effectively support a clustered solution, both the system and application administrators need to receive specialized training on how to use and managed this solution. Finally, and of perhaps greater importance, not all healthcare applications can be clustered.

For applications that cannot be clustered, real-time or close to real-time backup solutions should be considered. Basic system backups are required for any application and server. Usually incremental backups are scheduled to occur nightly, with full backups occurring over the weekends. The backup tapes are usually rotated and complete backup tapes stored off-site for protection. For healthcare solutions for critical systems, a backup solution may include both hardware and real-time data backups. In this approach, duplicate machines are built of the production systems, and the applications and operating system are imaged on the backup servers. Data is copied from the production machines to the backup machines as it is created, minimizing data availability should those systems be needed. This solution does require the purchase of specialized backup software, but several different applications are available from various vendors. In this configuration, if the primary system goes down, the backup system can be made available in a minimum amount of time. Alternative backup solutions are both available and, in some cases, viable, but may take more time to implement.

### Networks

Within the context of medical informatics, networks refer to one or more computers that are connected together using a shared set of mediums (such as wire and radio waves) for the transmission of data. There are several parallel areas of discussion that are needed to understand network concepts. These elements consist of the physical properties of the network, the data types, how the data messages are exchanged, the general types of networks, and the infrastructure devices used to facilitate the delivery of the data to the connected computers in an efficient and reliable manner. The following information provides a high-level review of the technology and is not meant to be complete. It is meant to provide the nontechnical manager with an entry-level understanding of the topic.

### Physical Mediums

The physical medium refers to the actual medium used by the network over which the data travels. There are three general classes of mediums. First are the copper cable solutions. Copper may refer to several types of cables, but the most common type found throughout the United States is the 8-conductor, category-5 type of cable. Most computers and servers come with the internal hardware needed to use these types of connections. These cables have the capacity to carry significant amounts of data, but have some limitations in terms of capacity and throughput. Capacity and throughput refers to the amount of data transmitted via the cable over a short period of time. Most copper cable can support transmission rates of 100 megabits per second, and with the proper equipment, 1 gigabit per second. Rates exceeding that level may result in the data being corrupted or lost in transit.

The second class is fiber optic or glass cables. These cables require special hardware on the servers and workstations to accommodate their use. This hardware is becoming more common and is considered a standard component on many business class systems. Fiber cables also require custom connections on various network devices. In general terms, fiber offers extremely high capacity and throughput, and is considered the most capable solution available. However, it is often more costly to deploy, so with a few exceptions (such as in radiology), it is limited to use as trunk lines, connecting multiple network devices together.

The third medium is the use of radio waves, commonly referred to as wireless networks. Wireless networks incorporate two-way radio transceivers, or wireless access points (APs), into a wired network. Almost all APs are designed to connect directly to copper-based systems and use standard connections to connect to network devices. Some specialized designs also allow power to be transferred to these devices—these require either network devices that provide power over specialized ports or aftermarket hardware to facilitate the power transfer. This configuration is referred to as power over ethernet (POE). The alternative to POE is to plug each AP directly into an AC (alternating current) wall outlet or other similar power source. To connect to an AP, a computing device must also have a transceiver built into it or pluggable into it. Several security requirements need to be addressed before these can realistically be used for business purposes, but these are the basic components of a wireless network.

### Data Types

Within healthcare, the types of data that are exchanged have the biggest impact on care delivery and related services. The data may consist of information in any form, including software applications, digital voice, and digital video. As hospitals continue to update their systems, it is common to see networks being asked to accommodate all of these data types. This combination of data types, referred to as data convergence, can potentially cause problems to the network if it is not built with the ability to accommodate their use. The volume or amount of information that can be carried across the network is referred to as the network's capacity.

In all networks, capacity utilization changes as different portions of it are used by different applications or devices. A video conference may need to utilize a large portion of a network's available capacity to deliver a high quality conference. Failure of the network to provide the needed capacity will cause problems, such as jumpy video or voice drops. From a utilization perspective, video conferencing is seldom an ongoing activity across most healthcare networks, so its requirements for network capacity are not constant.

Voice over Internet Protocol (VoIP) are basically telephone calls placed using computer data networks that, like video, cannot be delayed without significant quality degradation. For geographically dispersed organizations that already share data networks, these systems are increasingly popular as they can provide very significant cost savings over upgrading or maintaining standard telephone service private branch exchanges. These systems allow for calls to be routed over a healthcare organization's networks, not the telephone companies' networks. For organizations with facilities in different interexchange regions, such as Baltimore, Maryland, and Washington, D.C., a standard telephone call from one facility to the other using the telephone company's services will generate a long distance call charge. Using a VoIP solution, such a call would be routed across the organization's existing computer and data network, avoiding those charges. As an extension, assuming that both facilities have local exchange phone service (usually required for local emergency services at a minimum), the calls from one facility to numbers outside of the distant facility (but within that distant facility's local exchange) can also be made avoiding long distance charges. This is because the call enters the local exchange carriers' network as a local call. Though very cost effective, VoIP applications without sufficient bandwidth will be vulnerable to jitter, making a phone conversation difficult to conduct.

Computer data is often considered less critical in terms of timeliness. Nevertheless, in an emergency department, seconds waiting for specific clinical data do count. Studies sent from radiology may have priority equal to, or higher than, any video conference or phone call. Conversely, a normally scheduled synchronization of the EMR may be subservient to other uses of the network. Collectively, each of these requirements must be addressed and managed.

### Data Message Exchanges

Infrastructure communications are managed by devices that operate using a series of standards. Those standards are incorporated into the design of communications hardware systems and the applications that run on them. The essence of these standards is based on addressing information to certain locations, inside of each network and connections between networks. In the world of publicly networked computers, each location has a unique address. The challenge, then, is to know where those unique addresses are and how to get packets of information to certain addresses.

In a network environment, data is seldom sent in a constant stream. The larger the set of information that is sent, the longer it will take, and the more likely that some of the information will be lost or garbled, ruining the entire transmission. To nullify this problem, information that is to be sent a network from one computer to another is broken down into smaller packets of information. The disassembly and subsequent reassembly of data is performed by various applications on the computer, but their transmission and addressing is managed by a set of protocols known as the transmission control protocol and the Internet protocol (TCP/IP).

TCP enables two host computers or devices to establish a connection and exchange streams of data packets. TCP guarantees delivery of the data packets by confirming transmission and receipt as well as managing the disassembly of the message and its reassembly at the destination.[23] The IP is a set of data-oriented protocols that are designed to encapsulate data for delivery. It also applies a unique source and destination address associated with each unique device connected to the network (i.e., each device has its own number, similar in concept to a telephone number at an office desk). The details of the IP protocol are complex and beyond the scope of this chapter. Suffice it to say that it is incumbent upon healthcare managers to retain staff with the hands-on expertise in this area to support network operations and systems integration.

### Types of Networks

Networks can be described in several ways, and for referential purposes in this section, will be addressed in terms of physical dispersion. First, going from the smallest to the largest, is the local area network (LAN). LANs are found on single floors or wings within a building. This limitation on size is usually done to simplify management of the devices connected to it for exchanging data and information. The second type of network is the campus area network (CAN). A CAN is considered a collection of interconnected LANs, usually owned or managed by the same organization. CANs are usually dispersed across a group of buildings, usually in the same area. As an example, a hospital with one or more buildings residing in the same medical complex but sharing some common physical network attributes and resources (such as a shared Internet connection) could be considered a CAN.

The third type of network is the metropolitan area network (MAN). A MAN is often considered the connection of multiple LANs and CANs within the same geographic region. In a university teaching hospital where the same organization operates several hospitals and clinics within the same city, the connection between these different sites is usually provided by a third party, such as a telco common carrier. Often, a telco-managed MAN may be supplemented by communications mediums, such as line of sight communication lasers or radio connections, maintained by the facility or organization. These are sometimes deployed as cost-cutting measures. In those cases, the connection between each CAN or LAN is usually deployed as a private network, as opposed to the Internet or a public network. As such, these are purchased and maintained at a higher price than a basic Internet connection, yet provide higher reliability and security.

The fourth and final type of network is identified as a wide area network (WAN). A WAN covers a large geographic area, and in commercial healthcare organizations, uses transmission facilities provided by telcos. As in the case of the MAN, the connections between physical locations are usually accomplished through private connections or virtual private connections. A key difference is that over a wide area, one or more telcos may be involved with the connectivity. A major academic medical center with affiliated campuses around the world may use a WAN to ensure connectivity between environments. As with a MAN, costs are higher than basic Internet connectivity.

Within each of these classes of networks, wireless capabilities may be overlaid to provide mobile workers with the ability to use and access organizational information and resources, regardless of their location. To meet these needs, a supplemental solution to enhance mobility is often accomplished through the use of Wi-Fi networks and network cards. A Wi-Fi network is similar in nature to the wireless LAN in that both utilize radio transceivers. The key difference is that the Wi-Fi radios are managed by a telecom carrier and use that carrier's cell phone infrastructure and Internet connections into the organization to complete the communications connection. The Internet connection allows access to the organization's wired network. This remote access requires the implementation of a series of secure measures to be implemented. Unfortunately, not all Wi-Fi carriers provide acceptable services in all locations, and dead zones in coverage areas exist. As a result, care needs to be taken in validating a specific carrier's capabilities to meet the needs of mobile workers prior to entering into any long-term obligation.

### Network Devices

For networks, several types of devices are designed to support the management of data across the network to the end-point computers. In general terms, the core devices of any network are routers (which send data to end points and other networks) and switches (which optimize throughput for host-to-host and host-to-router traffic). In terms of healthcare solutions, building in redundancy and failover capability should be seriously considered in any deployment or network upgrade. The design and deployment of these types of network configurations requires staff with specialized skills. The specialization may warrant specific product knowledge and manufacturer certifications, such as a Cisco Certified Internetworking Engineer. Individuals with these skills are costly, but may be critical to the successful deployment and management of the network.

Ancillary to these core systems, the network may also need to support other solutions such as wireless LANs, video teleconferencing, VoIP, application layer switching, load balancing, and various security systems (firewalls, network and host-based intrusion detection, authentication, and monitoring). Larger and more complex network solutions require centralized management to facilitate their operation. Although there are alternative solutions available, they are seldom as effective as a more centralized management approach. It is incumbent on the IT manager to have access to the skilled resources needed to address the support of these systems throughout their planning and ongoing operations.

### Environmental Infrastructure

For IT systems, certain environmental controls need to be in place. The size and space will vary with the needs of an organization, but the basic requirements are the same. For sustainable and maintainable computing services, controls must be in place to regulate temperature, humidity, and particulate contamination within the operating environment. Most servers have automatic shutdown controls that engage if operating temperatures exceed approximately 100 degrees Fahrenheit. The lack of cooling air circulation, as a result of poor air conditioning or dust building up on cooling vents within the computer's case, may create this condition. Humidity-generated condensation (resulting from high humidity or unmanaged temperatures should the Heating, Ventilation, and Air Conditioning (HVAC) fail within the data center) may cause electrical shorts. Even in smaller facilities and clinics, environmental infrastructure is a legitimate concern—where placing the servers and related systems in an unused coat closet is not an unknown practice.

In addition to environmental controls, power to the data center is another design element that should be addressed. In most cases, hospitals have installed backup generators to ensure that operations are maintained in the event of local power failures. Additionally, most facilities also use uninterruptible power supplies (UPS) on many key systems to ensure that they do not fail in the event of a power interruption prior to the emergency generators coming on line. These key systems should include servers, but may primarily focus on clinical systems, such as patient monitoring or life support systems.

From an IT perspective, a major concern should be the sufficiency of the generator and UPS systems that are in use to support all systems using the local or facility power grid. Healthcare Chief Information Officers (CIOs) and managers need to be cognizant that a successful power failover test may not cover their systems. Many organizations conduct tests of only portions of the facility, such as a physical wing or floors of a building. In such tests, a circuit breaker is thrown for that portion of the complex, denying power to that area. When this occurs, the power management system senses the failure, switches to the battery backup on the UPS array, and initiates the automatic startup of the generator. Once the generator starts and begins generating full power, the power management system automatically switches from the UPS back to central power and the UPS is recharged. This cycle should take less than five minutes.

In many hospitals and clinics, their computing centers are designed to meet these and many other requirements. In all cases, these environmental constraints are key to the successful, long-term hosting of applications on servers. When examining any environment for hosting key resources, whether internal or external to your organization, asking detailed questions on humidity, cooling, power, and redundancy are all critical to ensuring the availability of the hosted solutions.

## Security

Security is not about the effectiveness of a firewall or an antivirus application. It involves many technologies, processes, and policies that are integrated into a cohesive plan that is implemented and maintained. Security is defined as the reduction and subsequent mitigation of risk to the point that the residual, or unmitigated, risk is at an acceptable level based on the value of the system or systems being protected. A cohesive plan measures the risks on a regular basis, identifies the value of the systems to the organization, and identifies cost-effective controls that are implemented to mitigate those risks to a level that is acceptable to the system owners.

Organizations need to perform a formal risk assessment and system valuation process for each system on a regular basis. Risk is defined as a combination of threats that have a relative probability of those threats exploiting certain known vulnerabilities associated with the system. Threats range from environmental factors (such as earthquakes, severe storms, and power and cooling failures) to human errors (including setup mistakes, patch installation errors, or simply spilling a drink onto a keyboard in the server room). For each threat that is identified, the system owner needs to determine if their system has exploitable vulnerabilities by those threats. They then need to determine the probability that the identified threat will occur and exploit the vulnerability in the next 12 months or some other measurable period. With these three pieces of information (the likelihood of a threat, the probability that it could exploit a vulnerability related to the system, and the probability that the exploitation will occur), a calculation can be made to determine the level of risk. Some threats, such as a data center being subjected to a cyber attack in the next 12 months has a definite probability of 1 while others, such as an EMR crashing the system it is hosted on, may be much lower, depending on many other factors. To optimize the determination of risk, a significant number of realistic threats should be considered and analyzed using this process.

The next step is to develop a realistic estimate on how long the organization can tolerate being without the system should an exploitation be successful. Some systems (such as a patient monitor in an ICU) cannot be down for more than a few minutes without risking patient safety, while other systems (such as a feedback blog page on an intranet Web site) can have a significantly longer outage without significantly affecting operations. As a word of caution, the use of arbitrary valuation methodologies is tempting but not very useful. Most system owners presume that their systems are critical to operations. The reality is not every system has the same value to the organization, nor are they all critical to the delivery of healthcare services. Asking all users of a system and averaging their responses may provide a more reasonable sense of value. If the majority of users consider a system of key importance to the performance of a certain percentage of their job, then the unavailability of that system can be determined using a cost analysis valuation.

The cost analysis valuation is associated with the impact of the system being unserviceable for some amount of time. It is not recommended to perform a valuation analysis on a partial system outage where only some of the functionality is available; an incremental value is not empirically useful when attempting to identify the associated value of the controls that would be used to mitigate risks. Calculating the value of the system to the organization should begin with an estimate of its complete replacement cost and a sound estimate of the lost productivity should the system become unavailable.[24] Lost productivity would be calculated on total user access or other metrics either calculated or analyzed from operational data.

As an example, if the e-mail system for a large academic medical center were to completely crash, the replacement e-mail system may cost $100,000 and may take five days to replace with the ordering of new hardware and related efforts. However, the valuation of that system must also include lost productivity for all of the users that rely on that e-mail system. If 10,000 employees are paid with a weekly payroll cost of $21 million and 10 percent of their work is dependent on e-mail, then a complete system loss for one week would cost the organization $2.1 million (or $12,500 per hour). Other losses, such as goodwill with the physicians and staff, as well as other less tangible costs like community relations, may also be factored in. With this cost estimate established, the system owners can make a reasonable estimate of the system's value.

With each threat and exploitable vulnerability, one or more controls should be in place to reduce the probability of the exploitation being successful. An accurate threat identification list will improve the likelihood that all of the needed controls will be deployed. In many respects, some controls may address multiple exploits. As an example, a firewall will restrict many cyber attacks and unauthorized access to the system. However, it is not designed to prevent someone from introducing a virus into the system via a thumb drive, the cooling system from failing, or someone spilling a drink in the data center. Disabling the USB ports on all workstations would address the thumb drive issue, while a policy disallowing open drink containers in the server room would address the third issue. Based on the probability of other events happening and the duration of the resulting outage, additional controls can be introduced or the risk of having the exploitation occurring can be accepted.

To complete the overall security assessment, a final value should be calculated; that is, the value of the controls used to mitigate the threats. If 100 percent of every conceivable technical and environmental threat were mitigated, the cost of those controlling mitigations could exceed the value of the system. To prevent this situation, the cost of the controls is also measured and balanced with the cost of the system and probability of a system failure. Using this methodology, an informed business decision can be made where security dollars can be allocated in the most efficient and cost-effective manner. In healthcare, budgets are tight and every dollar must count. Though tedious in approach, this methodology can help the medical informatics IT managers optimize their budgets and expenditures.[25]

There are multiple organizations that provide a wide range of guidance in this area, such as the National Institute of Standards and Technology (NIST), The SANS (SysAdmin, Audit, Network, Security) Institute, the IT Governance Institute, the Computer Security Institute, and the International Information Systems Security Certification Consortium ((ISC)²). All of these organizations provide multiple resources for developing comprehensive security programs. Individuals with the knowledge and experience in security should be retained or consulted with to develop and maintain an effective security plan.

## CONSTRAINTS AND CHALLENGES

In the areas of medical information systems, there are many issues that need to be addressed. One of the most critical issues is obtaining and maintaining funding for a specific project. First and foremost, a project needs to be aligned with the strategic goals of the organization. So long as the alignment is solid and the goals remain well founded, the basic success of the project has been established.

The participation and commitment of senior stakeholders to the project is also of great importance. This commitment is usually directly related to the benefit that they expect to receive once the project is completed. However, if the cost of supporting the project becomes too great versus the anticipated benefits, then their support will usually wane. This problem can be mitigated by communicating the status of the project to the stakeholders, making sure that it is running on schedule and to budget, and addressing problems aggressively as they occur.

A more fundamental success factor is the valuation of the project prior to or immediately after its inception. Valuation is the determination of complete system costs and the expected benefits over the entire life cycle of the project. The basis for investment must reside in sound business planning, performance, and measurable returns based on a quantifiable methodology. Investments in IT have become outcome based, with ROI usually being considered the key element in the decision making process.

The cost and benefit methodology should be the same as used for calculating any other capital investment within the organization. Managers should recognize that collecting project-specific cost and benefit data is a complex and time-consuming task. Due diligence requires a detailed, methodical approach to data gathering, so time needs to be allocated for the estimating process to be done correctly. It is also recommended that all estimates should use minimum, reasonable estimates for both costs and benefits. Managers must be careful not to allow individual estimators to pad their estimates independently. A structured basis for estimating should be followed to achieve the best results. From a cautionary perspective, using IT department estimates as a basis for financing a project will open the project to challenge from the finance department. It remains important to get multiple parties to participate in the estimating process.

The key to all of these aspects is for the estimating team to pay close attention to the many complex and interrelated details of a medical informatics solution. The technology is complex and expensive in terms of the procured items and the labor needed to make it work and then to maintain it. The technologies may be new to many IT departments, so recent past experience may not be available. The understanding of that technology, diligence, and attention to detail are the keys to making solid estimates for analytical purposes.

## CONCLUSION

This chapter describing some of the technologies used in medical informatics barely scratches the surface. Facility access control, the use of biometrics, identity management, power distribution, and even fire suppression are all areas worthy of review. The basic computing technologies needed by healthcare organizations have been developed over the last several decades and are finding their way into this environment. It should be expected that more and more manufacturers and consultants will offer their products and opinions on how things should be done.

Healthcare applications in informatics are becoming more capable with each new product or technology release. Many systems are being built using state-of-the-art development languages and tools. The result is that the current versions of many applications are functionally more capable than their predecessors. Of even greater importance is the diligence with which the new designers have engaged health professionals to assist them in developing the user interfaces and functionality needed to simplify use and improve performance. Collectively, the new languages and improved design interfaces will increase the popularity of these systems and provide for a more accelerated expansion into the healthcare market.

The medical informatics IT executive has significant and ongoing challenges. Budgets are tight and expertise with the depth of knowledge and experience is seldom readily available. To address these issues, the IT manager must take an aggressive approach to the political realities within the organization, the IT operations of the organization's environment, and informed decision making.

Healthcare IT management has at least two masters: the clinicians (especially physicians) and the other C-level executives (usually the chief financial officer and the chief executive officer). Knowing how to manage their expectations and their decision-making processes can be invaluable. The IT managers need to anticipate the needs and interests of these decision makers.

Staffing the operation with skilled resources is a challenge. Having those same people implement effective policies and procedures based on the industry's best practices can be close to impossible as other projects and tasks constantly interfere. Yet if those steps are achieved, there is a significant probability that system service will greatly improve. Technology updates, revisions, and changes are all part of IT. Addressing them in a logical and consistent manner can address many potential problem areas.

The formal analysis in support of decision making provides an excellent hedge against future risk and second guessing decisions. An extensive and accurate analysis that is performed correctly will generate supporting data that is difficult to question.

Informatics in healthcare will continue to change care delivery. It remains one major avenue where appreciable savings can be generated while improving the quality of care surrounding the patient. As the population ages, improvements in care are expected by patients. The application of IT services and solutions to the healthcare space can meet those expectations.

## NOTES

1. Collen, M. F. 1977. Preliminary announcement for the Third World Conference on Medical Informatics, MEDINFO 80, Tokyo, September 29, 1980.

2. Wikipedia. n.d. *Health Informatics*. Available at: http://en.wikipedia.org/wiki/Medical_informatics. Accessed October 1, 2006.

3. *Software Magazine*. 2004. "Standish: Project Success Rates Improved Over 10 Years." January 15. Available at: http://www.softwaremag.com/L.cfm?Doc=newsletter/2004–01–15/Standish. Accessed December 22, 2006.

4. Kaplan, R. S., and D. P. Norton. 1992. "The Balanced Scorecard: Measures That Drive Performance." *Harvard Business Review* (Jan/Feb): 71–80.

5. Balanced Scorecard Institute. 1998. *Balanced Scorecard*. Available at: http://www.balancedscorecard.org/basics/bsc1.html. Accessed December 31, 2006.

6. Nance, A. 2006. *ITSM Handbook*. Rotterdam, The Netherlands: ITpreneurs Nederland-BV, 19–20.

7. "ITIL Service Manager," from The ITIL Service Manager Workshop. Available at: http://www.itilsurvival.com/default.asp. Accessed December 20, 2006.

8. COBIT, or Control Objectives for Information and Related Technology, is a process very similar to ITIL, but focuses on industry-wide practices allowing for individual customization and implementation success to be reliant on the skills of the implementer. COBIT is a copyrighted process owned by the IT Governance Institute. For additional information, see http://www.ISACA.org.

9. ISO/IEC 20000–1:2005 is the formal specification, and defines the requirements for an organization to deliver managed services of an acceptable quality for its customers. It was issued in 2005 as the most current standard at that time by the

International Standards Organization, replacing standard BS (British Standard) 15000. It is administered by the itSMF (IT Service Management Forum).

10. Smithline, N. 2002. "Handheld, the Holy Grail of Healthcare?" Paper presented at the Healthcare Information Management Systems Society 2002 Conference, Atlanta, Georgia, January 27–31, 2002.

11. Role-based access is available at some level on all operating systems that are commercially available for either home or office use. The differentiation between user and administrator accounts is log-in based and may manifest itself as giving significantly fewer rights to the users. A common role-based access restriction allows only system administrators to install applications on desktop or laptop computers.

12. Vincent, C., S. Taylor-Adams, and N. Stanhope. 1998. "A Framework for Analysing Risk and Safety in Clinical Medicine." *BMJ* 316 (7138): 1154–1157.

13. PharmacyInformatics.com. n.d. *What Is Pharmacy Informatics?* Available at: http://www.pharmacyinformatics.com/informatics.html. Accessed February 21, 2007.

14. Dwight, J., M. Del Bewccaro, and M. Eisenberg. 2006. "CPOE at Seattle's Children's Hospital and Regional Medical Center." Children's Hospital and Regional Medical Center Seattle Washington Presentation sponsored by the Community Health Information Technology Alliance (CHITA). Material presented at the Seattle, Washington and Portland, Oregon sessions.

15. Wikipedia. n.d. *Digital Imaging and Communications in Medicine*. Available at: http://en.wikipedia.org/wiki/DICOM. Accessed February 28, 2007.

16. Wikipedia. n.d. *Laboratory Information System*. Available at: http://en.wikipedia. org/wiki/ Laboratory_information_system. Accessed February 28, 2007.

17. "An ALLSCRIPTS Case Study: Mount Carmel St. Ann's Hospital, Franklin County, OH," n.d., Available at: http://www.allscripts.com/siteresources/files/ casestudies/Mount%20Carmel.pdf. Accessed February 24, 2007.

18. Healthcare Information Management Systems Society. n.d. *EHR Electronic Health Record*. Available at: http://www.himss.org/ASP/topics_ehr.asp. Accessed February 21, 2007.

19. HIMSS Analytics. 2006. *EMR Sophistication Correlates to Hospital Quality Data: Comparing EMR Adoption to Care Outcomes at UHC Hospitals, Including Davies Award Winners, Using HIMSS Analytics' EMR Adoption Model Scores*. Available at: http://www.himss.org/content/files/UHCresearch.pdf. Accessed February 28, 2007.

20. Bates, D. W., L. L. Leape, D. J. Cullen, N. Laird, L. A. Petersen, J. M. Teich, E. Burdick, et al. 1998. "Effect of Computerized Physician Order Entry and a Team Intervention on Prevention of Serious Medication Errors." *Journal of the American Medical Association* 280 (15): 1311–1316.

21. Kaushal, R., A. K. Jha, C. Franz, J. Glaser, K. D. Shetty, T. Jaggi, B. Middleton, et al., and Brigham and Women's Hospital CPOE Working Group. 2006. "Return on Investment for a Computerized Physician Order Entry System." *Journal of the American Medical Informatics Association* 13 (3): 261–266.

22. U.S. Food and Drug Administration. 2006. *Ensuring the Safety of Marketed Medical Devices: CDRH's Medical Device Postmarket Safety Program*. Available at: http://www.fda.gov/cdrh/postmarket/mdpi-report.html. Accessed on April 18, 2007.

23. Webopedia. n.d. *What Is TCP?* Available at: http://www.webopedia.com/ TERM/T/TCP.html. Accessed March 5, 2007.

24. Staff Writer. 2005. "Technical Risk Assessment," Technical Support White Paper, Available from Riskwatch Customer Support Services, Riskwatch, Inc. Annapolis, MD.

25. Stoneburner, G., A. Goguen, and A. Feringa. 2002. "Risk Management Guide for Information Technology Systems," National Institute of Standards and Technology, Special Publication 800–30, dated July 2002. Available at: http://csrc.nist.gov/publications/nistpubs/800-30/sp800-30.pdf. Accessed April 18, 2007.

## REFERENCES

He, H.. 2003. *"Webservices Q&A"* published on the O'Rielly XML Web site on September 30, 2003. Available at: http://webservices.xml.com/pub/a/ws/2003/09/30/soa.html. Accessed September 10, 2005.

Jenkins, N., and S. Schatt. 1995. *Understanding Local Area Networks*. 5th ed. Indianapolis: SAMs Publishing.

Kohn, L., J .Corrigan, and M. Donaldson. 2000. *To Err is Human: Building a Safer Health System*. 1st ed. Washington, D.C.: National Academy Press.

Lewis, Chris. 2000. *CISCO TCP/IP Routing Professional Reference*. 3rd ed. Dallas, Texas: McGraw Hill Technical Expert Series.

Remenyi, D., A. Money, M. Sherwood-Smith, and Z. Irani. 2000. *The Effective Measurement and Management of IT Costs and Benefits*. 2nd ed. Oxford, United Kingdom: Butterworth-Hienemann.

Rogers, S., and S. Hendrick. 2005. *Oracle Builds a Comprehensive SOA Solution*. Available at: www.oracle.com/technologies/soa/idc_soa_platform.pdf. Accessed September 9, 2006.

Webopedia. n.d. *Webopedia: Online Encyclopedia that Provide Rapid Identification of Standard Information Technology Terms*. Available at: http://www.Webopedia.com.

# CHAPTER 6

# Complementary and Alternative Medicine and the Future of Healthcare in America

Chris D. Meletis

To understand the current role and placement of complementary and alternative medicine (CAM) in the hierarchy of the U.S. healthcare system, it is essential to appreciate the historical migration away from traditional healing methods to the allopathic, conventional model of medicine. It is equally important to objectively view how the current fragmentation of the U.S. model has been propagated and to seek insight into the rationale behind the economic and personal choice mandate made by the U.S. healthcare consumer toward CAM practices.

CAM is defined as everything that is not allopathic medicine; its practitioners provide naturopathic, chiropractic, acupuncture, massage, Ayurvedic (traditional medicine of India), nutrition, spiritual-based medical, and numerous other practices provided by the groups detailed in Table 6.1.

Historically, natural medicine practices have sustained humanity over the millennia as the only form of medicine until the advent of allopathic medicine. In many parts of the world, healthcare is not divided between allopathic and CAM but integrated in a collaborative model. From an historical perspective, the creation of the so-called new allopathic medical model began during the twentieth century with the advent of applied science, which triggered the rapid transformation of medicine in the United States. This series of events was formalized with the Flexner report in 1910, which established the allopathic medicine model as the new standard.[1]

Unlike other countries, which have maintained a fundamental appreciation of their traditional, natural medicine approaches and superimposed allopathic medicine, the U.S. healthcare system transitioned largely to replace traditional (CAM) practices. This is implied by the term itself—complementary and alternative—

Table 6.1
CAM Therapies Included in the 2002 NHIS

Acupuncture
Ayurveda
Biofeedback
Chelation therapy
Chiropractic care
Deep breathing exercises
Diet-based therapies
    Vegetarian diet
    Macrobiotic diet
    Atkins diet
    Pritikin diet
    Ornish diet
    Zone diet
Energy healing therapy
Folk medicine
Guided imagery
Homeopathic treatment
Hypnosis
Massage
Meditation
Megavitamin therapy
Natural products
    (nonvitamin and nonmineral, such as herbs and other products from plants, enzymes, etc.)
Naturopathy
Prayer for health reasons
    Prayed for own health
    Others ever prayed for your health
    Participate in prayer group
    Healing ritual for self
Progressive relaxation
Qi gong
Reiki
Tai chi
Yoga

*Source:* National Center for Complementary and Alternative Medicine, National Institutes of
Health. *The Use of Complementary and Alternative Medicine in the United States.* Available at:
http://nccam.nih.gov/news/camsurvey_fs1.htm#info#info.

suggesting that the role of traditional natural practices was to complement and/
or serve as an alternative to the established allopathic model.

There is no question that millions of lives have been saved by the application
and developments of allopathic medicine. The consequence has been better
understanding and appreciation of disease processes within the human body and
the sequential development of specialties and subspecialties.

But to appreciate the current state of the U.S. healthcare system and its
metamorphosis, we must assume that no healthcare model is beyond improvement. Many healthcare consumers seeking CAM healthcare believe the allopathic

model has become too focused on treating the parts of the body at the expense of treating the entire person. It is this shift away from whole-body medicine by the allopathic model, with its continuous movement to specialization, that has contributed to the surge in interest in CAM. It also explains the willingness of patients to spend money on services that are not presently reimbursed.

One can view consumer spending on CAM services as an expression of supply and demand. A combination of socioeconomic trends has led to a resurgence of interest in natural medicine. These include greater medical knowledge available via the Internet, the proliferation of medical newsletters, and the growing population of baby boomers who have discretionary income and do not readily embrace the concept of getting old.

A majority of healthcare consumers already use allopathic medicine in addition to treatments such as massage, acupuncture, chiropractic, and herbal remedies. As this chapter will show, allopathic medicine and CAM need not be mutually exclusive.

## THE EXTENT OF THE CAM REVOLUTION IN THE UNITED STATES

In the early 1990s, Dr. David Eisenberg analyzed market trends of the U.S. healthcare system relative to CAM. He estimated that there were 243 million more visits to CAM providers than to primary care allopathic physicians. Patients were paying for these visits with out-of-pocket discretionary dollars at a rate of $13 billion a year.[2] From 1990 to 1997, CAM expenditures grew to $27 billion, a 42 percent increase. With the shift towards shorter and more focused doctor-patient visits, a decline in the allopathic physician-patient relationship has occurred. The growth in CAM use is occurring across all age levels:

> Previously reported analyses of these data showed that more than one third of the U.S. population was currently using CAM therapy in the year of the interview (1997). Subsequent analyses of lifetime use and age at onset showed that 67.6% of respondents had used at least one CAM therapy in their lifetime. Lifetime use steadily increased with age across three age cohorts: Approximately 3 of every 10 respondents in the pre–baby boom cohort, 5 of 10 in the baby boom cohort, and 7 of 10 in the post–baby boom cohort reported using some type of CAM therapy by age 33 years. Of respondents who ever used a CAM therapy, nearly half continued to use many years later. A wide range of individual CAM therapies increased in use over time, and the growth was similar across all major sociodemographic sectors of the study sample.[3]

This trend is not a reflection on the level of innate caring or compassion possessed by the allopathic provider, but a reflection of the consequences of a move to managed care. In addition, in the 1990s, media attention to adverse drug reactions and hospital-acquired infections raised questions about quality and safety issues in modern medicine. Furthermore, the increased public awareness of the trends toward obesity, diabetes, cancer, and other degenerative chronic disease states primed the economic pump toward exercising personal choice. Moreover, there are some things modern medicine just does not address well, like chronic stress recognition and reduction. Yet, stress has been shown to be the second leading risk factor for heart disease after smoking.[4]

Thus, socioeconomic forces and healthcare education have shifted attention toward the CAM that focuses on empowered personal healthcare choices—choices that can be determined directly by the individual consumer, without gatekeepers or preapproval by an insurance company.

Quantifying this trend has been a challenge. Much of the healthcare interactions occurring in the realm of CAM are either not covered or only partially covered by medical insurance plans, making it difficult to collect quantifiable economic data. To date, the most reliable information of CAM use by Americans was released by the National Center for Complementary and Alternative Medicine (NCCAM) and the National Center for Health Statistics (NCHS, part of the Centers for Disease Control and Prevention) in May 2004. The data were compiled from the 2002 edition of the NCHS's National Health Interview Survey (NHIS), an annual study conducted that incorporates the health- and illness-related experiences of 31,044 adults aged 18 years or older, as described below.[5]

## UNDERSTANDING CAM

A culture of us versus them has begun to take hold on both sides of the fence between CAM providers/healthcare consumers and allopathic providers/healthcare consumers. As with all labeling of individuals in a culture, a subculture is established and identity is created as a result of being categorized.

As was pointed out by Pietroni in the *British Medical Journal* in 1992:

> To speak of "alternative" medicine is like talking about foreigners—both terms are vaguely pejorative and refer to large, heterogeneous categories defined by what they are not rather than by what they are. The analogy is apt: the current worldwide trend away from suspicion and hostility between "orthodox" and "alternative" medicine toward investigation, understanding, and consumer protection can be compared with the process by which Europeans have learnt to view each other as partners rather than foreigners. This shift in attitude is evident in the BMA's [British Medical Association] recent publication, Complementary Medicine: New Approaches to Good Practice,[6] and in the use of the term "complementary" rather than "alternative." We welcome this new spirit and believe it will benefit patients.[7]

> Even the term complementary medicine is not entirely satisfactory, lumping together as it does a wide range of methods with little in common except that they are outside the mainstream of medicine. The most accurate term may be "unconventional therapeutic methods."[8]

It is important to acknowledge that the separation of allopathic from nonallopathic is a gray line itself. When is CAM no longer CAM? The answer is when allopathic providers begin embracing it in their daily practice of medicine. The concept of allopathic medicine as the gold standard, to which all else is compared relative to its validity, is at the heart of the definition. Allopathic physicians have a history of incorporating natural products into their practices under the auspices of drug therapy. Examples would be foxglove, the origin of the heart failure drug digitalis; Madagascar periwinkle, the origin of the chemotherapy drug vinicristine; the chemotherapy drug Taxol from the Yew tree; the gout remedy Colchicine from Rauwolfia; and the statin drugs for lowering cholesterol from red rice yeast extract. Likewise, it is becoming a more common practice for nutraceuticals like EPA from fish oil, Coenzyme Q10 (CoQ10), and glucosamine sulfate to be recommended by allopathic physicians.

The reality is that a healthcare model that will be sustainable must be economically sound and deliver improved outcomes. Clearly, health maintenance, or wellness, must employ the strategic use of diet, exercise, and stress recognition and reduction at a far superior level than currently implemented in the United States.

Before we proceed further, a few definitions and an observation. Complementary medical practices are defined as those that are used with conventional/allopathic medicine, whereas alternative medicine is used in lieu of conventional medicine.

It is important to realize that until the advent of allopathic medicine, every practice of medicine would have been considered alternative. It is not until the differences among practitioners of allopathic and complementary and alternative medicine are transcended that true collaborative, holistic medicine can come to the forefront.

Having served as dean and chief medical officer at the National College of Natural Medicine (NCNM) in Portland, Oregon, I can attest that establishing a team approach among varied healthcare providers is both fruitful and essential. Many of NCNM's 16 teaching clinics incorporated varying degrees of integrated/collaborative medicine. The key in establishing an economically viable model is to establish a common focus for all the stakeholder providers that can best be summed as embracing patient-oriented wellness. It does not matter which therapy from a given discipline—CAM or allopathic—shifts the scales in favor of improved health. It is the end result that the team celebrates along with the patient it serves.

## VITAMIN THERAPY: CAM OR ALLOPATHY?

The majority of patients, according to the Eisenberg report, do not share with their physician that they are pursuing CAM therapies.[9] The inclusion of CAM into the healthcare setting would diversify income streams for clinics, hospitals, pharmacies, and integrated medical practices, while offering a more consistent delivery of these services by credentialed providers.

In 2002, according to the NHIS CAM survey,[10] 36 percent of U.S. citizens access CAM services. When megavitamin therapy and prayer are incorporated into utilization, this number rises to 62 percent. The *Journal of the American Medical Association* reported that as a tool to combat chronic degenerative diseases such as diabetes, cancer, and cardiovascular disease, a daily multivitamin would be a strong consideration:

> Vitamin deficiency syndromes such as scurvy and beriberi are uncommon in West-ern societies. However, suboptimal intake of some vitamins, above levels causing classic vitamin deficiency, is a risk factor for chronic diseases and common in the general population, especially the elderly. Suboptimal folic acid levels, along with suboptimal levels of vitamins B6 and B12, are a risk factor for cardiovascular disease, neural tube defects, and colon and breast cancer; low levels of vitamin D contribute to osteopenia and fractures; and low levels of the antioxidant vita-mins (vitamins A, E, and C) may increase risk for several chronic diseases. *Most people do not consume an optimal amount of all vitamins by diet alone. Pending strong evidence of effectiveness from randomized trials, it appears prudent for all adults to take vitamin supplements.* The evidence base for tailoring the contents of multivitamins to specific characteristics of patients such as age, sex, and physical activity and for testing vitamin levels to guide specific supplementation practices is limited. Phy-sicians should make specific efforts to learn about their patients' use of vitamins to ensure that they are taking vitamins they should, such as folate supplemen-tation for women in the childbearing years, and avoiding dangerous practices such as high doses of vitamin A during pregnancy or massive doses of fat-soluble vitamins at any age.[11]

Is vitamin therapy a CAM item or is it a non-CAM item? As we will discuss in the following paragraph, pharmaceutical companies are offering an array of vitamins and supplements. Natural medicines migrate into the realm of allopathy, such as fish oil for helping with lipid profiles and CoQ10 to support cardiac health, as well as glu-cosamine sulfate for osteoarthritis. What threshold will need to officially be passed for each of these to become regarded as non-CAM? Regardless of whether a natural prod-uct is recategorized, it is important that when CAM practices are incorporated into standard allopathic medicine, continuing medical education (CME) be provided to ensure proper training on dosing, administration, quality, and safety. To assume that all supplements are created equal and to recommend that a patient pick up a certain dose of CoQ10, glucosamine,, or any supplement off the shelves at the store would be a disservice to patient efficacy and safety. This issue was emphasized in *Comparative Guide for Nutritional Supplements*, which looked at the quality of supplements available to consumers. Of 1,000 multivitamins reviewed, 508 met the criteria for testing. Less than 1 percent of the total products compared exceeded a score of 90 percent.[12]

Though the following pharmaceutical companies are better known for the medications they manufacture, this small sample supports the idea that there is money to be generated through supplement sales, thanks to rising demand and no insurance reimbursement limits:

- *Wyeth:* Sells multivitamins under the brand name of Centrum.
- *SmithKline Beecham:* Sells nutritional and natural products under the labels Scott's emulsion, Eunova, Horlicks, Lucozade, Ribena, Cetebe, Abtei, and Alluna Sleep. SmithKline recently offered RemiFemin, a pop-ular herbal menopause supplement in Europe.

- *Pfizer:* Sells an array of natural medicine offerings, such as Lydia Pinkham, Nature's Bounty, Goldline, and vitamin E and glucosamine and chondroitin products. It has also diversified into pet vitamins, including Pet-Cal, Pet-Tinic, and Pet-Tabs Plus.

Consumers spend $21.3 billion on supplements, including multivitamins/minerals ($4.2 billion), single vitamins ($3 billion), single minerals ($1.8 billion), sports supplements ($2.2 billion), and botanicals/herbs ($4.4 billion).[13] All providers, CAM and non-CAM, generate strong sales in the pharmaceutical and nutritional supplement industry respectively, both from prescriptions and recommendations.

## PROFILING THE CAM CONSUMER BASE

What does a CAM user look like? What are the demographics that the physician, hospital, or clinic administrator need to understand to meet the needs of this growing consumer base? CAM utilization spans all socioeconomic sectors, yet there are demographics that display higher utilization[14]:

- Women more than men
- People with higher education levels
- People who have been hospitalized in the past year
- Former smokers

**Figure 6.1 CAM Use by U.S. Adults**

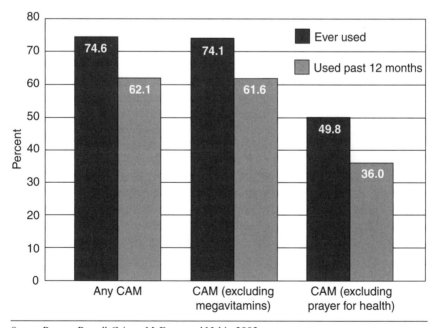

*Source:* Barnes, Powell-Griner, McFann, and Nahin 2002.

**Figure 6.2 CAM Use by Race/Ethnicity**

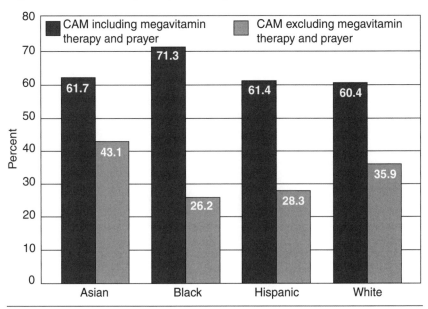

*Source:* Barnes, Powell-Griner, McFann, and Nahin 2002.

**Figure 6.3 CAM Use by Domain and Whole Medical Systems**

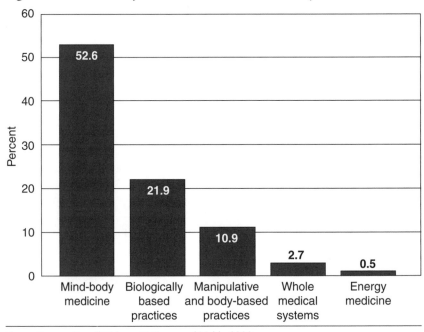

*Source:* Barnes, Powell-Griner, McFann, and Nahin 2002.

**Figure 6.4 10 Most Common CAM Therapies**

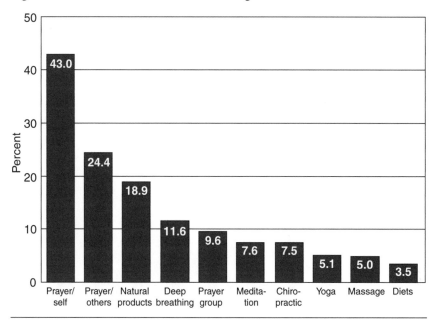

*Source:* Barnes, Powell-Griner, McFann, and Nahin 2002.

**Figure 6.5 Top 10 Natural Products\***

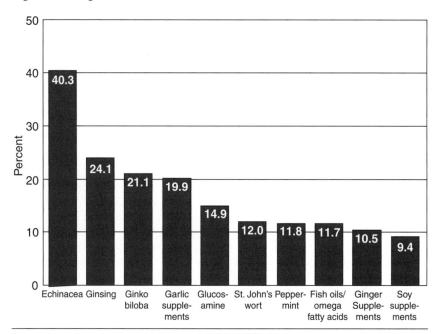

*Source:* Barnes, Powell-Griner, McFann, and Nahin 2002.

*The percentage for each product represents its rate of use among U.S. adults who use natural products.

Figure 6.6 Disease/Condition for Which CAM Is Most Frequently Used*

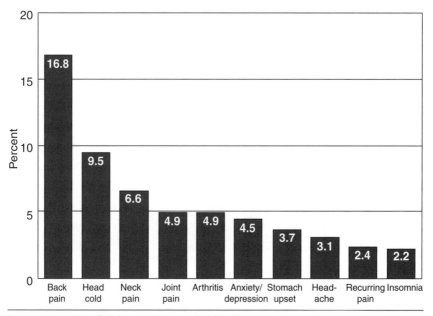

*Source:* Barnes, Powell-Griner, McFann, and Nahin 2002.
*These figures exclude the use of megavitamin therapy and prayer.

Prayer is the most commonly used CAM therapy. It is categorized as CAM since has not been embraced by the allopathic model as a tool in healthcare. When prayer is included in the definition of CAM, the mind-body medicine category becomes the most commonly used CAM category at 53 percent. Yet when prayer is not included, biological-based therapies, defined as substances found in nature, such as herbs, special diets, or vitamins at doses not used by conventional medicine, were used at a rate of 22 percent.[15]

## SELF-MEDICATION WITH NATURAL PRODUCTS AND POTENTIAL REPERCUSSIONS

Only 12 percent of the individuals using CAM report seeking the guidance of a licensed CAM provider when utilizing CAM therapies, raising the question of potential safety issues relative to self-prescribing. With nearly 20 percent of consumers of CAM reporting the use of supplements, it is worth noting that gingko, ginseng, garlic, fish oil, and ginger all possess blood-thinning properties. The number of individuals on prescribed blood thinners such as warfarin (Coumadin), heparin, Plavix, and aspirin illustrates the need for healthcare providers to become knowledgeable on potential interactions between CAM and allopathic medical therapies. Likewise, St. John's Wort ranked as the sixth most common supplement, has been shown to decrease blood levels of drugs metabolized by the

**Figure 6.7 Reasons People Use CAM**

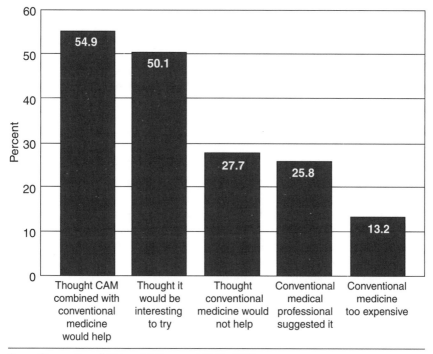

*Source:* Barnes, Powell-Griner, McFann, and Nahin 2002.

cytochrome oxidase P3A4 pathway (CYP3A4) by upwards of 50 percent.[16] These drugs include cardiac, immune, and psychiatric medications like amitriptyline* (Elavil), benzodiazepines alprazolam (Xanax), triazolam (Halcion), sertraline (Zoloft), and venlafaxine (Effexor).

## CAM UTILIZATION REFLECTS PRIMARY CARE MEDICINE

The health conditions that motivate patients to seek CAM therapies parallel those that motivate them to seek allopathic care: back, neck, head, or joint aches, and other painful conditions; colds; anxiety or depression; gastrointestinal disorders; and sleeping problems. The leading driver of CAM interventions appears to be pain.

## WHAT ARE THE ECONOMIC IMPLICATIONS?

The accounting for CAM expenditures is incompletely understood, since transactions are frequently being made outside of customary medical channels and third-party reimbursement. It is estimated that the U.S. public spent $36 billion to

$47 billion on CAM therapies in 1997 (the latest year for which data are available). Approximately $12 billion to $20 billion was paid out of pocket for the services of professional CAM healthcare providers.[17] The significance of these numbers is that CAM professional fees exceed the total amount paid for out-of-pocket expenses for hospitalizations in 1997 and represent about half of the amount paid for out-of-pocket physician services. Revenues continue to grow in nutraceutical purchases, including herbal remedies, vitamins, and other supplements, at a rate of $5 billion of out-of-pocket spending per year.[18]

## CREATING A CAM HEALTHCARE TEAM

What follows is an investigation into how CAM professionals function within America's healthcare terrain and their economic impact. Additionally, general concepts of how collaborative medicine can increase safety and financial viability will be discussed. A focus will be placed on the four largest CAM professional groups, chiropractors, naturopathic physicians, acupuncturists, and massage therapists, to reflect overall trends in CAM utilization. Each of these groups has been accepted as integrated services within hospitals and outpatient clinics and has varying levels of insurance reimbursement.

As the dean of naturopathic medicine and chief medical officer at NCNM, the supervision, growth, and management for 16 clinics, incorporating varying levels of integrated medicine, was my primary focus. Clinical faculty included naturopathic doctors (NDs), medical doctors (MDs), osteopathic physicians (DOs), chiropractic physicians (DCs), and Chinese medicine providers, including Master of Oriental Medicine and licensed acupuncturists. A growing number of medical models have incorporated a patient oriented and collaborative medicine model that works at both a clinical and economic level and as discussed below.

## CAM PROVIDERS

Thus far, we have discussed CAM trends from the consumer side of the healthcare services model. Yet, there are well-established CAM medical models that represent a strong constituent group in the shaping of the evolving American healthcare system. To understand current and future economic trends and to be able to project future areas of growth, it is important to appreciate the educational backgrounds, scope of practice, and current economics of these professionals.

Lobbying efforts of all medical professions, scope of practice, insurance issues, and other legal and governmental regulatory processes are at play along with consumer spending patterns. The positioning for growth or strategizing to maintain market share are continuously influencing the American healthcare landscape. Legal skirmishes are routinely occurring at the state level across the United States, among CAM professionals, and between CAM and allopathic lobbyists as well.

## Chiropractic Economics, Evidence, and Education

There are over 53,000 chiropractic physician according to statistics from the U.S. Bureau of Labor. In general, chiropractors complete four years of chiropractic medical school after graduating college. Chiropractic educational programs in the United States are approved by an accrediting agency recognized by the U.S. Department of Education. Prior to practicing, chiropractic trainees must demonstrate competency and public safety knowledge by passing national board examinations and they must obtain state licenses.[19]

Most chiropractors go into solo practice and are self-employed. Some chiropractors choose not to practice full-time and work in academic teaching positions, perform research, or offer their services to hospitals, insurance companies, or natural medicine companies.[20]

Chiropractic physicians can be found in all 50 states and the District of Columbia. Scope of practice varies from state to state, with some serving as primary care physicians offering generalized, though somewhat limited, family medicine practices. The concept of a chiropractor as being limited in scope of practice to manipulation or adjustment of the spine is a misnomer. In the state of Oregon, chiropractic physicians can order laboratory and diagnostic imaging tests, perform physical exams, and perform minor surgery. With the aging population, the need for noninvasive treatments for mechanical and structural problems will continue to rise.

Chiropractic medicine embodies the growing acceptance of CAM providers by both the allopathic medical community and insurance companies. Chiropractics was once perceived as having little scientific evidence supporting its claims. But well-designed studies have clearly documented efficacy. Examples:

- Two hundred and fifty-two patients with low back pain secondary to osteoarthritis were randomly assigned to either the treatment group (moist hot pack plus chiropractic care) or the moist heat group subjects who attended 20 treatment sessions over several weeks. Chiropractic care combined with heat is more effective than heat alone for treating osteoarthritis-based lower back pain. Pain reduction occurs more rapidly and to a greater degree, and range of motion increases more rapidly and to a greater degree.[21]
- Flexion distraction is a commonly used form of chiropractic care with chiropractor utilization rates of 58 percent as seen in a study of 235 subjects who were randomized to either chiropractic care (flexion distraction) or physical therapy (exercise program). During the year after care, subjects who received chiropractic care (flexion distraction therapy) had significantly lower pain scores than subjects who received physical therapy (exercise program).[22]
- A randomized, double-blind clinical trial with 192 subjects experiencing low back pain of two to six weeks' duration were randomly allocated to three groups with interventions applied over two weeks. Interventions

were either chiropractic adjustments with placebo medicine, muscle relaxants with sham adjustments, or placebo medicine with sham adjustments. The Visual Analog Scale for Pain, Oswestry Disability Questionnaire, and Modified Zung Depression Scale were used. Chiropractics was more beneficial than placebo in reducing pain and more beneficial than either placebo or muscle relaxants in reducing global impression of severity scale.[23]

Current findings have shown that chiropractic medicine reduces pain, decreases medication, rapidly advances physical therapy, and requires very few passive forms of treatment, such as bed rest.[24]

A growing number of insurance plans cover chiropractic services, yet the extent of coverage varies greatly between plans; thus consumers must be savvy as to how to access care within the confines of their plan. Limits to a certain number of visits or spending limits per annum are still common.

For salaried chiropractors, the median income was approximately $69,910 in May 2004. The middle 50 percent earned between $46,710 and $118,280 a year. In a survey conducted by *Chiropractic Economics* magazine in 2005, the mean salary for chiropractors was $104,363. Factors affecting income include number of years in practice, location of practice relative to patient density, the number of other chiropractors in area, and local socioeconomic demographics.

The predominant reason for a chiropractic visit is back-related pain. This should not be surprising, since 31 million Americans experience low-back pain at any given time.[25] According to survey evidence, 50 percent of all working Americans report having back pain symptoms each year, and 80 percent will experience back pain sometime during their life.[26] Furthermore, back pain is one of the most common reasons for missed work, second only to upper-respiratory infections. The economic impact of back pain in the United States is staggering, with at least $50 billion spent annually.[27] Thus, the addition of chiropractic services into an integrated practice incorporating allopathic and other services provides the potential for increased income while helping to ensure continuity of care.

With the rise in the aging population, high level of sedentary jobs, increasing rate of obesity, and high-stress living, the need for chiropractic medicine in the field of medicine fills a gap in the current healthcare needs of Americans. The question arises within the ranks of CAM providers of whether their profession will go the way of DOs and that absorption into the allopathic model will occur.

Upon reviewing the current level of evidence-based medical studies, the Agency for Health Care Policy and Research, a federal government research organization, made the recommendation that individuals suffering from low-back pain begin with the most conservative care first, with spinal manipulation as a safe, effective, drugless form of initial professional treatment for acute low-back problems in adults.[28] Chiropractic physicians spend an equal amount of classroom and clinical hours (minus residency) in their training as allopathic physicians.

### Naturopathic Economics, Evidence, and Education

Naturopathic medicine in the United States has grown out of traditional healing practices from around the world. Of CAM providers, the licensed naturopathic physician (ND) is the most broadly trained primary care healthcare provider. There has been a resurgence in naturopathic medicine. Currently there are only about 3,500 licensable NDs in North America—those in jurisdictions offerings NDs the ability to hold a license to practice naturopathic medicine. There are currently only five accredited schools offering four-year postbaccalaureate doctorate degrees:

- Bastyr University (Kenmore, Washington)
- Canadian College of Naturopathic Medicine (North York, Canada)
- National College of Natural Medicine (Portland, Oregon)
- Southwest College of Naturopathic Medicine & Health Sciences (Tempe, Arizona)
- University of Bridgeport College of Naturopathic Medicine (Bridgeport, Connecticut)

The majority of states have licensed naturopathic medicine at different times since its formation as a distinct American medical profession in 1902, yet only 14 states currently license NDs: Alaska, Arizona, California, Connecticut, Hawaii, Idaho, Kansas, Maine, Montana, New Hampshire, Oregon, Utah, Vermont, and Washington. Additional NDs are licensed in the District of Columbia, U.S. Virgin Islands, and Puerto Rico.

It is important to differentiate between four-year ND medical school graduates and the graduates of correspondence schools that can often use the initials ND or NMD behind their names in unlicensed states. Thus, inquiring about the school an ND has graduated from is an important question to understand the level of training received. The term ND is used here to designate licensed four-year graduates of one of the five naturopathic medical schools who have passed national licensure exams.

Naturopathic physicians are trained in basic sciences the first two years, while the last two years are spent in a blend of clinical training and classroom instruction. Naturopathic physicians enjoy a broad scope of practice in such states as Arizona, Washington, and Oregon. Collaborative professional relationships between conventional medical doctors and licensed NDs are becoming more common. NDs are broadly trained in botanical medicine, nutrition, supplements, manipulation of the spine, minor surgery, standard physical exam, diagnostic blood work, and imaging studies. NDs also have prescription-writing privileges and can apply for U.S. Drug Enforcement Administration numbers to prescribe narcotics and sedatives, as determined by each state's licensure guidelines.[29] Naturopathic physicians spend an equal amount of classroom and clinical hours (minus residency) in their training, as do allopathic physicians.

The guiding principle for naturopathic physicians is *Vis Medicatrix Naturae* (The Healing Power of Nature). This concept guides NDs as they access healthcare interventions, prioritizing the least invasive approach over more aggressive and potentially more risky procedures.

---

### Guiding Principles of Naturopathic Physicians

- The healing power of nature.
- First do no harm.
- Treat the whole person.
- Treat the cause.
- Prevention is the best cure.
- The physician is a teacher.

---

Naturopathic physicians generally do not work within the hospital setting, practicing instead alone, in group practices, or in integrated clinical settings. NDs routinely work with allopathically trained primary care physicians, internists, and specialists in comanaging patients, as appropriate, to access additional diagnostic and therapeutic expertise, much the same as a family medicine physician makes referrals.

A national survey on Americans' use of CAM, published in 2004, reported that less than 1 percent of the 31,000 survey respondents had used naturopathy.[30] Though the 1 percent number seems low, it is important to remember that there are only 3,500 naturopathic doctors licensed in 14 states, compared with over 50,000 chiropractors and nearly one million medical and osteopathic doctors licensed in 50 states. The survey noted above demonstrates the following rationale for utilization of ND services:

- Sixty-two percent believed that naturopathic medicine combined with conventional medicine would help.
- Fifty-three percent believed conventional medical treatments would not help.
- Forty-four percent thought naturopathic medicine would be interesting to try.
- Twenty-eight percent responded that conventional medicine was too expensive.
- Seventeen percent were referred to a naturopathic doctor by a conventional medical professional.

Almost 75 percent of all naturopathic visits were for chronic health conditions, such as fatigue, headache, and back symptoms. In a comparison among naturopathic practices between the east coast (Connecticut) and the west coast (Washington), the following prescription trends were noted: botanical medicines (51 percent of visits in Connecticut, 43 percent in Washington), vitamins (41 percent and 43 percent), minerals (35 percent and 39 percent), homeopathy, which is the use of dilute amounts of specially prepared natural substances that are not sufficiently concentrated to be considered a botanical, vitamin, or mineral (29 percent and 19 percent), and allergy treatments (11 percent and 13 percent). The mean visit length was about 40 minutes. Approximately half the visits were paid for directly by the patient.[31]

Visits in Connecticut were slightly more likely to be covered by insurance than visits in Washington, 60 percent versus 49 percent of visits.[31] More than 70 percent of visits included examinations or the ordering of diagnostic or screening tests, most often assessment of vital signs and upper respiratory exams related to infection.[31]

Naturopathic practice also involves significant amounts of patient counseling and education. On average, naturopathic physicians spend more than twice as much time with patients as conventional physicians at each visit, 40 minutes versus 14 minutes, permitting greater time to address health concerns and build the foundation for a deeper doctor-patient relationship.[32]

A common patient motivation observed by naturopathic physicians is a level of concern and frustration among people that getting an annual physical, basic blood work, and cholesterol count is still not sufficient to avoid deadly health trends—such as seen in recent diabetic statistics[33]:

- *Total:* 20.8 million people—7 percent of the population—have diabetes.
- *Diagnosed:* 14.6 million people.
- *Undiagnosed:* 6.2 million people.

People thus often go to naturopathic doctors in an attempt to get a fuller picture of their overall health and to become personally empowered regarding their level of wellness. A growing concept is to focus on wellness care versus healthcare, since wellness is descriptive of a heightened level of health.

The average naturopathic physician's salary varies greatly depending on the location of their practice, insurance reimbursement, chosen field of self-specialization, and practice style. Salaries range from $75,000 to $150,000 and up for full-time physicians in eclectic practices.

### Acupuncture Economics, Evidence, and Education

There are currently about 16,000 acupuncturists in the United States, and it is estimated that this number will increase by 10 percent per year over the next decade. Although acupuncturists earn approximately $40,000 to $90,000 per year, experienced acupuncturists have been able to earn as much as $10,000 to $20,000 per month.[34] State licensure and national board exams are required to demonstrate and maintain competency.

Acupuncture has grown in popularity in the United States during the last twenty years. The report from a Consensus Development Conference on Acupuncture held at the National Institutes of Health (NIH) in 1997 stated that acupuncture is being widely practiced—by thousands of physicians, dentists, acupuncturists, and other practitioners—for relief or prevention of pain and for various other health conditions.[35]

In addition, the 2002 National Health Interview Survey estimated that 8.2 million U.S. adults had used acupuncture, and an estimated 2.1 million U.S. adults had used acupuncture in the previous year.[36]

Acupuncture originated in China more than 2,000 years ago. The term *acupuncture* describes a group of medical procedures used to stimulate anatomical points on the body. The most heavily researched form of acupuncture is the technique that involves penetrating the skin with thin, solid, metallic needles that are manipulated by the hands or by electrical stimulation.

The theory of acupuncture cannot be readily defined in Western medicine terms. Rather, it's important to understand the unique concepts of traditional Chinese medicine (TCM), such as qi (chi) and meridians.

Qi refers to the energy emanating from within and flowing throughout the human body. The flow of qi in the body is often compared with the nervous system or circulatory system, yet the concept of meridians, which are the paths through which qi travels, are completely unique to TCM and there are no exact comparisons. The performance of the body is dependent upon qi, and there can be no function without qi and no qi without function. Qi is also considered the life force, or the vital force, and with its total absence there is death.

Meridians were described over 2,000 years ago by Chinese physicians who posited the presence of 14 major channels that serve as the conduits of qi. Meridians comprise an intricate and invisible network transporting and directing qi to every part of the body. Through empiric observation, the destinations of the meridians have been quantified to 361 regular acupuncture points on the major meridians where qi can be accessed and stimulated as clinically indicated.

Blocked qi can lead to health maladies. Both external and internal substances and circumstance can lead to an imbalance of the flow of qi. These include poor nutrition, impure food, toxic air or water, infectious agents, organ disease, and traumatic events or overuse injuries.

Research indicates that acupuncture releases endorphins and other pain inhibitors, and it decreases inflammation. There are many well-designed studies on the benefits of acupuncture that meet the standards of the allopathic model:

- Forty-nine patients with temporomandibular joint dysfunction (TMD) were treated with a combination of acupuncture and manual therapy two or three times a week at the hospital. The pain and maximal mouth opening (MMO) were assessed before and after one and four weeks of treatment. The combination therapy produced significant changes in pain levels and mouth opening. These findings suggest that combining manual therapy and acupuncture decreases the pain level and increases the MMO of TMD patients.[37]
- A random, controlled trial of 570 patients with osteoarthritis of the knee had 23 true acupuncture sessions over 26 weeks. Controls received six two-hour sessions over 12 weeks or 23 sham acupuncture sessions

over 26 weeks. Primary outcomes were changes in the Western Ontario and McMaster Universities Osteoarthritis Index (WOMAC) pain and function scores at 8 and 26 weeks. Secondary outcomes were patient global assessment, six-minute walk distance, and physical health scores of the 36-Item Short-Form Health Survey (SF-36). Participants in the true acupuncture group experienced greater improvement in WOMAC function scores than the sham acupuncture group at 8 weeks. At 26 weeks, the true acupuncture group experienced significantly greater improvement than the sham group in the WOMAC function score. The conclusion is drawn that acupuncture seems to provide improvement in function and pain relief as an adjunctive therapy for osteoarthritis of the knee when compared with credible sham acupuncture and education control groups.[38]

Current spending on acupuncture services is approximately $500 million per year. Conditions treated by acupuncture include pain, stress, insomnia, addictions, arthritis, digestive disorders, headaches, fatigue, and allergies.[39]

## Massage Therapy Economics, Evidence, and Education

According to the U.S. Department of Labor, employment for massage therapists is expected to grow faster than average, at a rate of 18 to 26 percent, with 97,000 massage therapists working in 2004. About two-thirds were self-employed.[40] Currently, consumers visit massage therapists about 114 million times every year. The percentage of American adults receiving one or more massages from a massage therapist in the previous year (18 percent) more than doubled since 1997 (8%).[41]

Massage therapists can specialize in over 80 different types of massage techniques. A sampling includes Swedish massage, deep tissue massage, reflexology, acupressure, sports massage, and neuromuscular massage. In simple terms, massage therapy is a hands-on manipulation of the soft tissues of the body, including muscles, connective tissue, tendons, ligaments, and joints. The principle goal is to improve the circulation, speed the removal of metabolic waste products from tissues, support healthy lymphatic flow, and relax the body. Additional benefits include increased flexibility of muscles, ligaments, and other soft tissues, pain relief, and warming up before a sporting event.

Here is a description of a few common types of massage techniques:

- *Deep tissue massage* is used to release chronic muscle tension through slower strokes and more direct pressure, or friction, applied across the grain of the muscles. Techniques employing breath and movement are also used for releasing muscular congestion.
- *Shiatsu* is a Japanese form of massage. It can used to assist with specific injuries, overall health, and to support relaxation. The philosophy underlying Shiatsu is that qi energy flows throughout the meridians. The

goal of the Shiatsu practitioner is to employ a variety of techniques to improve energy flow. These may include gentle holding; pressing with palms, thumbs, fingers, elbows, knees, and feet on the meridians; and, when appropriate, more dynamic rotations and stretches.

- *Swedish massage* is a collection of gentle techniques designed primarily to relax muscles by applying pressure to them against deeper muscles and bones and massaging in the same direction as the blood flows to the heart. The concept is that the lymph system and veins (which carry blood back to the heart) both rely on muscle action, rather than heart pump pressure, to keep the lymphatic system flowing.

Prior to a massage therapy session, an interview with the patient occurs to find out about the person's medical history. This helps screen patients that may not be medically appropriate for massage therapy, because massage can increase circulation, disrupt underlying structural or pathological conditions, spread infection, and aggravate inflammatory processes.

Massage therapists work in private offices, hospitals, nursing homes, fitness centers, and sports medicine facilities. Due to the physical nature of the work and time needed in between sessions to clean and prepare rooms, massage therapists who give massages from 15 to 30 hours per week consider themselves to be full-time workers.

Each state has varying requirements for massage therapists to practice. In 2004, 33 states and the District of Columbia passed laws regulating massage therapy. Most of the boards require massage therapists to complete a formal education program and pass the national certification examination or a state exam. There are roughly 1,300 massage therapy postsecondary schools, college programs, and training programs in the United States. Massage therapy training programs are generally accredited by a state board or other accrediting agency. Approximately 300 programs are accredited by a state board or department of education–certified accrediting agency.

After completing a training program, many massage therapists opt to take the national certification examination for therapeutic massage and bodywork administered by the National Certification Board for Therapeutic Massage and Bodywork.

Median hourly earnings of massage therapists, including gratuities earned, were $15.36 in May 2004. The highest 10 percent of massage therapists earned more than $32.21 per hour. Actual income may be higher, since massage therapists in private office settings typically charge between $60 and $90 per session.

## MANDATE FOR A HEALTHIER UNITED STATES: HINTS FROM EUROPE

The Institute of Medicine (IOM) presented a review of the role of CAM in 2004 to integrate CAM into allopathic medical practice. The recommendation was that allopathic professional training programs incorporate adequate information so that graduates could advise patients on appropriate access to CAM services.[42] Adopting an approach that embraces diverse approaches to healthcare as practiced in European countries was encouraged. A study reported the following findings in Germany:

> The goal was to chart the use of complementary medications compared with conventional treatments among practitioners and patients in Germany. A cohort study of 4178 patients presenting with chronic as well as acute symptoms by 218 practitioners at 218 centers was reviewed at clinics that focused on either conventional medicine, complementary medicine, or both. The results were clear that complementary medicine was preferentially prescribed over conventional medicine in patients <18 and >65 years old, in women, and in patients with chronic symptoms. The decision to incorporate complementary medicine was based on both the patient's and the practitioner's wishes in 40.8% of the cases compared with 25.8% of the cases of conventional therapies. Tolerability and satisfaction with treatment appeared greater with complementary than with conventional therapies. The conclusion read, Patients receiving complementary medicine appear to be more closely involved in the decision process and more satisfied with treatments than conventionally treated patients.[43]

CAM treatments are used by many therapists throughout Europe.[44] The major forms are acupuncture, homeopathy, spinal manipulation, and botanical medicine. Consumer surveys consistently show positive public attitudes to complementary medicine, with about 60 percent of the public in the Netherlands and Belgium[45] stating that they are prepared to pay extra for insurance premiums for it, and 74 percent of the British public favoring it being available in the National Health Service.[46]

In European countries where statistics are available, CAM therapies are used by 20 percent to 50 percent of the population. The popularity of complementary medicine is growing rapidly. For instance, in 1981, 6.4 percent of the Dutch population visited a therapist providing complementary medicine, a number that increased to 15.7 percent in 1990.[47] Though current data are not readily available, it is estimated to have experienced a similar growth to that seen in the United States during the same period.

One of the challenges in comparing the European and U.S. healthcare consumer is the differences in services available, definitions of CAM, and overall attitudes relative to healthcare and cultural preference for therapeutic modalities. For instance, in France, homoeopathy is the most popular form of CAM therapy, and it rose from utilization by 16 percent of the population in 1982 to 36 percent in 1992.[48]

In the United Kingdom, members of the Consumers Association who visited a nonallopathic practitioner in the preceding 12 months rose from 14 percent in 1985 to almost 25 percent in 1991.[49] The United Kingdom has among the lowest per capita spending in the European Union for over-the-counter homeopathy, but the British market is growing by 20 percent a year. Countries such as Greece and Portugal with low per capita spending have even more rapid growth—30 percent a year[50]

## GOVERNMENTAL RESEARCH INTO CAM TRENDS AND ALLOCATION OF RESOURCES

The United States Congress passed legislation in 1991 that allowed the National Institutes of Health (NIH) to establish the Office of Alternative Medicine (OAM) with an annual budget of $2 million to coordinate research on CAM practices.

In 1998, Congress established the National Center for Complementary and Alternative Medicine (NCCAM), with an annual budget of more than $68 million, to supersede OAM. NCCAM's mission is to support basic and applied CAM research and inform both the public and healthcare providers.

Within the first five years, NCCAM achieved the following results:

• Over 780 projects at 123 institutions were funded.
• Over 700 scientific publications were generated by funded research.
• The enrollment of nearly 40,000 participants in clinical protocols was supported.
• 1.5 million visitors visited its Web site (http://www.nccam.nih.gov) annually.
• The search engine CAM on PubMed lists nearly 400,000 articles on CAM topics.

Though great strides have been made via NCCAM, the $122.6 million allocated in fiscal year (FY) 2006 is not sufficient to meet the expansive needs to conduct research in the fields of CAM and to educate the public on efficacy and safety.

## INTEGRATED MEDICINE IN ACADEMIA

The National Institutes of Health has fostered healthcare collaboration through NIH–sponsored R-25 grants. The goal of each grant is to expose medical students and faculty to CAM concepts as part of an institutional medical curriculum. A spirit of appreciation has grown between CAM and non-CAM providers through lecture series and CAM curriculum discussions of actual patient care. Portland, Oregon, the location for this NIH grant, provides a unique setting for this level of academic collaboration. Within the confines of the metropolitan area, there is OHSU (allopathic medical school), NCNM (naturopathic medical school), OCOM (Chinese medicine school), and WSCC (chiropractic medical school), giving faculty and students from each institution an opportunity to interview and work with patients in a collaborative fashion, comanaging the cases. Shortly after the beginning of this grant, the Center for Women's Health at OHSU brought CAM providers delivering naturopathic, chiropractic and acupuncturist services on board.[51]

## INTEGRATED MEDICINE AT WORK

Cancer Treatment Centers of America (CTCA), a network of hospitals dedicated to the holistic treatment of patients with cancer, serves as a role model for blending comprehensive healthcare by having skilled professionals from CAM fields work side by side with their allopathic colleagues.

> Physically, CTCA is a network of cancer treatment hospitals and facilities. But it's much more than that. CTCA programs can be a cancer patient's greatest ally when it comes to fighting cancer. Because we understand that cancer doesn't just affect one part of your body—it affects all of you and everything in your life. So that's how we treat it. Top to bottom, inside and out, it's total care for your mind, body and spirit.
>
> At CTCA, we assemble a dedicated team of experts who provide comprehensive, personalized treatment. Your team will fight your cancer on many fronts, through an integrated combination of medical, nutritional, physical, psychological and spiritual therapies.[52]

Naturopathic physicians, pastoral services, acupuncturists, and dieticians work together in a patient oriented manner, focusing on the individual needs of each patient to strengthen the mind, body, and spirit.[53]

When a collaborative team of healthcare professionals join forces in the pursuit of excellence in healthcare with the single focus on patient-oriented wellness, the barriers of personal and philosophical bias can be shelved for the greater good and the true calling of all healers can be fulfilled to serve humanity without prejudice.


## CONCLUSION

In the United States, we live in a melting pot of cultures; yet, with the immersion into the U.S. Westernized culture, the health practices of the majority of Americans have been based on allopathic medicine. Over the course of the last few decades, U.S. citizens have fallen prey to epidemics of obesity, diabetes, depression, heart disease, and stress-related diseases, despite the current level of healthcare delivery and focus on preventive medicine. The current system is not only bankrupting America, it is not sustaining its people with the robust health of a technologically advanced and wealthy country. We can do better. In short, CAM and allopathic practitioners need to work together with respect, an open mind, and the intent to help support the patient in achieving their health goals in a safe and positive fashion.

The current healthcare system is not sustainable. The United States has a growing, aging population that will continue to need healthcare resources. Medicare and private insurance companies cannot sustain the current level of expenditure without significant premium rate hikes or a decrease in services offered.

It is time that the fragmented healthcare system in America embrace a more collaborative and holistic model of care. Currently, an estimated 38 million U.S. adults are using botanical medicine, 29 million are using relaxation techniques, and 15 million U.S. adults are using chiropractic. Among CAM users, 41 percent used two or more CAM therapies during the prior year. CAM is here to stay. Healing of America's healthcare system will promote healing of its people.

Key Concepts

- CAM is most often used to treat back pain, colds, neck pain, joint stiffness, and depression.
- The percentage of patients who believe that combining CAM with conventional healthcare approaches provides added benefits is 54.9 percent.
- Licensed CAM providers are qualified healthcare providers that graduate from accredited schools and share a common goal of protecting the patient from harm and assisting them with their health needs.
- European countries, organizations, and academic settings have demonstrated that patients' desire to access CAM services and allopathic services in a parallel fashion is not only possible, but results in improved patient and family satisfaction.
- United in a collaborative spirit, CAM and conventional medicine can serve individual patient needs, promote continuity of care, and deliver superior care.

## NOTES

1. Flexner, A. 1910. *Medical Education in the United States and Canada: A Report to the Carnegie Foundation for the Advancement of Teaching*. New York: Carnegie Foundation.

2. Eisenberg, D. M., R. C. Kessler, C. Foster, F. E. Norlock, D. R. Calkins, and T. L. Delbanco. 1993. "Unconventional Medicine in the United States: Prevalence, Costs, and Patterns of Use." *New England Journal of Medicine* 328 (4): 246–252.

3. Kessler, R. C., R. B. Davis, and D. F. Foster. 2001. "Long-term Trends in the Use of Complementary and Alternative Medical Therapies in the United States." *Annals of Internal Medicine* 135 (4): 262–268.

4. Rosengren, A., S. Hawken, S. Ounpuu, M. Sliwa, W. Zubaid, K. Almahmeed, C. Blackett, H. Sitthi-amorn, S. Sato, and S. Yusuf. 2004. "INTERHEART Association of Psychosocial Risk Factors with Risk of Acute Myocardial Infarction in 111,119 Cases and 13,648 Controls from 52 Countries." *Lancet* 364 (9438): 953–962.

5. "CAMBASICS, 2007." Available at: http://nccam.nih.gov/. Accessed May 15, 2007.

6. British Medical Association. Complementary. 1993. *Medicine: New Approaches to Good Practice*. Oxford: Oxford University Press.

7. Pietroni, P. 1992. "Beyond the Boundaries: Relationship between General Practice and Complementary Medicine." *British Medical Journal* 305 (6853): 564–566.

8. Fisher, P., and A. Ward. 1994. "Medicine in Europe: Complementary Medicine in Europe." *BMJ* 309 (6947): 107–111.

9. Eisenberg, D., R. B. Davis, S. L. Ettner, S. Appel, S. Wilkey, M. Van Rompay, and R. C. Kessler. 1998. "Trends in Alternative Medicine Use in the United States, 1990–1997: Results of a Follow-up National Survey." *Journal of the American Medical Association* 280 (18): 1569–1575.

10. Ewers, H-H. 2001. *Children's Rights in Literature*. Available at: http//www.goethe.de/os/hon/kiju/ewemod.htm. Accessed May 6, 2002.

11. Fletcher, R. H., and K. M. Fairfield. 2002. "Vitamins for Chronic Disease Prevention in Adults." *Journal of the American Medical Association* 287 (23): 3127–3129.

12. MacWilliams, L. 2003. *Comparative Guide to Nutritional Supplements.* Northern Dimensions Publishing. Vernon, British Columbia, Canada.

13. "NIH, 2007." Available at: http://ods.od.nih.gov/pubs/fnce2006/What DietarySupplementsAreUSChildrenTaking_Picciano.pdf. Accessed May 15, 2007.

14. "NIH, 2007," Available at: http://nccam.nih.gov/news/camsurvey_fs1.htm. Accessed May 15, 2007.

15. "NIH, 2007." Available at: http://nccam.nih.gov/. Accessed May 15, 2007.

16. Meletis, C., and T. Jacobs. 2005. *Interactions between Drugs and Natural Medicines.* 2nd ed. Sandy, OR: Eclectic Medical Publishing.

17. Eisenberg, D., R. B. Davis, S. L. Ettner, S. A. Wilkey, M. Van Rompay, and R. C. Kessler. 1998. "Trends in Alternative Medicine Use in the United States, 1990–1997: Results of a Follow-up National Survey." *Journal of the American Medical Association* 280 (18): 1569–1575.

18. Centers for Medicare and Medicaid Services. n.d. *1997 National Health Expenditures Survey.* Available at: http://www.cms.hhs.gov/statistics/nhe.

19. Meeker, W., and H. Haldeman. 2002. "Chiropractic: A Profession at the Crossroads of Mainstream and Alternative Medicine." *Annals of Internal Medicine* 136 (3): 216–227.

20. U.S. Department of Labor Bureau of Labor Statistics Occupational Outlook Handbook. Available at: www.bls.gov/oco/ocos071.htm#emply. Accessed May 15, 2007.

21. Beyerman, K. L., M. B. Palmerino, L. E. Zohn, and K. Foster. 2006. "Efficacy of Treating Low Back Pain and Dysfunction Secondary to Osteoarthritis: Chiropractic Care Compared with Moist Heat Alone." *Journal of Manipulative and Physiological Therapeutics* 29 (2): 107–114.

22. Cambron, J. A., M. R. Gudavalli, D. Hedeker, M. McGregor, J. Jedlicka, M. Keenum, A. J. Ghanayem, A. G. Patwardhan, and S. E. Furner. 2006. "One-Year Follow-up of a Randomized Clinical Trial Comparing Flexion Distraction with an Exercise Program for Chronic Low-Back Pain." *Journal of Alternative and Complementary Medicine* 12 (7): 659–668.

23. Hoiriis, K. T., B. Pfleger, F. C. McDuffie, G. Cotsonis, O. Elsangak, R. Hinson, and G. Verzosa. 2004. "A Randomized Clinical Trial Comparing Chiropractic Adjustments to Muscle Relaxants for Subacute Low Back Pain." *Journal of Manipulative and Physiological Therapeutics* 27 (6): 388–398.

24. Pain M. B., H. Heart, M.C.H. Failure, and E. Parenting, 2003. "Time to Recognize Value of Chiropractic Care? Science and Patient Satisfaction Surveys Cite Usefulness of Spinal Manipulation." *Orthopedics Today* 23 (2): 14–15.

25. Jensen, M., M. N. Brant-Zawadzki, N. Obuchowski, M. T. Modic, D. Malkasian, and Jeffrey S. Ross. 1994. "Magnetic Resonance Imaging of the Lumbar Spine in People Without Back Pain." *New England Journal of Medicine* 331 (2): 69–116.

26. Vallfors, B. 1985. "Acute, Subacute and Chronic Low Back Pain: Clinical Symptoms, Absenteeism and Working Environment." *Scandinavian Journal of Rehabilitation Medicine,* Supplement 11: 1–98.

27. This total only represents the more readily identifiable costs for medical care, workers compensation payments, and time lost from work. It does not include costs associated with lost personal income due to acquired physical limitation resulting from a back problem and lost employer productivity due to employee medical absence.

Project Briefs: Back Pain Patient Outcomes Assessment Team (BOAT). In MEDTEP Update, Vol. 1 Issue 1, Agency for Health Care Policy and Research, Rockville, MD, Summer 1994.

28. Bigos, S., O. Bowyer, G. Braen, K. Brown, R. Deyo, S. Haldeman, J. L. Hart, E. W. Johnson, R. Keller, D. Kido, and M. H. Liang. 1994. *Acute Low Back Problems in Adults. Clinical Practice Guideline No.14. AHCPR Publication No. 95–0642.* Rockville, MD: Agency for Health Care Policy and Research, Public Health Service, U.S. Department of Health and Human Services.

29. Boon, H. S., D. C. Cherkin, J. Erro, K. J. Sherman, B. Milliman, J. Booker, E. H. Cramer, M. J. Smith, R. A. Deyo, and D. M. Eisenberg. 2004. "Practice Patterns of Naturopathic Physicians: Results from a Random Survey of Licensed Practitioners in Two US States." *BMC Complementary and Alternative Medicine* 4: 14.

30. Barnes, P. M., E. Powell-Griner, K. McFann, and R. L. Nahin. 2004. "Complementary and Alternative Medicine Use Among Adults: United States, 2002." *CDC Advance Data from Vital and Health Statistics* 343: 1–20.

31. Dunne, N., W. Benda, L. Kim, P. Mittman, R. Barrett, P. Snider, and J. Pizzorno. 2005. "Naturopathic Medicine: What Can Patients Expect?" *Journal of Family Practice* 54 (12).

32. Ibid.

33. National Diabetes Information Clearinghouse. Available at: http://diabetes.niddk.nih.gov/dm/pubs/statistics/index.htm#7. Accessed May 15, 2007.

34. American College of Acupuncture and Oriental Medicine. Available at: http://www.acaom.edu/en/cms. Accessed May 15, 2007.

35. Culliton, P. D. 1997. "Current Utilization of Acupuncture by United States Patients." Abstract presented at the National Institutes of Health Consensus Development Conference on Acupuncture. Bethesda, Maryland.

36. Barnes, P. M., E. Powell-Griner, K. McFann, and R. L. Nahin. 2004. "Complementary and Alternative Medicine Use Among Adults: United States, 2002." *CDC Advance Data from Vital and Health Statistics* 343: 1–20.

37. Shin, B. C., C. H. Ha, Y. S. Song, and M. S. Lee. 2007. "Effectiveness of Combining Manual Therapy and Acupuncture on Temporomandibular Joint Dysfunction: A Retrospective Study." *American Journal of Chinese Medicine* 35 (2): 203–208.

38. Manheimer, E., B. Lim, L. Lao, and B. Berman. 2006. "Acupuncture for Knee Osteoarthritis—A Randomised Trial Using a Novel Sham." *Acupuncture in Medicine* 24 (Suppl.): S7–S14.

39. "NIH, 2007." Available at: http://www.nih.gov/news/pr/nov97/od-05.htm. Accessed May 15, 2007.

40. U.S. Department of Labor/Bureau of Labor Statistics. Available at: http://www.bls.gov/oco/ocos295.htm. Accessed May 15, 2007.

41. National Holistic Institute, 2007. Available at: http://www.nhi.edu/massage-therapy-careers.html. Accessed May 15, 2007.

42. Committee on the Use of Complementary and Alternative Medicine by the American Public, Board on Health Promotion and Disease Prevention, and Institute of Medicine of the National Academies. 2005. *Complementary and Alternative Medicine in the United States.* Washington, D.C.: National Academic Press.

43. Schneider, B., J. Hanisch, and M. Weiser. 2004. "Complementary Medicine Prescription Patterns in Germany." *The Annals of Pharmacotherapy* 38 (3): 502–507.

44. Fisher, P., and A. Ward. 1994. "Medicine in Europe: Complementary Medicine in Europe." *British Medical Journal* 309 (6962):107–111.

45. Sermeus, G. 1991. "Alternative Health Care in Belgium: An Explanation of Various Social Aspects." In *Complementary Medicine and the European Community*, eds. G. Lewith, and D. Aldridge. Saffron Walden, Belgium: CW Daniel.

46. Fisher, P., and A. Ward. 1994. "Medicine in Europe: Complementary Medicine in Europe." *BMJ* 309 (6962):107–111.

47. Van Dijk, P. 1993. *Geneewijzen in Nederland*. Deventer, The Netherlands: Ankh-Hermes.

48. Fisher, P., and A. Ward. 1994. "Medicine in Europe: Complementary Medicine in Europe." *BMJ* 309 (6962):107–111.

49. Consumer's Association. 1992. *Regulation of Practitioners of Non-Conventional Medicine*. London: Consumer's Association.

50. Fulder, S., and R. Munro. 1992. *EEC Market for Homoeopathic Remedies*. London: McAlpine, Thorpe and London.

51. OHSU Center for Women's Health. Available at: http://www.ohsuwomens health.com/services/doctors/alt_consult.html. Accessed May 15, 2007.

52. Cancer Treatment Centers of America. Available at: www.cancercenter.com. Accessed May 15, 2007.

53. Cancer Treatment Centers of America. Available at: www.cancercenter.com. Accessed May 15, 2007.

# CHAPTER 7

# The Next Frontier in Addressing Clinical Supply Costs in Hospitals

Anand S. Joshi

Supply costs represent an important element of the business of healthcare from a number of different perspectives. From the macro viewpoint, clinical supplies are big business, and a review of the Fortune 50 makes that abundantly clear. Of these top 50 companies by revenue, five are major healthcare supply-related business, including pharmaceutical companies, medical device manufacturers, and distributors.[1] Cumulatively, clinical supplies utilized in hospitals account for roughly 10 percent of the $1.9 trillion spent on healthcare in the United States in 2004, and quite a few suppliers—Johnson & Johnson, Pfizer, Medtronic, for example—are truly household names.[2]

Similarly, from the micro viewpoint of individual acute care hospitals, supply costs for clinical items account for a significant piece of their expense base. While the exact proportion of spending on clinical supplies can vary tremendously based on the types and volumes of cases performed, it often represents, after labor-related costs, the largest category of expenses in an acute care hospital's profit and loss statement.[3] Indeed, given the increased financial pressures faced by acute care hospitals across the country over the last decade, the issue of addressing clinical supply costs in hospitals has become a more pressing challenge. This challenge has been highlighted not only in the relatively narrow field of hospital supply chain, but also more broadly in the popular press.[4]

The purpose of this chapter is to highlight cutting-edge approaches being taken by hospitals to lower supply chain costs on clinical supplies. Special attention is given to the challenges related to addressing costs associated with supplies whose use is driven primarily by physician preferences.

## RECENT ADVANCES IN HOSPITAL
## SUPPLY CHAIN PRACTICE

Given the scope and importance of addressing clinical supply costs, there have already been advances over the years. A lot of the progress has come from applying basic supply chain concepts, honed in other industries, to the hospital supply chain. For example, the emergence of the GPOs (group purchasing organizations) that represent hundreds, or even thousands, of hospitals derive a significant portion of their value by consolidating the spending base of these hospitals. This consolidation allows the group to approach suppliers with more leverage from a volume standpoint than a single institution could hope to amass. Although the business models of many of the nation's GPOs, such as Novation and Premier, have morphed to include other value-added elements for their hospital members,[5] such as focused utilization reviews on specific product categories and standardization analytics driven by information technology (IT), the model is still very much like the cooperatives established by farmers, independent grocers, and retail hardware stores to gain purchasing power.[6]

Another related supply chain concept that has its roots in the supply chain dogma of other, more industrial, businesses is standardization. Here, too, the relatively straightforward concept of one is better than two and two is better than three, whether it comes to number of suppliers involved in supplying a particular product or the number of actual products used, created value in the hospital supply chain when initially implemented. For example, gone are days where hospitals operated with multiple types of exam gloves from multiple suppliers or two different IV pumps, each with its own tubing and accessories. Standardization in these areas has resulted in more efficient, less costly, supply chains.

Finally, data has emerged as a significant force within the hospital supply chain. Relative to other industries, healthcare has always been hampered by an inadequate investment in IT.[7] By extension, it should come as no surprise that historically, hospital supply chain data were extremely difficult to obtain, analyze, and act on. Over the past several years, however, many hospitals, with the assistance of their GPOs, have become more adept at understanding their supply chain procurement costs.[8] For the most part, hospitals no longer need to rely on suppliers' databases to understand their own purchase history for a specific product. Rather, that information is readily available, accessible, and usable within a hospital's procurement database for helping address supply costs.

When placed in the context of "how things used to be," the advances highlighted above in the realm of supply costs are tremendous. The pace of change is often slow in the hospital environment, and departure from the status quo comes only with an enormous amount of effort and perseverance. However, returning to a macro perspective on the issue, numerous indicators suggest significant room for improvement. For example, the margins for earnings before interest, tax, depreciation, and amortization (EBITDA/total revenue) for major publicly traded hospitals over the past six years have trended downwards from approximately 18 percent to 15 percent from 2000 through 2005, with their supply expense ratios (supply expenses/total revenues) rising through that time period from less than 14 percent to more than 15 percent.[9] On the other hand, a view of major suppliers' gross margins (revenue generated from product sales minus the costs of making their actual products) shows that the majority of these suppliers have seen gross margins increase over the past several years.[10] Also, EBITDA margins of major publicly traded medical device manufacturers grew from 30 percent to 31 percent between 2002 and 2005.[11] Two conclusions can be drawn from these trends. One is that hospitals still face a significant operating margin challenge, driven at least partially by increased supply costs, making the need to address supply chain costs important. The second is that efforts at reducing hospital supply costs to date have certainly not whittled supplier margins to the bone—so, there is still work to be done.

To achieve further gains in addressing hospital supply costs, however, will not require merely further application of the methods and strategies described above, which are derived from successful supply chain approaches in other industries. To establish the next frontier in hospital supply cost reduction, the industry will have to establish a broader armamentarium of supply chain tools and techniques, unique to the hospital environment. Granted, this next frontier is already being established in some hospitals and hospital systems, but by no means has it been fully defined. The core elements of the emerging next frontier are hospitals taking a more nuanced view of the hospital supply base to inform cost-reduction strategies and more active engagement of physicians who utilize a great majority of the high-expense items in a hospital supply chain. As was the case with earlier advancements in addressing hospital supply costs, moving hospitals to embrace the new approaches highlighted below will not be an easy task. However, without these advancements, the progress seen within hospital supply chains over the past decades will likely stall and erode as suppliers fine-tune their own competitive strategies.

## CASE PRESENTATION

### Introduction

Pacemakers and automatic implantable cardiac defibrillators (AICDs) account for a significant amount of spending in any hospital with a sizeable electrophysiology (EP) program, and with unit costs ranging as high as $30,000 for top-of-the-line AICDs, the costs can add up quickly. The marketplace for these extremely complicated devices is dominated in the United States by three manufacturers—Medtronic, St. Jude, and Boston Scientific (formerly Guidant Corporation)—who introduce next generations of technology for each of the product segments of EP implants almost on a quarterly basis.[12] Hospital procurement departments struggle to control costs in this arena for several reasons. The companies and their representatives have, over the years, invested significant time and resources to establishing strong relationships with electrophysiologists. Also, given the complexity of the technology and the rapid introduction of similar devices with slightly enhanced features, the intrinsic value of these devices is hard to determine. Finally, there are no clinical trials demonstrating the superiority of one supplier's products over another's. In this setting, some hospitals attempt to standardize a significant percentage of their use of these devices to one supplier as a strategy to achieve the lowest pricing from the primary supplier. It is often difficult, however, to implement such a strategy, because hospitals have a difficult time engaging electrophysiologists on cost-related issues. Also, because each supplier routinely comes out with technology that may be perceived to be slightly better than the other suppliers' products, even those hospitals that have a compliance contract in place with one supplier often see the savings from that contract erode due to the volume of purchases made with the non-primary suppliers.

### Crosswalk Strategy

Hospitals that have been able to implement more progressive supply cost management strategies can have more success in controlling costs for electrophysiology implants. One academic medical center (AMC) in the northeast began by initiating a dialogue several years ago with electrophysiologists to categorize the roughly equivalent technologies sold by each supplier, stressing the value of pursuing a crosswalk strategy that would allow for physicians to access devices from any of the three primary suppliers. The key element of the dialogue was the development of an understanding that physicians would try to reduce their utilization of products that were priced at an unwarranted premium to similar competitive products. With this credible threat to potentially increase or decrease business based on relative pricing, the procurement officials of the hospital initiated negotiations with each of the suppliers. The hospital stressed that it was *not* interested in committing its physicians to utilize any specific volume of a suppliers' products. Rather, the hospital committed to routinely communicating any price differentials between competing products to physicians.

At the outset, the approach had a dramatic impact on pricing, since the physicians had heretofore rarely been engaged or involved in discussions when the hospital negotiated its EP implant contracts. Suppliers, faced with a united front from the hospitals and physicians working in concert, reduced their prices by approximately 20 percent (roughly $5 million in savings), without any commitment by the hospital to buy a specific amount of any particular supplier's product. Recognizing that suppliers' new product introductions could rapidly erode any reductions in price on previous models, the hospital procurement group and physicians routinely reviewed all new products being introduced by suppliers and ensured pricing was in line with the competition, updating the original crosswalk over time. When a supplier balked at lowering its prices, citing the value of its new technology, the hospital and physicians, armed with a solid fact base about comparative pricing and a credible threat to not utilize technology that was not fairly priced, were successful in maintaining a cap on the price increases associated with new technology. In the long term, utilizing the crosswalk strategy, the hospital was able to maintain very tight control over one of its largest and most complicated spending categories and allow its physicians the flexibility to utilize different suppliers' technologies for specific patients.

## CASE ANALYSIS: A NUANCED VIEW OF THE HOSPITAL CLINICAL SUPPLY BASE

Traditionally, the predominant strategy employed by hospitals to address supply costs has focused on standardization and utilizing GPO contracts that achieved lower prices based on commitments of such standardization.[13] The "standardization mantra" has become synonymous with hospital clinical supply cost reduction. A survey of hospital executives and supply chain managers published by the Healthcare Financial Management Association in 2002 ranked "involving clinicians in *standardization*" and "reducing operating room costs through *standardization*" as the two top future opportunities.[14] (emphasis added) Hospital procurement departments utilized the same approach in addressing spending on garbage bags, needles, and syringes, or interventional radiology guidewires.

Standardization strategies were only as effective as they were applicable to a particular spending category being reviewed. To overcome this challenge, hospital supply chain administrators have begun to segment their hospitals' spending base, and employ different strategies to address overall supply costs. Given the breadth of clinical supplies utilized in the hospital, there are a number of dimensions along which they could be divided—supplier, spending volume, and hospital department where primarily used. However, one of the most critical dimensions has heretofore *not* been a key driver of supply category designation. Operational stickiness refers to the extent to which a supply is built into the operations of the unit or units where it is utilized and, by extension, the difficulty created by changing supplies or having multiple types of similar supplies available. For instance, intravenous (IV) tubing and extension sets have a high level of operational stickiness. The notion of having multiple types of tubing available and needing to in-service nursing staff every few months with new IV supplies is unfathomable for most organizations. Likewise, many operating room (OR) implant sets (i.e., hips, knees, spinal fusion, etc.) have a high degree of operational stickiness in that the familiarity of the nursing staff in the ORs with specific trays and their components can significantly improve procedure flow and decrease operation time. For these types of categories (that is, those with significant operational stickiness), establishing a standard for use across the hospital, or a significant percent of use in the ORs, can lower the total cost of ownership in two ways:

- More efficient operations through increased familiarity with a standardized supply to reduce a hospital's costs
- Decreased personnel training costs for suppliers, leading to increased hospital discounts if these lowered expenses are shared with the hospital

A number of categories score lower on the operational stickiness scale, such as the guidewires or stents used by interventional cardiologists or radiologists.

Having a number of different suppliers' products is not challenging from an in-servicing perspective because a limited number of clinicians utilize these products, all of whom are proficient at using several different suppliers' products. While there may be inventory-holding costs for holding multiple suppliers' products, if the approximate pattern of usage of suppliers' products is known, excess inventory should be minimal. For instance, a catheterization lab that utilizes 50 guidewires a day by one supplier and wants to hold two days worth of inventory would carry 100 guidewires. Another lab that uses 20 guidewires a day of supplier A and 30 of supplier B that wants to maintain two days' worth of inventory would also need to hold 100 guidewires—40 from supplier A and 60 from supplier B. Certainly, organizing one shelf versus two shelves may be easier; however, the traditional view of narrowing the supplier base to lower inventory holding costs is often overstated for situations like this.

Interestingly, from a supplier standpoint, the cost structure to support a specific volume of sales in nonsticky categories is likely to be different from operationally sticky categories. For example, proportionally speaking, in a typical hospital setting, supplier representatives are physically present for many fewer cases that utilize guidewires and stents than in those utilizing spinal implants or orthopedic implants. Also, while suppliers of nonsticky categories are often willing to establish a consignment of product for a particular area in the hospital, the inventory turns (number of times per month the total value of product inventory gets used completely) on their consignment volume are much greater than in sticky categories, and hence, as a percent of sales, their working capital investment (value of products that a supplier has created but has not been paid for by a hospital) is often less.

The scale advantage for a supplier when a hospital standardizes to a single supplier for a particular nonsticky product category is significantly less than it is for a supplier of an operationally sticky product category. The cost to manufacture the product does not change if a single hospital chooses to standardize to a particular guidewire, and the proportion of a representative's time spent at an account relative to sales volume will likely increase or stay the same. Given these realities for both hospitals and suppliers, though, many hospitals still continue to utilize the same standardization approach to addressing costs in nonsticky categories, and suppliers continue to play along—offering the largest discounts to those customers who can commit to purchasing a large percentage of a particular supply from them.

## THE CROSSWALK STRATEGY FOR NONSTICKY PRODUCT CATEGORIES

Some hospitals are developing different strategies for handling nonsticky product categories—approaches that are more in line with the operational and fiscal realities for both suppliers and the hospital. One method involves maintaining a constant competitive marketplace for nonsticky product categories in which actual use of a specific product in a particular case can be influenced by the pricing. Executing the strategy essentially involves establishing crosswalks for a particular product category. A crosswalk is a grid of similar products within a category offered by different suppliers that demonstrates pricing differentials between competing suppliers' products. A well-constructed crosswalk built with input from the clinical community and then routinely communicated to physicians can help ensure that cost is at least partially taken into consideration in making product use choices. When contracting under this strategy hospitals must ensure that product pricing is *not* tied to any specific volume or share commitment to purchase a particular product.

For many nonsticky categories, the crosswalk strategy can be effective at lowering a hospital's cost base—and has several distinct advantages over contracts that require a commitment of volume or share to a particular company. In nonsticky categories like interventional cardiology or interventional radiology, numerous suppliers routinely introduce slight variations on the same technology. If compliance or volume contracts are in place with a supplier that falls behind in this constant leapfrogging process, hospitals must either deny access to a potentially more attractive technology or lose discounts from a primary supplier. On the other hand, if a hospital is employing a crosswalk-based strategy with no commitments (except to provide pricing transparency to clinicians), a new technology could be utilized, where appropriate, without jeopardizing other pricing—as long as the new technology is fairly priced. In fact, if appropriately executed, hospitals may be able to negotiate with a supplier looking to introduce a new technology into the hospital at a discount relative to incumbent product pricing. If this discounted pricing does drive increased usage of the new product, it also creates competitive pressure for the incumbent to lower prices to preserve or regain share. For example, in the relatively crowded interventional radiology/vascular surgery marketplace, some suppliers have done just that for new stents. Also, because hospitals typically get reimbursed for inpatient cases at a fixed rate, regardless of whether they use one supplier's product for the case or another supplier's, having competitive pricing across various suppliers for a particular procedure better aligns a hospital's revenue streams to its costs for a particular procedure.

In the current paradigm, where most significant contracts are based on compliance or volume commitments, medical device companies' research and development (R&D) strategies are driven by the goal of creating a broad product line, where hospitals could reasonably commit a significant volume or share, and less by a desire to gain share by offering products at extremely competitive prices. The current compliance- or volume-based contracting stifles competition from smaller companies who may be able to compete on price for specific products but often do not have the resources to develop and market a complete line of products. Hospitals with compliance- or volume-based contracts often cannot entertain these suppliers' products because of the impact on their compliance contracts within a category.

## CHALLENGES IMPLEMENTING THE CROSSWALK STRATEGY

Implementing the crosswalk strategy offers several challenges. First, developing a crosswalk and maintaining it in the face of continuous new product introductions in complicated product categories takes dedicated supply chain personnel who can keep abreast of changes in products, pricing, and features within specific product categories. Second, hospitals that attempt to utilize a crosswalk strategy with suppliers that are not accustomed to competing in this manner will face significant resistance establishing fair pricing without making a commitment to purchase a specified volume or share. Finally, the greatest challenge rests on the ability of the hospital to engage its clinicians. Establishing the credible threat of clinicians making price the decision-driving attribute when they are clinically indifferent between specific products is vital to how receptive suppliers will be to provide fair pricing without a volume commitment. A supplier that sees its sales drop significantly with the introduction of a clinically similar product by a competitor that is less expensive incentivizes the incumbent supplier to try to earn back share with lowered pricing or truly improved features. Because many devices cost only 25 to 40 cents on the dollar to manufacture, providing some discount on a product to ensure its sale is better for suppliers than not making the sale at all. Thus, if the challenges described above can be overcome, the crosswalk approach could be effective at not only lowering prices, but also ensuring physician access to a wide array of clinical technology.

For a hospital that is looking to improve its cost-containment strategy, understanding its cost base in a more nuanced way than just spending by category or spending by vendor, and then taking different strategies in addressing different categories of spending is vital. The above discussion related to sticky and non-sticky categories and associated crosswalk strategy is a significant departure from the standardization approach that has characterized hospital supply cost reduction efforts to date. The ongoing competitive pressure on suppliers that this strategy can create resembles more the competitive forces created by retailers on manufacturers in the retail industry than the type of competition medical device companies typically face. Michael Porter and Elizabeth Teisberg writes, "The wrong kinds of competition have made a mess of the American health care system."[15] Although their thesis does not explicitly address hospital clinical supply costs, the same concept applies. By redefining the nature of competitive strategy for certain nonsticky product categories, hospitals can improve supply cost management by bringing the right competition to bear.

## ENGAGING CLINICIANS ON CLINICAL SUPPLY COSTS

Clinician engagement is not only a valuable element of implementing the crosswalk strategy, as described above, but is a requisite element for success regardless of what strategy is utilized to address costs in any category of supplies. Identifying the importance of engaging the end user is not revolutionary. Any centralized procurement group, regardless of the industry or particular commodity group in question, is continuously challenged to develop a close working relationship with its internal clients. For example, centralized procurement functions in a consumer packaged goods or pharmaceutical company will often face challenges in their efforts to engage these companies' sales and marketing divisions for their major advertising contracts. A vice president (VP) of marketing and an interventional cardiologist will likely voice the same concerns when faced with the prospect of working with a procurement professional on a purchasing project: "Purchasing doesn't understand the complexity of what I need to do," or, "Purchasing is only viewing cost as an important criterion."

In the advertising scenario above, both the VP of advertising and the procurement professional are typically employed by the same entity, whereas in many hospitals, physicians are not employees of the hospital while the procurement professionals are. For the most part, the analogy is accurate, and in both cases, the challenge of engagement of end users must be addressed in order to lower costs.

Some hospitals have already taken steps to engage clinicians. Over the last decade, a number of hospitals and GPOs have hired nurses as part of their procurement arms to connect with clinicians on procurement-related activities.[16] Nurses play a significant end-user role in the hospital, utilizing a vast amount of supplies for the day-to-day care of patients. Having similarly credentialed professionals within hospital procurement helps to address end user fears that "purchasing doesn't understand the complexity of what I need to do and is only concerned about costs." Much of the progress in lowering supply costs in hospitals over the last decade has centered on general medical-surgical floor supplies utilized by nursing. Supply categories like needles and syringes, drapes and gowns, exam gloves, bandages and gauze—often termed general medical-surgical supplies—are typically no longer viewed as sources of concern within the clinical supply cost base. For these general medical-surgical supply categories, having nurses who can connect with patient care nurses was an important element of the hospitals' success controlling costs in this area.

## THE IMPORTANCE OF PHYSICIAN STAKEHOLDERS

Lowering clinical costs within a hospital must involve successfully addressing the increasing proportion of a hospital's supply base that is driven by technologically advanced supplies utilized by physicians—primarily in the operating rooms and interventional suites of a hospital. For many medical centers whose business model is driven by its physicians performing procedures on patients in these venues, physician preference supplies can be a greater proportion of the clinical spending base than general medical-surgical supplies and typically represent a greater savings opportunity.[17] While the importance of these subsets of supplies within the scope of the clinical supply cost base has been clearly identified, actual engagement of physicians as partners in the effort to address these costs, however, has been difficult to achieve for many hospitals. One of the barriers to hospitals working effectively with physicians to lower costs is the perceived relationship between physicians and the suppliers from whom hospitals procure products. Whether these relationships are focused on consulting activities, where physicians offer their expertise to suppliers in marketing a particular product, or research activities, where physicians offer their expertise to suppliers as they develop their next generation devices, hospital supply chain professionals view them as a necessary evil. These relationships have been sensationalized in the lay press and in the hospital materials management literature as creating a significant conflict of interest that aligns physicians' interests with suppliers' interests, more so than with a hospital's interests.[18]

However, this type of conflict is not dissimilar to the conflict created with suppliers in any industry that utilizes their sales and marketing dollars to influence decision makers within an organization. To return to the VP of marketing analogy, no doubt many of his or her suppliers/advertising agencies court his or her favor through dinners, outings, and other promotions, and any effective efforts at procuring the most cost-effective advertising agency require overcoming any potential impact or conflict of interest created by such activities. Given the intense scrutiny medical device manufacturers face related to their sales and marketing approaches with physicians,[19] hospital procurement organizations might actually be better positioned not to allow those types of conflicts to interfere than in other industries. For example, the Advanced Medical Technology Association (ADVA-MED), the largest trade association representing medical device manufacturers, recently updated its "Code of Ethics for Interactions with Health Care Professionals" to reflect growing concern within the healthcare sector about the appropriateness of various relationships between medical device companies and healthcare professionals.[20] While promulgating this code does not eliminate the potential influence that relationships between medical device companies and healthcare professional may have, it does, at a minimum, set some commonly understood expectations for these activities.

## THE DIFFICULTY IN COMPARING MEDICAL DEVICES

One of the challenges raised by hospital procurement organizations is the difficulty in determining whether a particular device is better than or equivalent to another. The intrinsic value of a certain device relative to others can be difficult to gauge for a nonphysician, and as such, choices made by a particular physician to utilize one device versus another are difficult to understand in the context of price differentials between the two devices.[21] Similarly, hospital procurement officials feel challenged to understand why standardizing a certain product category to one supplier is not possible. Unfortunately, this difficulty in understanding nuanced clinical differences between products on the part of hospital procurement professionals, in the setting of the perceived conflicts created by the physicians' relationships with suppliers, creates the conditions for mistrust between these parties. However, in many cases, the mistrust is not warranted and gets in the way of making progress in addressing supply costs. Again, the analogy of advertising service procurement is apropos. The nuanced differences in the approach, areas of expertise, and experience of a particular agency for a specific promotional campaign may be incomprehensible to a procurement professional who does not have a background or experience in that field. But for a VP of marketing, these differences could be worth a premium. The problem, and solution, in both instances is less about the specialized products and services that are being procured and more about the mindset of the procurement organization. If there is no effective dialogue and desire to gain an understanding of the complexities, for example, of one guidewire versus another or one stent versus another, it is highly unlikely that a hospital procurement organization will be very effective in developing an approach to manage the costs of guidewires and stents.

Given the difficulty in understanding the differences between similar supplies sold by different vendors, there has been significant desire to use outcomes evidence to help distinguish between supplies' performance in an objective fashion.[22] In a similar vein to a marketing group tracking the return on investment on their specific advertising investments with a particular agency, hospital administrators, in the areas of procurement and quality, view clinical trial results as a helpful tool in understanding the intrinsic value of specific devices. Unfortunately, for proponents of evidenced-based discussions related to procurement of physician preference items with physicians or suppliers, there is scant evidence in the literature about any of the device categories that are significant expenses in the supply cost base of a hospital. There are a number of reasons for this (see sidebar, below). The actual volume of patients who might be eligible to participate in a trial between so-called similar devices is relatively small, especially when compared with a pharmaceutical trial. For example, the number of patients enrolled in trials of the cholesterol lowering drug Lipitor, one of the most widely studied pharmaceuticals on the market, is greater than 800,000,[23] while one of the most closely studied medical devices, the Taxus drug-eluting stent by Boston Scientific has pooled trial data on 3,445 patients.[24]

Also, unlike pharmaceuticals, clinical device trial results can be significantly impacted by the actual operator involved in the trial. The highly skilled, experienced, trained senior physician may achieve better outcomes using any guidewire for a particular case relative to a less skilled or less experienced physician. Likewise, a physician accustomed to utilizing a particular product for decades to perform a specific procedure may see a drop in quality or outcomes if he or she switches to utilizing a different product for the same procedure, regardless of the relative quality of the two products. Controlling for these types of variables is extremely difficult and requires significantly larger studies. As a result of these difficulties, few true outcome-based studies have demonstrated clear superiority of one particular type of device versus another in the same class of product. In the largest head-to-head device versus comparable device trials conducted, investigators examined outcomes differences between two competing drug-eluting stents—Cypher, manufactured by Cordis, a division of Johnson and Johnson, and Taxus, manufactured by Boston Scientific. The *REALITY* trial randomized 1,386 patients across 90 centers worldwide to receive either a Cypher or Taxus stent, but the results were inconclusive. The principal investigator in the trial, Dr. Marie-Claude Morice, comments, "There are not enough data to select one drug-eluting stent over the other. They are both very durable and very efficient to prevent restenosis....There is no one good and one bad, one ugly and one marvelous. The reality's not there. We are in small differences and I think we need much more data to dramatically change the practice."[25]

The converse—that no data to support the superiority of one device over another implies the devices must be equivalent—is not appropriate either. The lack of evidence, again, may be a function of the challenges inherent in actually conducting a trial of this nature and may not be a function of the superiority or equivalence of any particular device. In the case of a physician in any hospital choosing one drug-eluting stent versus another for a specific patient, factors such as specific patient anatomy, experience deploying one stent versus another, and availability of a particular size stent are all factors that may play into decision making. Despite evidence showing the two stents to be equivalent, physicians faced with choosing a specific stent for a specific lesion are often forced to make decisions that rely on their own clinical judgment and not on any documented study result.

---

**Difficulties Making Evidence-Based Comparisons between Medical Devices**

- Inadequate volume to power statistically significant trials
- Outcomes are operator dependent to begin with
- Changing supplies often involves a learning curve
- Operator based clinical judgment *is* relevant

---

## FURTHERING THE DIALOGUE ON SUPPLY COSTS WITH PHYSICIANS

Engaging physicians about their use of high-expense items involves moving beyond some of the misconceptions described above and developing a more robust trust- and transparency-based dialogue on the decision-making and financial impact of specific device selection. All too commonly, the preconceived notions of physicians' decisions being driven by nefarious supplier relationships and hospital procurement's decisions being driven by a mindless drive towards standardization to a single supplier dominate and, ultimately, doom this dialogue to failure. Also, misinterpretation and utilization of evidence in discussing product choice can also create situations where physicians and hospital procurement are talking past one another and not with one another.

Some hospitals, however, have begun to take the dialogue to new levels, in particular, while utilizing the crosswalk strategy described above. This strategy involves providing pricing transparency for relatively similar products to physicians in an organized manner to gain physician champions' support to shift greater usage toward lower-priced, clinically equivalent products. Over time, other than creating a continuous downward pressure on pricing, the approach engenders a trust-based working relationship that allows hospital procurement professionals to understand clinical product selection in an ongoing manner and allows clinicians to see their input reflected in the hospital's contracting approach.

Some hospitals have begun employing physicians in their sourcing departments or increasing the involvement of administrators with medical credentials (i.e., chief medical officers and chief quality officers) to reduce hospital supply costs. All of these approaches are aimed at fostering the development of a productive relationship between hospital procurement officials and physicians who utilize physician preference items. As medical device technology continues to advance, driving more of the hospitals clinical cost base towards physician preference items, efforts to build the foundation for effective physician engagement will be well rewarded.

## CONCLUSION

In the current environment, the size of suppliers' gross margins (total sales – cost to manufacture their products) do not provide a strong incentive to improve operating efficiency. Suppliers whose research and development, manufacturing, or sales and marketing activities are inefficient can compete in today's hospital supply marketplace by masking their inefficiency with high prices that go effectively unchallenged in many hospitals. However, if hospitals become more effective at improving supply cost management, the resulting pressure to provide competitive pricing for clinical supplies will force suppliers to improve their efficiency in all areas in order to maintain profitability. Increased pricing pressure in what have been typically viewed as technology-driven markets will cause suppliers' R&D groups to orient their activities less around minor technical advances for a product and more around approaches to reducing the cost of manufacturing a product. Currently, there is very little reason for this type of R&D manufacturing-process focus because suppliers have typically been able to extract higher prices from hospitals for products of each successive device generation. Ultimately, creating the impetus for process efficiency improvements and reallocation of resources within the supplier base now could lower the growth trajectory in this large segment of U.S. healthcare spending. While suppliers may not find this scrutiny and pricing pressure pleasant, this result would be welcomed by most healthcare stakeholders given the unsustainable cost pressures on our healthcare system.

## Key Concepts

- Although clinical supply cost management is an important element of a hospitals' financial performance, progress to date has been primarily based on utilizing basic sourcing tools and techniques common to many industries.
- To achieve a greater impact, however, in the higher cost physician-preference categories such as electrophysiology implants or drug-eluting stents, hospitals must apply different strategies and establish greater engagement with the physicians who utilize these products.

- Hospitals fostering greater pricing pressure on medical device companies could help spur improvements in medical device companies' operating efficiencies in sales and marketing and reorient R&D activities to focus on lowering manufacturing costs of healthcare technology.


Glossary

- *GPO:* Group purchasing organization—an organization that aggregates purchases of various products for member hospitals with the aim of negotiating discounted pricing on behalf of its members.
- *Operational stickiness:* Refers to the extent to which a supply is built into the operations of the unit or units where it is utilized and, by extension, the difficulty created by changing supplies or having multiple types of similar supplies available.
- *Crosswalk strategy:* Describes an approach to lower supply costs by maintaining a constant competitive marketplace useful in specific product categories where a grid of similar products within a product category (a crosswalk) is utilized to demonstrate pricing differentials between competing suppliers' products and help drive usage toward lower cost products.
- *Commitment-based contracts:* Contracts typical in many medical device product categories where suppliers provide specific discounts based on a hospital's commitment to purchase a certain volume (units) of a particular product, or maintain a certain percentage (share) of the suppliers' products in relation to competitors' products in the same category.
- *Gross margins:* Financial ratio characterized as the total sales for a product minus the cost of producing the product, divided by the total sales of a product.
- *Internal clients:* Term used within procurement departments to describe colleagues from other parts of their organization whom they assist in making purchasing or contracting decisions.


## NOTES

1.   Cable News Network LP, LLLP. A Time Warner Company. 2006. "Fortune 500, 2006: Our Annual Ranking of America's Largest Corporations," *Fortune,* April 17, 2006. Available at: http://money.cnn.com/magazines/fortune/fortune500/. Accessed January 2, 2007.

2.   California Healthcare Foundation. 2006. *Snapshot: Health Care Costs 101.* Available at: http://www.chcf.org/documents/insurance/HealthCareCosts06.pdf. Accessed December 15, 2006.

3.   Schneller, E. S., and L. R. Smeltzer. 2006. *Strategic Management of the Healthcare Supply Chain.* San Francisco: Jossey-Bass, 2.

4. Brin, D. W. 2005. "Hospitals Look to Pare Costs, Share Savings With Physicians." *Wall Street Journal*, March 29. Available at: http://users2.wsj.com/lmda/do/checkLogin?mg=wsj-users2&url=http%3A%2F%2Fonline.wsj.com%2Farticle%2FSB111204797928891196.html%3Femailf%3Dyes. Accessed January 25, 2007.

5. Schneller and Smeltzer, 215–227.

6. Hendrick, T. E. 2007. *Purchasing Consortiums: Horizontal Alliances Among Firms Buying Common Goods and Services; What? Who? Why? How?* Available at: http://www.capsresearch.org/Publications/pdfs-public/hendrick1997es.pdf. Accessed November 15, 2006.

7. Bower, A. G. 2005. "Federal Investment in Health Information Technology: How to Motivate It?" *Health Affairs* 24 (5): 1263–1265.

8. Schneller and Smeltzer, 53.

9. Citigroup Investment Research, Health Care Facilities Group. Personal communication, September 11, 2006.

10. Healthcare Financial Management Association. 2006. "Should You Be Negotiating More Aggressively with Medical Device Companies?" *Supply Chain Solutions* 2 (4): 12.

11. Bloomberg Financial. 2006. *Summary Financial Report for Medtronic, Boston Scientific, St. Jude, Guidant, Bard, Baxter, Edwards, Zimmer, Becton Dickinson, Alcon, FY 2002–2005.*

12. Medtronic. 2006. *Medtronic News Releases.* Available at: http://wwwp.medtronic.com/Newsroom/NewsReleases.do?category=category.businessunit&subcategoryId=1095197591862&lang=en_US. Accessed January 25, 2007.

13. Schneller and Smeltzer, 72.

14. Healthcare Financial Management Association. 2002. *Resource Management: The Healthcare Supply Chain 2002 Survey Results.* Available at: http://www.hfma.org/NR/rdonlyres/B35AA31C-D1BE-4BD5-B41A-569B864F8A17/0/scsurvey.pdf. Accessed September 15, 2006.

15. Porter, M. E., and E. Olmsted Teisberg. 2004. "Redefining Competition in Health Care." *Harvard Business Review* (June): 65–76.

16. Schneller and Smeltzer, 81.

17. Joshi, A. S. 2007. "NYPH Reduces Physician Preference Costs by $40 Million with a Homegrown Approach." *Supply Chain Solutions* 3 (1): 8–10, 12.

18. Abelson, R. 2006. "Whistle-Blower Suit Says Device Maker Generously Rewards Doctors." *New York Times-Business,* January, 24, 2006. Available at: http://www.nytimes.com/2006/01/24/business/24device.html?ex=1295758800&en=fda96725616cb077&ei=5088&partner=rssnyt&emc=rss. Accessed December 14, 2006.

19. Jones, J. W. 2005. "Medical Device Manufacturer Relationships." *Physician's News Digest.* Available at: http://www.physiciansnews.com/law/205jones.html. Accessed December 1, 2006.

20. Advanced Medical Technology Association: Advamed. 2005. *Code of Ethics for Interactions with Health Care Professionals.* Available at: http://www.advamed.org/publicdocs/coe_with_faqs_4–15–05.pdf. Accessed December 15, 2006.

21. Schneller, and Smeltzer, 39.

22. Ibid., 82.

23. Pfizer Corporation. 2006. *Lipitor: Important Facts.* Available at: http://www.lipitor.com/cwp/appmanager/lipitor/lipitorDesktop?_nfpb=true&_pageLabel=lipitorFactsAbout. Accessed September 15, 2006.

24. Baim, D. S. 2006. "Update—DES Stent Thrombosis and Long-Term Safety Profile." *Letter to Colleagues*, September 20, 2006. Available at: http://www.taxus-stent.com/usa/BaimPhysicianLetterThromb09202006.pdf. Accessed November 20, 2006.

25. Angioplasty.org. 2005. *Drug-Eluting Stent Trials at the 2005 ACC Scientific Session*. Available at: http://www.ptca.org/articles/acc2005_summary_f.html. Accessed October 15, 2006.

# CHAPTER 8

# Liability Risk Management: Saving Money and Relationships

Kathryn K. Wire

Unlike medical specialties or financial services, risk management is a difficult activity to define. It has evolved haphazardly in healthcare, and while there are healthcare risk-management organizations, they do not spell out scope of practice or standards of practice. To understand risk management in today's healthcare environment requires some general background, some historical study, and a willingness to look in a new direction: at our patients instead of ourselves.

## THE 20,000-FOOT VIEW

Generic risk management has five fairly simple steps. Knowing them can add to a deeper understanding of the other concepts discussed below. Applying this framework can also assist providers contemplating a new or changed risk in their practice environment.[1] The five steps:

- *Identify and analyze loss exposures.* Traditional healthcare risk management defined loss as a malpractice indemnity payment or expense.[2] An exposure is the source of the loss. For example, the loss is a payment to parents of a brain-damaged newborn and the birth of the child is the exposure. Insurance companies and actuaries measure potential losses by counting exposure units, including inpatient days, bed counts, outpatient procedures, the number of covered physicians, emergency department visits, and so forth. Exposures can be further subdivided into specific groups, such as counting newborn deliveries and identifying the number of high-risk births, or counting surgeries and further quantifying the number of bariatric procedures. Different exposures present different sorts of possible losses, or risks.

- *Examine risk reduction techniques.* Often, several paths can lead to reducing or eliminating a financial risk. Five are typically used, alone or in combination.

    - The most clear-cut method is the complete *avoidance of the exposure.* A hospital that admits no patients cannot incur malpractice exposure. A hospital with no obstetrics unit or emergency room would similarly avoid some risk. A physician who no longer performs surgery has avoided surgical risk exposure. A freestanding clinic may contract with a specialized provider to perform all radiology studies, thereby avoiding the risk of incorrect reading. This approach has obvious disadvantages, in that it limits available healthcare and also constrains revenue to providers.
    - Providers can also engage in *loss prevention*, which reduces the likelihood of an adverse event in the course of encountering a risk. For example, time-out protocols before procedures are designed to prevent wrong-site surgery. Sponge and instrument counting during surgery prevents inadvertent retention of foreign objects.
    - Another approach is *loss reduction*, in which the provider takes steps to mitigate the effect of an event once it occurs. Saving placentas for later analysis is an example. If a newborn does badly, the placenta may be evidence to show the inevitability of the injury, potentially reducing the extent of the loss. Routine postoperative X-rays to detect retained objects in high-risk surgical cases do not prevent the adverse event, but they can significantly reduce the injury resulting from a retained object like a sponge. Postincident event management, including outcome disclosure and negotiation, is another form of loss reduction.
    - *Segregation of loss exposures* consolidates a risk in one location or department so a provider can maximize both loss-prevention and loss-reduction strategies through specialization and/or development of special protocols. For example, a company with long-term care facilities may keep all of its ventilator-dependent patients in one building. Segregation can also put selected high-risk activities in preferred judicial venues, where judges and juries have found more favorably in past malpractice cases.
    - *Contractual transfer of exposures* occurs when one party compensates another to assume a risk. The financial risk shifts through either contractual indemnification provisions (in which one party agrees to compensate the other for loss) or the purchase of insurance. In either case, the parties negotiate a transaction in which one assumes certain liabilities that might otherwise fall on the other.

- *Select the best technique for the identified risk exposure.* Often this step presents significant challenges. Many techniques have grown out of patient safety work in the last decade that looked at system analysis and redesign. They can be helpful. Examples include failure mode and effect analysis, human factors study, and various tools for statistical examination.
- *Implement the selected technique.* At this point, the effort changes from investigation and planning to change management and operational leadership. More than the other steps, implementation requires multilevel support in the organization to facilitate the necessary changes. Selection of suitable training and learning methods can be critical at this point.
- *Monitor, evaluate, and improve the program.* Is it accomplishing the desired improvement? If not, fix it.

This outline of possible approaches to risk hints at a number of areas typically involved in a comprehensive risk management program: insurance management, contract review, incident review and analysis, claim management, staff education, and performance improvement techniques. All are relevant in any risk management program.

Healthcare presents unique issues that merit more extensive consideration. Most arise from the dual nature of the patient/provider relationship. Patients are consumers of our services, but they expose themselves physically and emotionally to healthcare providers in a manner that differs greatly from, say, buying a car. The special provider-patient relationship leads to a unique trust in healthcare providers, far more comprehensive than trust in other service suppliers.[3] Research is demonstrating that a provider's malpractice risk profile changes dramatically if the provider and staff nurture and protect that relationship, and healthcare risk management has started to evolve as a result. Later sections of this chapter discuss those developments in more detail.

## RISK MANAGEMENT IN HEALTHCARE

Risk management in healthcare has always involved aspects of clinical loss prevention, event management, claim management, education, and insurance oversight. In a facility or practice, the risk manager handles some or all of those tasks. However, the specific characterization of the risk management function remains a moving target. Often, it helps to begin defining risk management by what it is not.

### Risk Management Is *Not* Patient Safety

The twenty-first century advent of the patient-safety movement has confused the risk-management picture. Though critically important, the systematic improvement of patient care promoted by patient safety advocates does not currently address most of the risks that lead to malpractice losses. Accordingly, it remains a separate discipline from risk management, though they are clearly related and often accomplished by the same department using some of the same tools.

Risk managers identify the patient-care issues that generate claims. These often differ from patient-safety concerns raised by regulatory or reimbursement agencies (such as Joint Commission for the Accreditation of Healthcare Organizations [JCAHO] core measures, the 100,000 Lives initiative, etc.). While those issues may drive patient outcomes in a general sense and may impact hospital earnings by reducing unnecessary cost, they are often not the source of malpractice suits. Patient-safety efforts have independent value, but they often do not meet risk-management needs. The two disciplines have to be considered separately.

### Risk Management Is *Not* Clandestine

Historically, risk managers worked in dark corners, conducting confidential investigations they could not share out of fear that sharing the lessons learned would generate additional liability. Incident reports and the valuable data they contained were hidden in filing drawers. Attorneys discouraged risk managers from discussing cases until they had been resolved, often many years after the underlying event.

Now, research indicates that the source of most malpractice suits is a broken relationship with patients and their families.[4] When a perceived poor outcome occurs together with a problematic relationship, a claim often results.[5] Claim-reduction processes must focus on the patient/family relationship *and* the care, but fixing the relationship will have the greatest impact. This requires communication and trust, not secrecy; this is why risk managers have to become broad-based educators and facilitators of disclosure. Prompt efforts to identify and solve care problems are essential to keeping the patient relationship intact.

### Risk Management Is *Not* Enforcement

As healthcare in the United States rushes toward a major shift in the twenty-first century to transparency and patient-centered care, risk management's role will change. In the past, risk management often functioned like the principal's office—staff members hesitated to report things, fearing that they would get in trouble. Risk managers educated providers in their facilities by invoking fear of lawsuits, not other benefits of low-risk care. Because the healthcare community believed malpractice risk arose primarily from dangerous clinical practices, risk managers were viewed as the enforcers of good care.

We have learned that inducing change in clinical practice requires much more than a lecture from risk management and that clinical practice seldom related to the likelihood of a suit, anyway.[6] Slowly, risk managers' tools are changing from fear and threats to collaboration and partnership. Education has moved far beyond, "If you don't document it, you didn't do it." Risk management education in the twenty-first century will focus proactively on interpersonal relations, not on documentation of past events or deposition preparation. Rather than making providers afraid of their patients, the new wave of risk managers will help providers engage in dialogue with their patients, embracing the uncertainty and conflict necessary for healthy and productive resolutions. To understand how that change will occur, it is important to look at the history of the still young field of healthcare risk management.

## THE BEGINNING

Prior to the mid-1960s, medical malpractice was a relatively rare concern. Nonprofit healthcare institutions were protected by charitable immunity (for-profit systems were rare if they existed at all), and malpractice suits were filed against physicians personally. Courts did not recognize a legal duty on the part of the hospital, holding instead that the physician managed the care and had legal responsibility for meeting the standards. Both the legal and medical climates inhibited large jury awards against physicians; insurance adequacy and cost were not issues.[7]

In the 1960s, states began to hold hospitals liable for their own negligence, either for the acts of their employees or for failing to act where there was a clear problem with the patient's care by others,[8] and states began to reduce the protections of charitable immunity.[9] Changes in reimbursement models made healthcare providers more conscious of costs, so they behaved more like businesses. The resulting institutional behaviors and the increasingly frequent presence of large organizations as defendants made suits less personal, and claims against physicians and hospitals became more common and more successful.

By 1975, malpractice insurance had become an unattractive product for the insurance industry. The policies issued by malpractice carriers typically provided *occurrence*-based coverage—they covered the insured for any event that occurred during the policy period. Most statutes of limitation don't begin to run until a patient reaches the legal age of majority, or adulthood; most also have some provision to keep the limitations period from expiring before the plaintiff even becomes aware of the injury. When these provisions apply to medical malpractice cases involving children or very subtle injuries, they can create very long tails—the delay between an occurrence and the ultimate determination of liability. Insurers found they were dealing with losses on policies issued years and sometimes decades before, purchased at lower premium levels based on the perceived exposures in that earlier era. This is still a problem for malpractice insurers, and has led to the predominance of the "claims made" policy, which covers only *claims asserted* during the policy period.

Premiums began to go up, and many of the large hospitals and growing health systems initiated self-insurance programs in the mid-1970s, while physicians began to form physician-owned or mutual companies.[10] The risk management profession first appeared during this period, largely driven by the need to control burgeoning professional liability exposures, now borne increasingly by the healthcare providers themselves. Facing more financial responsibility for their own risk, facilities and physician groups began to appoint so-called experts to reduce that exposure: risk managers.

Risk managers come from a variety of backgrounds, and the focus of a risk management program often depends on whether the designated individual had a legal, insurance, administrative, or clinical background. However, the risk managers and insurance companies all looked in one direction for early guidance. To protect themselves from malpractice losses, they reasoned, they needed to talk to the people involved in those losses—their attorneys.

Attorneys told the healthcare providers why they lost trials. The risk management field became very adept at identifying factors that made lawsuit defense difficult: poor documentation, witnesses who do not present well, bloody or disturbing medical presentations (where a picture is worth a thousand words and some dollars), or a smoking gun document such as an altered medical record.

But risk managers failed for decades to examine the more important questions. How can we avoid the litigation process altogether? What behaviors will render the quality of our employees as witnesses irrelevant, allowing us to focus instead on their quality as providers of care? How can we relate to our patients so they don't feel the need to sue? Attorneys took a weak stab at this relationship issue with their platitude, "People don't sue doctors they like." While risk managers everywhere understood the basic truth of this concept at some level, they rarely took it farther. Eventually, it became apparent that healthcare's risk management focus on documentation and retrospective clinical improvement was not working. The mid-1980s brought another crisis in coverage availability and cost, as loss frequency and severity mounted.

Researchers began to search for the factors that actually caused patients and their families to sue healthcare providers. Two related factors jumped out of their research. First, the malpractice litigation system did not work very well.[11] It was slow to resolve issues, the results were not very accurate,[12] the occasional unfounded verdict encouraged baseless lawsuits, and physicians afraid of suits began to practice defensive medicine.[13]

One key finding came out of the early research at Vanderbilt University: the incidence of claims and suits rarely related to the underlying quality of the medical care provided by the defendants. As one of the researchers described his motivation:

"[T]he challenge is to identify what can be done to reduce the number of unfounded claims while simultaneously permitting legitimate claims to proceed." Although a bad outcome was often present and presumed to have caused the lawsuits, something else distinguished the patients who sued—they could not get what they needed at a personal level. Put another way, the healthcare providers had destroyed their trust.[14]

## IMPROVING RELATIONSHIPS: THE PATH TO
## REDUCING LAWSUITS AND LOSSES AND
## IMPROVING CARE

Curious about the true causes of suits, Gerald Hickson, a professor of pediatrics, and his colleagues at Vanderbilt University began by questioning families who had filed claims against Florida obstetricians. He and his fellow investigators found that less than 25 percent of the families asserted a claim because they needed money. An equal number indicated they filed because they recognized a coverup. Many reported failed communication resulting from physicians who would not listen or talk openly, attempted to mislead them, and/or did not talk to them about the long-term prospects for their children.[15]

Hickson has established the following key factors about malpractice claims:

- The quality of care delivered by high-claim and low-claim doctors is indistinguishable.[16]
- Doctors with high-claims experience generate more complaints when their patients are surveyed.[17]
- Doctors with many patient complaints tend to have many malpractice claims regardless of the quality of care.[18]
- A substantial portion of complaints were relationship based, not clinical.[19]
- Patients with complications affecting their clinical outcome are more likely to complain.[20]

Essentially, Hickson and his colleagues have given us a picture that shows most suits or claims relate to poor communication or relationship skills, not the quality of care. They do, however, correlate to poor outcomes. A poor outcome, when combined with a previously difficult relationship or one that fails after the adverse event, plants the seed for a suit.[21] Poor outcomes in the absence of relationship problems are much less likely to generate a claim. None of these indicators points to a poor quality of care as a definitive factor, just poor outcomes. Because healthcare providers can expect unavoidable poor outcomes to continue in spite of quality medical care, it makes sense to focus on the thing that *does* differentiate high-claim versus low-claim scenarios: relationships.

Hickson and his colleagues found that malpractice claims experience, though unrelated to the quality of care, was predictably higher for physicians who had unsolicited complaints in four areas, as further broken down by the study's authors[22]:

- Communication (poor communication, did not listen, poor doctor to doctor communication, doctor jousting, who's in charge)
- Care and treatment concerns (treatment problem, diagnosis problem, adverse outcome whether or not caused by the medical practitioners)
- Availability (waiting, rushing, calls not returned, refused recommended care)
- Humaneness of the physician (rudeness, angry, yelled at patient)

In a similar vein, Wendy Levinson and colleagues studied communication patterns by recording patient/physician interactions.[23] Their research indicated that low-claim physicians (but not surgeons) had the following characteristics:

- They engaged the patients more in the communication process, soliciting their opinions, checking their understanding, and encouraging them to talk.
- They did more to orient the patient, educating them about what to expect and how their contact during the visit would flow.
- They laughed and used humor more than high-claim physicians.
- They spent about three minutes more on average with each patient. (The visit length had an independent impact on the likelihood that a physician had claim activity.)[24]

When researchers studied tapes of surgeons' conversations with patients, they identified particular voice tones that correlated strongly with malpractice experience rather than other communication patterns. Specifically, the surgeons who routinely exhibited more dominance and less concern or anxiety for the patient had demonstrably higher levels of malpractice claim activity.[23]

Research has also demonstrated that patient satisfaction with healthcare providers increases when the provider introduces discussion of difficult but important topics such as domestic violence[25] and end of life issues,[26] whether or not the issue is resolved.

Though their research did not compare behaviors to claim activity, Scheitel et al. found that patients tend not to process information very well during a visit to a physician; for example, a high percentage do not remember many details of the diagnosis.[27] As a result, incongruent priorities can result from the encounter. In fact, their research was the basis for the National Health Council's advertising slogan, "Most People Suffer a 68% Hearing Loss When Naked."[28] That campaign encouraged patients and physicians to overcome the problem by taking specific steps to improve communication and the retention of information, such as giving written summaries to patients at the end of visits.

All these findings indicate that when physician behaviors encourage comfort and communication, both the quality of the medical exchange and the patient's trust level can improve. Presumably, both factors impact the claims experience of physicians and may go far to explain why fewer than 10 percent of the physicians can account for up to 85 percent of complaints and nearly 50 percent of suits.[29]

This research addresses only physicians, in part, because of the difficulty in isolating factors in the more complex environment of hospital care. However, risk managers find that bad things almost never happen in isolation, and there is often a collection of events and communication failures contributing to a claim situation. Other clinical and support staff can improve a physician's risk by substituting their own relationship efforts, or they can make the situation worse by their own failures. Conversely, a physician who handles patient relationships well can mask problems with a patient's relationship with other providers. Effective efforts to improve loss experience must address all the players.

## Case Study: The Impact of Trust

### *Postoperative Pressure Sores: Closed versus Transparent Approach*

In the following actual occurrence, the family did not sue, probably because the complication did not become the life-altering problem it might have. However, the family (prominent in their community) shared their negative experiences with anyone who would listen, a result which also bears significant cost. The case demonstrates the many small ways that healthcare providers of all kinds can contribute to a frustrating, dysfunctional, and unresponsive communication experience for patients.

### *Facts*

Barbara, 75, needed a hip replacement. Her doctor sent her to an orientation class at the hospital where she would have surgery; she met the nurses and saw the rooms. She began to feel more comfortable about the upcoming ordeal.

Her nurse helped her out of bed on her first postop day (Day 2), and noticed two very large open blisters high on her buttocks. The staff put Duoderm (gel) bandages on them. There was no further discussion of the issue with her family that day. On Day 3, her daughter (a healthcare provider) arrived to help. After the day shift had left, the daughter learned of the wounds. She finally tracked down Barbara's nurse at about 9 P.M. The nurse on that shift knew nothing of the sores, or of any care plan to take care of them. The bandages had shifted, leaving the sores exposed and very painful. (Barbara's hip precautions forced her to scoot to get out of bed.) The nurse changed them to large gauze bandages, complaining that there was no care plan and she had no idea what the doctors or her supervisors wanted her to do. However, she was very sympathetic and attentive as she dressed the wounds. Otherwise, the hip was recovering well.

The next morning, the surgeon's physician assistant visited, as did Barbara's internist's partner. (Because it was Saturday, her real doctors were off.) The internist assured her that the hospital's wound care specialist would visit—on Monday. Meanwhile, the gauze had bunched up and was still in place. Because the nurses were transferring Barbara from her inpatient room to the rehabilitation unit, no one addressed the bandage issue until mid afternoon, when the family finally insisted that someone adjust or change them. The nurse commented that the gauze bandages were not the correct type, and put the original gel type of bandages in place. She again indicated that the wound care specialist would be available on Monday. The nurses obtained an air mattress to reduce pressure on the sores. Otherwise, the hip recovery was going well.

On Sunday, no one looked at the sores or discussed them. As Barbara began to recover from her surgical pain and became more active, the pain from the sores was an increasing problem.

The nurse on the unit was obviously flustered all day Monday with a number of new admissions. By afternoon, the family became more insistent, and Barbara's nurse finally paged the wound care nurse at 2 P.M. When she arrived, the specialist first pointed out that she managed stage three and four wounds, and Barbara's were documented as stage one and two. However, she did look at the wounds, rebandage them, and explain that the bandages would stay on up to a week and that the home health nurses would check the sites. Because Barbara had been discharged to rehab, her doctors did not visit, only the rehab doctor.

### Additional Facts

1. The hospital later explained, in its defense, that they have a standard care plan for skin breakdown on the computer, and the nurses just have to print it and put it in the chart. Each unit has a trained point person for wound care who is supposed to help the staff manage stage one and two wounds. The family never learned of this, much less met such a person, and was highly skeptical about the existence of this structure, at least on the days they needed it.

2. Barbara's surgeon never discussed the issue with her. When her husband brought it up at their second postop visit, the doctor mumbled that extra weight can do that and tossed a prescription at them.

3. No one ever addressed the cause of the wounds with Barbara. Their placement and timing is highly unusual. Barbara remains suspicious, though she is not sure of what. Her daughter believes Barbara developed pressure sores from a device used to support her in the lateral position for surgery. The family doesn't know if the hospital has changed its procedures or if they had similar experiences before.

4. Several months after her surgery (covered by Medicare and supplemental insurance), Barbara received a statement, her first from the hospital, which indicated that she owed $38,000 and to please contact the hospital about payment arrangements.

5. No one from the hospital ever called Barbara to talk about the issue. Her daughter complained to risk management about the lack of information for Barbara and the family. In response, the risk manager sent a letter which outlined facts one and two above and summarized the medical record. The letter referred to facts in the medical record that the family are pretty sure never happened. Neither the surgeon nor the hospital suggested a meeting.

6. Barbara recovered from the hip well and continues to improve, though she has scars. The wounds were painful for months. Barbara's husband told the facts of this disappointing experience to everyone who asked about her.

## A Better Way

Barbara, 75, needed a hip replacement. Her doctor sent her to an orientation class at the hospital where she would have surgery; she met the nurses and saw the rooms. She began to feel more comfortable about the upcoming ordeal.

Her nurse helped her out of bed on her first postop day (Day 2), and noticed two very large open blisters high on her buttocks. The staff put Duoderm (gel) bandages on them. She printed the computerized care plan for pressure sores so she could begin implementation, and she completed a report so an investigation of the cause could begin.

The unit had a specially trained nurse who managed stage one and two wounds, and she reviewed the report and the chart. These were unusual, and she would need to support the investigation into the cause. She approached Barbara and her husband, explaining that the sores appeared to be pressure related, but that they were unusual. She asked for permission to photograph them so the staff on the unit and in the operating room could try to identify the cause, either from pressure or an electrical grounding problem. She discussed the care plan, and told the family what to watch for. She updated all the unit's records so all subsequent nurses caring for the patient would know what to do. She discussed using an air mattress, but she and Barbara decided the surface would be too unstable for a day or two and they would reconsider it later. She did bring in a special pressure-relieving surface.

Each time the nurses moved Barbara, they checked the bandages, replacing them when Barbara's scooting across the bed dislodged them. When the doctors visited, they asked about the wounds and confirmed to the family that there was no need for new orders. (Before the surgery, her surgeon had educated her about the follow-up hospital care, which would involve visits from a physician's assistant who was qualified to check her progress and incision.) By the weekend, when the surgeon and Barbara's regular internist were off duty, she and her family were comfortable with the management of her underlying care and her wounds.

Though Barbara and her husband knew that there was a full-time wound specialist for the hospital, they did not need to see her because the wound nurse on the unit continued to communicate with them daily about the status and progress of the wounds. She continued to follow Barbara with a brief daily visit during her stay on the rehab unit. She assured Barbara that the home health nurses who would follow her twice weekly after discharge had extensive experience with pressure sores; in fact, Barbara found the home health nurses very helpful.

A week after Barbara's discharge, the hospital risk manager called her and explained that the hospital had completed an investigation into the development of her wounds. The cause, a mechanism used to support her on her side during surgery, would be adjusted or padded in the future to try and avoid similar developments. There had not been any similar problems in the past, and they were continuing to examine what factors in Barbara's situation had triggered the development of the wounds to avoid that outcome for other similar patients. Though she didn't tell Barbara, the risk manager had contacted the billing office to make sure that there were no charges related to the wounds, either from the hospital or home care, and that the billing process went smoothly.

When Barbara visited her surgeon, he asked about the wounds and told Barbara that the hospital had notified him of the results of the investigation. He would work with them to make sure that the orthopedic surgeons evaluated the need for any additional precautions in other patients.

### Case Analysis

1. The nurses and/or physicians should have a frank and open discussion with the patient and family as soon as they notice an unusual situation. If facts remain to be developed, then say so and commit to a time for further discussion.
2. Identify, if possible, the cause of *any* unanticipated outcome and share it with the patient, as well as efforts in place to prevent it in the future. The complexity of the process will vary with the nature of the issues involved.
3. Share with the patient and family how the situation will affect care, including assessment modalities, treatment, and prognosis.
4. The goal is to get the patient and family all the information they need either when they need it or as soon as it can reasonably be available.
5. Implement support systems to make sure those in contact with the patient have the information they need—and make sure they use it.
6. The providers have to address conflict and frustration as part of the process.
7. The clinical care plan (including physician's orders) should be open and should constitute the foundation for all clinical discussions of care.
8. Control the billing process and use it as part of your event management. Patients often view it as part of the problem.
9. Educate patients about transitions between providers, such as weekend coverage or to the rehabilitation staff. Who will be available to them?
10. Avoid blaming the event on the patient. In this case, even though Barbara was an overweight mild diabetic with sensitive skin, those were background facts to be evaluated, not a defense. In tort law, you take your plaintiffs as you find them.

The research by Gallagher and Levinson and their colleagues supports the content of this communication. Hickson's research findings on physician demeanor and availability underlie this whole process. If the physicians and staff are cold, unfeeling, or hard to reach, or do not share important information, the communication process simply cannot work well. While Hickson's research only addresses physicians, assuming that it also applies to other providers can generate no harm.

Query: How would the end of the story differ if the wounds and the implanted joint became infected? What would the disclosure discussion look like in each of these scenarios, either when the patient needed six weeks of intravenous antibiotic treatment or when the implanted joint had to be removed?

## HOW DOES DISCLOSURE FIT?

### The JCAHO Mandate

Partially in response to a perceived conspiracy of silence about errors and poor medical outcomes, the JCAHO in 2001 promulgated a standard mandating, "Patients and, when appropriate, their families are informed about the outcomes of care, including unanticipated outcomes.[30] This sentence created a firestorm of discussion and activity, even though its simple intent, as described by the JCAHO, was hardly controversial: The responsible licensed independent practitioner or his or her designee clearly explains the outcome of any treatments or procedures to the patient and, when appropriate, the family, *whenever those outcomes differ significantly from the anticipated outcome.*" (Emphasis added)

Though many feared that unanticipated outcome disclosure would significantly increase claims activity, it has, in fact, had the opposite effect in many well-publicized trials, when combined with prompt and straightforward claim resolution.[31] In keeping with the findings that patients want open, respectful communication with their providers, they often responded to disclosure discussions with a willingness to listen and resolve differences reasonably amicably. Some malpractice insurance companies have actually incorporated disclosure and early resolution into special programs that include guidance for physicians as they go through the process.[32]

The American Society for Healthcare Risk Management (ASHRM) published three monologues to help healthcare providers deal with disclosure of unanticipated outcomes.[33] Many independent experts and educators have produced books, videos, and seminars to help providers understand disclosure and accomplish it effectively.

With disclosure developing as an apparent improvement over past approaches and with its support from the JCAHO, the next wave of research focused on the willingness to disclose, skill levels for disclosure, and sources of resistance to disclosure in healthcare providers. Studies have demonstrated that patients want full disclosure regarding unanticipated outcomes, including errors. Only recently has the research focused on the provider side of the disclosure discussion.

Gallagher et al.[34] found that patients simply want a complete discussion of errors and outcomes that will have an effect on them. The primary attributes patients want in a disclosure process:

- What happened.
- The implications for their health.
- Why it happened.

- How it will be corrected.
- How future similar errors will be prevented.
- They want information supplied to them voluntarily; they don't believe they should have to ask.

As simple as the process sounds, it becomes more complicated in the application. While physicians superficially endorse disclosure, they often find reasons not to disclose.[35] They often define errors differently than patients, including only deviations from the standard of care. Patients, on the other hand, include nonpreventable adverse events, poor service quality, and "deficient interpersonal skills of practitioners"[36] as errors. Physicians also report fear of liability as an impediment to disclosure; however, recent studies indicate that liability concerns actually constitute less of a barrier than reported by the physicians. Canadian physicians, who have much less malpractice exposure, disclose in very similar patterns to their U.S. colleagues.[37] Gallagher et al.[38] proposed that physicians have deeply embedded attitudinal blocks to disclosure and discussion of errors (or patient-perceived errors) that do not directly arise from litigation fear. Their study concluded that fear of malpractice has a relatively small impact on physician attitudes about disclosure. Rather, the training and the culture of medicine have not prepared them for talking about errors, and they lack the skills to do it comfortably. Gallagher points out that his survey demonstrates "how early we are in a culture of transparency."[38]

Risk managers are usually central to the management of disclosure processes. Perhaps because they are more involved in disclosure, risk managers are generally supportive of the concept. However, in practice, they tend to be conservative about what information they would disclose to a patient or family, and are uncomfortable with full disclosure of the five informational elements listed by patients as essential. Though they will discuss the simple facts of the case, they hesitate to disclose "lessons learned," and are still noticeably squeamish about apology.[39] This hesitancy may well result from decades of influence from trial lawyers, who have forbidden any discussion of subsequent action that might indicate a preexisting problem and who still often advise clients not to apologize unless the apology will stay out of court.[40]

The two concepts, disclosure and apology, are clearly related, and it is hard to envision any disclosure of an error without a sincere apology. Unfortunately, as the next section explains, an incomplete apology can leave the aggrieved party less satisfied than no apology at all. As research continues, risk managers will learn whether partial disclosure, in fact, exacerbates patient and family frustration.

## APOLOGIES

Based on their survey of patients, Gallagher et al. recommend that providers reveal and describe errors and offer an apology.[41] Apologies, however, have become a contested point due to both fears of their impact and questions about their appropriateness when both the existence and the definition of error are in doubt.

Focus-group research indicates, however, that an appropriate apology, in fact, facilitates the fair and prompt resolution of a malpractice claim. Jill Robbennolt[42] tested participants with three civil liability scenarios: one with full apology, one with partial apology (sympathy for pain/inconvenience, but no responsibility), and a third with no apology at all. She found that the outcome depended on the nature of the underlying facts of the event that led to the injury. If there was clear liability or clear error, then a full apology increased the chances for a reasonable settlement, and partial apology was worse than none at all. However, if liability was unclear or the injury minor, a partial apology (sympathy) was effective and achieved more settlements than no apology.[42]

Robbennolt's research addresses a point of concern for many participants in disclosure and apology conversations—what if liability is unclear? No one (except perhaps no-fault proponents) has advocated assuming liability where none exists. But from whose vantage point do we make that determination? If the patient's willingness to abandon litigation is the desired outcome, and the response to a particular type of apology depends on the patient's perception of liability or error, the effectiveness of an apology (and the related disclosure) will depend on the *recipient's* understanding of the facts.

How can providers impact the patient's perception of the event? They must put themselves in the patient's shoes and imagine both what has already been shared, intentionally or not, and why the patient might believe what he or she already does believe. Has the disclosure to date been complete? Providers need to watch for situations in which they find themselves saying things like, "I'm sorry but I can't discuss that privileged information," or, "I can't share anything about our response to this event," or, "I am not allowed to talk with you about that," or, "Our rules don't allow you to see your medical record right now." Does the provider's behavior convey a message of secrecy, even though the words don't?

Providers and risk managers also often view situations through defense-colored lenses, discussing facts without acknowledging apparent problems in care or with defensive explanations. They ignore the patient's view of liability. If a patient presents to the emergency department with chest pain and then dies at home after discharge, his family will not appreciate a technical explanation of how the hospital met the standard of care. Yet, often, that is how providers have responded. Instead of acknowledging the patient/family's pain and frustration and anger, the system explains its defenses without validating or even seriously acknowledging the patient/family experience. To know how to apologize, we have to understand their viewpoint and move from there.

So far, providers have directed their efforts at the content of the disclosure, not at the relationship skills inherent to understanding the patient's perspective and building trust. Hickson's research, outlined above, identifies a bad relationship as a cause of lawsuits; undoubtedly it will also impede the effectiveness of efforts at post-event management. A patient who believes that the providers have erred in providing care will expect an acknowledgement and an apology. One who trusts the provider, in spite of disappointment, is more likely to listen to explanations and react accordingly.

## THE CRITICAL ROLE OF TRUST IN PATIENT CARE, DISCLOSURE, AND APOLOGY

The effectiveness of any disclosure conversation will depend directly on the patient/family's willingness to believe what they are told. If they fear a cover-up or posturing, then the disclosing providers will have a much harder job. An apology in the context of perceived insincerity hurts more than it helps. Yet these conversations typically take place after an unanticipated bad outcome, and must incorporate the existing pre-event relationship to providers. This leads back to close the circle on Hickson's previously discussed findings about caring relationships.[15-19]

Effective exchange of information, both personal and clinical, and mutual respect improve the malpractice picture on many levels. They result in better clinical care, because the physician and patient each have better data. The relationship between providers and patients is healthier if an adverse event occurs. Assuming that the disclosure discussion also includes effective trust building communication practices, then the parties will more likely share a common understanding of the event itself and related liability. Any apology is more likely to achieve the desired healing effect.

On the other hand, picture a disclosure discussion in the absence of trust and respect. If a patient has encountered trust roadblocks—perceived an uncaring affect from nurses, waited without food for scheduled procedures, survived minor care problems such as untimely medications, unsuccessful attempts to meet with doctors, and perceived a lack of appropriate resources—a sudden gush of caring and concern during a disclosure conversation will certainly want for sincerity. The patient and family are likely to believe that the niceness and honesty is a ploy to manipulate them.

In short, without basic respect and trust, a disclosure may meet regulatory requirements, but it will not achieve any risk management goals. So an effective risk management program must also address the foundations of the underlying relationship and how to improve it. Risk management professionals increasingly focus on how to impart skills such as emotional intelligence, active listening, and daily conflict management.

## MANAGING THE FINANCIAL SIDE OF DISCLOSURE: CLAIM HANDLING

Unfortunately, some active proponents of disclosure as a risk management tool are so supportive of the approach that they may leave an impression that disclosure and apology could eliminate financial losses completely. However, a more accurate analysis would look at the impact of those activities on the ability to resolve a claim promptly, for a reasonable sum, and with a minimum of resources devoted to the process. How does disclosure impact total claim costs, and how must claim managers (as opposed to risk managers) respond to support disclosure?

Our current malpractice litigation system fails both providers and patients in several respects. While most settled claims involve some questionable care, the groundless claims cost money to defend. The total cost of just operating the system, including attorney fees, expert fees, and court costs is over 50 percent of the total expended for professional liability. Many truly injured and deserving parties do not recover anything. Some undeserving parties recover too much.[43] Because of the secrecy of litigation, any clinical learning that results from an event is unavailable for years—many risk managers do not talk to staff about events and the lessons learned from them until the resulting claims have been resolved.

Providers' ability to promptly follow disclosure discussions with an equally collaborative discussion of financial settlement is severely hampered by the fact that insurance companies and self-insured entities have designed their claim management programs around the litigation structure. Some require expert witness opinions and depositions in many cases before they can consider settlement, especially where large sums are involved. Because the decision makers have traditionally had drawers full of information before settlement discussions arose in earnest, many remain extremely uncomfortable making a judgment early, based on internally derived information. Many claim committees meet quarterly, and rules forbid any settlement until a matter has been before the committee.

Earlier discussion of events with patients, as triggered by the disclosure requirement and more advanced risk-management practices, will require changes in this bureaucratic and inflexible claims management structure.

A number of structural and professional factors add barriers in the process. The "disclosure to claim resolution" quagmire derives from these process-related factors, among others:

- Often, several providers and carriers are involved in the underlying events, and they disagree about evaluation and/or apportionment.
- Defense attorneys are accustomed to pinning down every possible fact before evaluating a case.
- Decision makers rely on lengthy group processes to justify payment decisions and do not empower front-line claims experts. Rigid, hierarchical decision-making structures cannot serve a need for fast-paced resolution. Claim professionals often use standardized valuation structures that only acknowledge economic damages as real damages. Like our early disclosure discussions, this process fails to validate the emotions and noncompensable experience of the patient. It minimizes life disruption, fear, disappointment, anger, and other very real factors that influence patients at this difficult time. Over time, the valuation system may need to adapt and consider these factors if claims are to be resolved early.
- Disclosure discussions can generate a momentum toward resolution as they lead to openness and provide a vehicle for identifying the claimant's true needs. Many claim management processes do not appreciate the value of that momentum.

- Decision makers will not acknowledge the full value of the claim early; they still require more time to adjust.
- The healthcare provider wants to settle, but the insurance carrier does not, or vice versa.
- If plaintiff attorneys are involved at this stage, they often expect a full fee of one-third to 40 percent of the settlement despite the substantial reduction in both risk and work required to achieve early resolution.
- Defense attorneys, who are compensated based on hours of preparation time, will lose a substantial portion of their livelihood. Accordingly, even the most forward-thinking malpractice defense lawyers have an inherent conflict unless they can concentrate their practice on alternative resolution processes.

If we can address these challenges, we can dramatically change the path and nature of medical professional liability claims.

## DISCLOSURE, APOLOGY, AND LITIGATION: ARE WE GIVING AWAY THE FARM?

Even the most effective disclosure and mediation process will sometimes fail to bring the parties to a resolution. Will the fact that they went through the process create unwarranted litigation risk in the subsequent lawsuit? Both focus group outcomes and a growing body of real-world results indicate that the answer is a resounding, "No!"[44]

Because case variables make it impossible to take two similar cases and handle one with disclosure and early resolution efforts and one without (the classic medical research model), we have to look at indirect indicators of the potential outcomes of so-called new risk management programs. The first is focus groups. When preparing for trial, attorneys will often hire consultants to assist with mock trials to test different trial strategies. When a case that involved disclosure is tested with disclosure as part of the defense of the case, the results are better than when the defense does not talk about disclosure. The consultants who perform the test conclude that disclosure has a favorable impact on juries because it meets their expectations. Though they may still find liability, juries do not increase the award because of the fact of disclosure, and may reduce it.[45]

The second method of analyzing a disclosure-based approach is to study results of the organizations using it. The Pew Charitable Trust has funded such an effort in Pennsylvania, which they describe as a mediation-based model. The reports from that project generally support the financial success of the model.[46]

Some have expressed fear that disclosure will lead to more suits because without it, the patient would not have realized that anything was wrong. While this argument has some initial appeal, it assumes that people with bad outcomes will not sue anyway. Risk managers know that healthcare providers do not get away with much anymore. This argument also flies in the face of the research that distinguishes injured patients who sue from those who do not based on communication and trust. In fact, the research, as outlined above, indicates that communication and information reduce the likelihood of a suit with any given outcome.

## THE QUANDARY: HOW TO IMPROVE BEHAVIORS?

Healthcare environments are notorious for implementing management programs of the week, the latest tool for management excellence. Employees who have survived such a two-day seminar know that explaining how to behave is one thing, but actually influencing behavior is much more difficult and complex.

Gerald Hickson has proposed that physician behavior can best be altered by introducing an objective system of measurement, together with peer-based interventions.[47] His program, which has operated successfully at Vanderbilt to reduce patient complaints about targeted physicians, relies on helping relationship-challenged physicians by exposing them to better practices, with a high dose of peer support. Physician behaviors are measured by counting independently generated patient complaints (not surveys), and trained coders categorize the complaints. Statistical comparisons show which physicians have an exceptional number of complaints, and trained physician peers then counsel the outliers. He attributes the success of the program to the relative absence of subjectivity in identifying the target physicians and using peers for the intervention process.

Gallagher et al.[48] suggest that physicians have trained and worked in a culture that simply doesn't deal well with the concept of errors or transparency, and thus imply that a cultural shift must take place to change their behaviors, not just training. Their more recent research with risk managers supports this concept and also suggests that discomfort with openness and transparency goes beyond physicians and, in fact, is ubiquitous in the healthcare structure.[48]

As providers move to a culture of safety, they will also need to embrace a culture of transparency that encourages emotional intelligence and conflict management. The new open culture for patient safety and risk management will help the disciplines support each other, so implementing the efforts side by side should be helpful. Patient safety efforts will help providers develop a greater understanding of systems and process improvement, reducing adverse events and enabling providers to better understand and explain the failures that impact patients. As risk managers and clinical providers learn more from patients in open discussions, that information can feed back into the process improvement efforts.

One comprehensive study endorses the systematic use of traditional mediation and alternative dispute resolution skills in the early event management process to reduce claims activity and maximize the benefit of disclosure.[49] Those conflict management skills overlap with basic change management practices designed to soften resistance to change, such as listening to the resistors and meeting their needs.[50] As providers and administrators around them adopt these interpersonal conflict management practices in both the risk management arena and operations and patient safety, the synergy between the processes can grow.

## ENTERPRISE RISK MANAGEMENT

Risk management began as a financial effort—to reduce losses due to malpractice liability. Over time, executives in other industries (and some in healthcare) have realized that the risk of substantial financial loss spreads beyond liability situations, and can arise from, for example, operations, supply chains, human resource issues, the environment, regulatory compliance, and financial markets. A good example of an issue that presents dramatic risk for healthcare providers in several of those areas is the nursing shortage. It can impact costs in many ways, and expenditures that improve hiring and retention can have benefits at many levels.

As risk analysis tools are accepted as essential in more legal, financial, and operational areas, some healthcare providers have begun to incorporate risk management into a much broader range of decisions. Accordingly, chief risk officers have appeared and are included in senior executive circles to bring risk analysis and control concepts into play on a broader variety of issues.

The move to enterprise risk management has also generated more complete analysis of classic risk issues. Instead of telling the risk manager to stop the losses in a service line, which may or may not be possible, the losses are balanced against the benefits of the line and the cost of controlling the risk. For example, the department that generates the most liability cases may also have an otherwise stunning margin. Previously, few healthcare organizations took such a broad view of loss control.

A similar broad view can demonstrate the potential benefit of early resolution programs. The cost of early resolution, in other words, settling a few things that may not have been settled in a more aggressive defense environment, may well be balanced by improved patient satisfaction and higher quality that arise from more transparent event management practices that incorporate early lessons learned back into patient safety.

## RISK MANAGEMENT CLASSICS: DOCUMENTATION AND INFORMED CONSENT

It is hard to picture a complete discussion of risk management without some mention of documentation and informed consent. However, they are easy to comprehend if one considers them in the framework discussed above: transparency and emotions.

The medical record and any related documents serve one purpose. They communicate—to other providers, to insurance companies, to patients and families, and to lawyers. If a lawsuit develops, they communicate to juries. If providers consider this role in conjunction with the findings about patient and jury expectations for complete communication, medical record preparation becomes much simpler. Is the event/finding related to the patient's condition? Is it important for other caregivers to know? Might it impact how another caregiver interacts with the patient? If so, it belongs in the record.

Comments or behavior indicating that the patient is disappointed or angry can be very relevant to those coming into the chain of future care. Information on the root cause of an error is not; it needs to be distributed in a different pathway for maximum patient safety impact. Because more patients are asking to see their records, caregivers must record information with an assumption that it will be reviewed by the patient or the family.

Informed consent (perhaps more accurately viewed as patient education) remains important for loss control, but not because a piece of paper signed by the patient has legal significance. The paper simply serves to confirm that the patient has experienced a discussion with his or her physician about the underlying condition, options for treatment, and the risks and benefits of treatment. The communication process is the legally critical piece and also most important for the underlying relationship. Informed consent and disclosure also seem to wind up as two sides of the same coin. If a patient knows the risks of treatment decisions, then outcomes will less likely be unanticipated, and the post-event conversations will flow much more easily. Both documentation and informed consent are part of an inclusive education and communication process which will reduce risk in both surgical and nonsurgical care situations.

Documentation and informed consent go beyond physician relationships. How does the patient decide whether to cooperate with the nurse who is asking for early, painful ambulation? How does a physical therapist deal with a patient resisting important therapy because of pain? Those are important care decisions, much like the decision to undergo surgery. In fact, they may be more important to the patient's ultimate outcome. Often, nonphysician staff just charts "noncompliant with ambulation" or "refuses therapy." Conversations and notes about the patient's background condition and the risks and benefits of that decision offer both fuller communication and understanding.

Communication that covers all relevant areas of patient concern (and documentation that confirms those conversations) still has a large role in reducing healthcare liability risk.

## CONCLUSION

Healthcare liability risk will be a fact of life for all providers for the foreseeable future, for patients will have disappointment and unpredictable outcomes. By managing their relationships with their patients—generating trust and strong communication—providers can significantly improve their experiences in this risky domain. However, the best results come from addressing conflict and concerns with the patients and their families directly, a process that, for many, will require new skill development and support from risk managers, educational systems, and professional organizations.

Key Concepts

- Loss identification and prevention (avoiding adverse outcomes) remains an important component of risk management. Efforts in this area should be coordinated with the patient-safety movement.

- Risk management requires openly addressing both real adverse outcomes and potential problems identified through incident and outcome reporting processes.
- Simply enforcing rules for good clinical practice will not eliminate the majority of claims and suits.
- Most lawsuits and claims arise from patient dissatisfaction with the patient-provider relationship, usually coupled with a disappointing medical outcome. The statistically significant factor is the relationship, not the quality of care. Patients do not split out their relationships, and all providers during a course of care are part of the experience.
- Significant risk reduction for high-claim providers requires attention to behavioral and communication issues, as well as clinical quality and outcomes.
- Patients and families want open, honest, and voluntary discussion of disappointing encounters and outcomes, as identified by them. Providers have to address these events as identified by the patients with the patients, not just what the medical field defines as errors. Discussion should include education about the event, steps to prevent it in the future, and in most cases an apology.
- Clinical documentation and informed consent processes need to support the transparent culture.

## REFERENCES

1. Carroll, R., ed. 2004. *Risk Management Handbook for Healthcare Organizations*. 4th ed. San Francisco: Jossey-Bass

2. A later section of the chapter discusses the broader concept of enterprise risk management, which encompasses financial, regulatory, and other operational risks.

3. Hall, M. 2002. "Law, Medicine and Trust." *Stanford Law Review* 55 (2): 463–527, 474.

4. Hickson, G., C. Federspiel, J. Pichert, C. Miller, J. Gauld-Jaeger, and P. Bost. 2002. "Patient Complaints and Malpractice Risk." *Journal of the American Medical Association* 287 (22): 2951–2957; Levinson, W. D. Roter, J. Mullooly, V. T. Dull, and R. Frankel. 1997. "Physician-Patient Communication: The Relationship with Malpractice Claims among Primary Care Physicians and Surgeons." *Journal of the American Medical Association* 277 (7): 553–559.

5. Hickson, G., cited in A. Robeznieks. 2002. "Being Open May Avoid Lawsuits." *American Medical News* (June 10). Available at: http://www.ama-assn.org/amednews/2002/06/10/prsb0610.htm.

6. Hickson, G., J. Pichert, C. Federspeil, and E. Clayton. 1997. "Development of An Early Identification and Response Model of Malpractice Prevention." *Law and Contemporary Problems* 60 (1): 7–29.

7. Mohr, J. 2000. "American Medical Malpractice Litigation in Historical Perspective." *Journal of the American Medical Association* 283 (13): 1731–1737.

8. *Darling v. Charleston Community Memorial Hospital*, 33 Ill.2d 326, 211 N.E.2d 253, 14 A.L.R.3d 860 (1965).

9. *Va. Code Ann.* § 8.01–38; Danzon, Patricia, 1984. "The Frequency and Severity of Medical Malpractice Claims." *Journal of Law and Economics* 27 (1): 115–148.

10. U.S. General Accounting Office. 1993. *Medical Malpractice: Multiple Factors Have Contributed to Increased Premium Rates.* Washington, D.C., 38–39. Available at: http://www.gao.gov/new.items/d03702.pdf.

11. Brennan, T., and M. Mello. 2002. "Deterrence of Medical Errors: Theory and Evidence for Malpractice Reform." *Texas Law Review* 80: 1595, 1599–1600, 1618.

12. O'Connell, J., and A. S. Boutros. 2002. "Treating Medical Malpractice under a Variant of the Business Judgment Rule." *Notre Dame Law Review* 77: 373, 377.

13. Hickson, James, Federspeil, and Clayton, 8.

14. Ibid.

15. Hickson, G., E. Clayton, P. Githens, and F. Sloan. 1992. "Factors that Prompted Families to File Medical Malpractice Claims Following Perinatal Injuries." *Journal of the American Medical Association* 267 (10): 1359–1363.

16. Hickson, Pichert, Federspeil, and Clayton, 12.

17. Hickson, G., E. Clayton, S. Entman, C. Miller, P. Githens, K. Whetten-Goldstein, and F. Sloan. 1994. "Obstetricians' Prior Malpractice Experience and Patients' Satisfaction with Care." *Journal of the American Medical Association* 272 (20): 1583–1587.

18. Hickson, Pichert, Federspeil, and Clayton, 12.

19. Hickson, Federspiel, Pichert, Miller, Gauld-Jaeger, and Bost, 2955.

20. Murff, H. J, D. J. France, J. Blackford, E. L. Grogan C. Yu, T. Speroff, J. W. Pichert, and G. B, Hickson. 2006. "Relationship between Patient Complaints and Surgical Complications." *Quality and Safety in Health Care* 15: 13–16.

21. Hickson, G., cited in A. Robeznieks. 2002. "Being Open May Avoid Law-suits." *American Medical News* (June 10). Available at: http://www.ama-assn.org/amednews/2002/06/10/prsb0610.htm.

22. Hickson, Federspiel, Pichert, Miller, Gauld-Jaeger, and Bost, 2955.

23. Ambady, N., D. LaPlante, T. Nguyen, R. Rosenthal, N. Chaumeton, and W. Levinson. 2002. "Surgeons' Tone of Voice: A Clue to Malpractice History." *Surgery* 132 (1): 5–9.

24. Levinson, Roter, Mullooly, Dull, and Frankel, 553–559.

25. Rhodes, K., M. Drum, E. Anliker, R. Frankel, D. Howes, and W. Levinson. 2006. "Lowering the Threshold for Discussions of Domestic Violence." *Archives of Internal Medicine* 166: 1107–1114.

26. Wolosin, R. 2005. "How Safe Do Patients Feel?" *Patient Safety and Quality Healthcare e-newsletter* (November/December). Available at: http://www.psqh.com/novdec05/how-safe.html.

27. Scheitel, S., B. Boland, P. Wollan, and M. Silverstein. 1996. "Patient-Physician Agreement about Medical Diagnoses and Cardiovascular Risk Factors in the Ambulatory General Medical Examination." *Mayo Clinic Proceedings* 71 (12): 1209–1210.

28. Public Health Advertisement from United Health Foundation. Available at: http://www.unitedhealthfoundation.org/tips/doc_ad.pdf. Accessed July 27, 2007.

29. Hickson, Pichert, Federspeil, and Clayton, 15, 22.

30. Joint Commission for the Accreditation of Healthcare Organizations. 2002. *Comprehensive Accreditation Manual for Hospitals: The Official Handbook.* Chicago: Joint Commission Resources, RI-10. (RI refers to the section on Patient Rights, Ethics, and Institutional Responsibility.)

31. Boothman, R. 2006. "Apologies and a Strong Defense at the University of Michigan Health System." *The Physician Executive* (March–April): 7; Kraman, S., and G. Hamm. 1999. "Risk Management: Extreme Honesty May Be the Best Policy." *Annals of Internal Medicine* 131 (12): 963.

32. COPIC Insurance Company. 2006. *COPIC 3Rs Program* 3 (1). Available at: http://www.callcopic.com/resources/custom/PDF/3rs-newsletter/vol-3-issue-1-jun-2006.pdf.

33. American Society for Healthcare Risk Management. 2003. *Disclosure (Parts 1-3)*. Available at: http://www.ashrm.org/ashrm/resources/monograph.html. Accessed July 29, 2007.

34. Gallagher, T., A. Waterman, A. Ebers, V. Fraser, and W. Levinson. 2003. "Patients' and Physicians' Attitudes Regarding the Disclosure of Medical Errors." *Journal of the American Medical Association* 289 (8): 1001.

35. Gallagher, T., and M. Lucas. 2005. "Should We Disclose Harmful Medical Errors to Patients? If So, How?" *Journal of Clinical Outcomes Management* 12 (5): 253.

36. Gallagher, Waterman, Ebers, Fraser, and Levinson, 1003.

37. Gallagher, T., A. Waterman, J. Garbutt, J. Kapp, D. Chan, W. C. Dunagan, V. Fraser, and W. Levinson. 2006. "U.S. and Canadian Physicians' Attitudes and Experiences Regarding Disclosing Errors to Patients." *Archives of Internal Medicine* 166 (15): 1605–1611; Pierce, O. 2006. "Why Docs Don't Say I'm Sorry." *United Press International*. Available at: http://www.upi.com/archive/view.php?archive = 1&S toryID = 20060815–120236–5629r.

38. Pierce.

39. Gallagher, T., G. Brundage, K. Bommarito, E. Summy, A. Ebers, A. Waterman, V. Fraser, and C. Dunagan. 2006. "National Survey: Risk Managers' Attitudes and Experiences Regarding Patient Safety and Error Disclosure." *Journal of Healthcare Risk Management* 26 (3): 11.

40. Zimmerman, Rachel. 2004. "Doctors' New Tool to Fight Lawsuits: Saying 'I'm Sorry.'" *Wall Street Journal* (May 18): A1; Butcher, Lola. 2006. "Lawyers Say 'Sorry' May Sink You in Court." *The Physician Executive* (March–April): 20.

41. Gallagher, Waterman, Ebers, Fraser, and Levinson, 1006.

42. Robbennolt, J. 2003. "Apologies and Legal Settlement: An Empirical Examination." *Michigan Law Review* 102: 460.

43. Studdert, D., M. Mello, A. Gawande, T. Gandhi, A. Kachalia, C. Yoon, A. Puopolo, and T. Brennan. 2006. "Claims, Payments and Compensation Payments in Medical Malpractice Litigation." *New England Journal of Medicine* 354 (19): 2024–2033.

44. Boothman, 7. 2005. "Product Liability—Pro-Active Protection." *IndustryWeek.com*. Available at: http://www.industryweek.com/ReadArticle.aspx?ArticleID = 10902.

45. Popp, P. 2003. "Disclosure: A Legal View: How Will Disclosure Affect Future Litigation?" *Journal of Healthcare Risk Management* 23 (1): 5.

46. Liebman, C., and C. Hyman. 2005. *Medical Error Disclosure, Mediation Skills, and Malpractice Litigation: A Demonstration Project in Pennsylvania*. Available at: http://www.pewtrusts.com/pdf/LiebmanReport.pdf.

47. Hickson, Pichert, Federspeil, and Clayton, 25.

48. Gallagher, Waterman, Garbutt, Kapp, Chan, Dungan, Fraser, and Levinson, 1605–1611; Gallagher, T., A. Waterman, A. Ebers, V. Fraser, and W. Levinson. 2006.

"National Survey: Risk Managers' Attitudes and Experiences Regarding Patient Safety and Error Disclosure." *Journal of Healthcare Risk Management* 26 (3): 11.

49. Liebman and Hyman.

50. Maurer, R. 1996. *Beyond the Wall of Resistance: Unconventional Strategies That Build Support for Change*. Austin, TX: Bard Press.

CHAPTER 9

# Pastoral Medicine:
# The Impact of Pastoral Care

Samuel Miller

Pastoral medicine is not easily defined. It is the warmth and caring that nurtures and supports patients and their families, as well as the caregiver staff. It provides emotional and spiritual support in a compassionate way. In its broadest sense, pastoral medicine is practiced by doctors, nurses, technicians, chaplains, friends, family, and other spiritual and medical caregivers.

The use of prayer and other spiritual practices to improve health dates back thousands of years, to Hippocrates and Maimonides. Using spirituality in ancient medicine was a way for doctors of the day to approach care for their patients. It was not because they did not have diagnostic tools or medicines. Even though they were very different from today's modern technology, they did possess medicines and tools for diagnosis and treatment.

Maimonides wrote, "May I never see in the patient anything but a fellow creature in pain."[1] The essence of this quote indicates the need for caregivers to be equal with those whom they are treating. Medicine, and especially pastoral medicine, should be a partnership filled with humility. Pastoral medicine embraces the idea of treating the patient as a person rather than as a medical condition. It also includes treating the whole person, body, mind, and spirit. The purpose of this chapter is to define spirituality and spiritual assessment and to present case histories of pastoral medicine interventions.

## SPIRITUALITY AND HEALING

The concept of spirituality is at the core of pastoral medicine. Many practices may help a person to develop spiritual connectedness and balance, including prayer, journaling, yoga, and meditation.

These practices may be done alone, with a group, or in a community. All of these practices provide a way for a person to achieve internal clarity. The most profound effects of these techniques happen when they become part of a daily routine.

Spirituality and religion are not the same thing. Spirituality is what the divine gives to us, and religion is what we have made it into. Prayer is often thought of within the context of religion, but prayer can be practiced outside of its context. When pastoral medicine is practiced well, it meets people where they are, whether they are within a religious context or outside of it.

## SPIRITUAL ASSESSMENT

Spiritual assessment is used by nurses in the hospital and completed at the beginning of each shift. It consists of three questions:

- Does a patient have meaning and purpose in her life?
- Does he or she have a sense of love and belonging?
- Does he or she have freedom from guilt and shame?

If the patient answers yes to all three questions, he or she has the emotional and spiritual balance to move forward in the healing process. When he or she answers no to any of the three questions, his or her nurse determines if this area of the patient's life is hindering the patient's medical treatment or imposing a barrier to recovery. Barriers represent an opportune time to consult the pastoral medicine service. The following case presentations are examples of pastoral medicine.

---

### Case Presentation: Atypical Chest Pain

Jack was a 48-year-old man who arrived at the emergency room complaining of chest pain and shortness of breath. The emergency department physician immediately performed an electrocardiogram (EKG), chest X-ray, and blood tests. The EKG showed no evidence of heart attack, and blood tests revealed no heart muscle damage. However, Jack continued to complain of chest pain, and was admitted to the hospital for serial testing and observation.

Within 12 hours, Jack had earned a reputation for being a noncompliant, abusive, belligerent patient. The nursing staff on his unit began coming early to make certain *not* to have him as one of their patients.

For a day and a half, Jack refused to allow staff to draw blood tests. He also refused to take any medications or allow any intravenous needles to be inserted. When a nurse saw a hospital chaplain in the hall, she asked, "Glenn, I have a patient that I really need help with! Please see Jack in room 3111."

---

It took Jack almost 45 minutes to vent before he could talk about his situation:

Glenn:   "What kind of work do you do?"

Jack:    "I drive an 18-wheeler—a brand new, customized Kenworth Diesel with leather interior and chrome magnesium wheels on both the tractor and my tanker trailer. I haul 10,000 gallons of jet fuel to the rural airports in the mountains. I love my truck! I have the best job in the world."

Glenn:   "What seems to be bothering you the most?"

Jack:    "I am scared that I am going to get fired from my job. And my wife has left me for the fourth time. This time she is threatening to get a divorce."

As Jack shared his story, he grew calmer. He realized that he described his truck in more loving terms than he described his wife. The chaplain said, "Jack, I am not a clinical person, but your EKG did not show any evidence of a heart attack. It may be that the stress in your life is causing your chest pain. Unless you allow the hospital staff to complete the necessary tests, you will not be able to learn whether you really have any heart problems."

The chaplain left Jack's room, and Jack changed his attitude. When his nurse returned, he used appropriate language, stated that he was ready to take his medicine, and allowed staff to draw blood tests. By the next day, the nurses asked Glenn, "What did you do to Jack? He is a different patient—cooperative and not swearing. He is even letting us help him get better."

### Case Analysis

Numerous studies indicate a correlation between spirituality and health. Considering the spirituality of patients informs, enhances, and adds a new dimension to clinical practice.[2] Abundant evidence indicates a change in outcomes when principles of pastoral medicine are used. The broader concept of a person's spiritual, emotional, and mental health affecting physical health continues to gain momentum in Western medicine.

## Case Presentation: A Near-Death Experience

A Western cardiologist recalled a lesson that he learned over 20 years ago at the bedside of a patient who was in cardiogenic shock. After three hours, he had done everything he could think of to save her life without success. He ended the resuscitation and prayed. He left the hospital and expected to hear that she had died. Instead, the woman survived. She told him that as she lay near death, she had heard a choir of praying voices, including his.

"It went against everything I had been taught. Her numbers were incompatible with life. Over and over again, I see a divine hand in the lives of my patients."

### Case Analysis

Modern medicine can dehumanize patient care. A hospital gown and semiprivate room limit patients' privacy. Furthermore, an average patient may have no clue what high-tech machines do. The healing environment demands high touch. VanDecreek[3] documented the beneficial outcomes for patients in whom pastoral medicine works in conjunction with clinical practice. The partnering of high tech with high touch is the healing environment where science and spirit blend. High touch includes:

- connecting with patients emotionally;
- reassuring them with a pat on the arm, shoulder, forehead, or back;
- reaching them spiritually with prayer or meditation;
- actively listening to their concerns and empathically trying to put oneself in their frame of reference; and
- providing a calming presence.

## Case Presentation: Overcoming Anxiety

A woman who volunteered at a hospital walked into the chaplain's office and said, "I told the radiology department that they would have to wait because I had to see the chaplain before I go in for my MRI [magnetic resonance imaging] exam. I know that I can do it because I had an MRI before, but I am very claustrophobic, and I hate that thumping sound. Will you please pray with me and for me, so that I can calm down and get this done?" After a brief conversation followed by prayer, the patient was ready for her MRI.

### Case Analysis

Competent pastoral medicine balances and blends physical and spiritual assessments. Optimal care represents not an either-or, but a both-and perspective.

## Case Presentation: Reframing Perspectives

Kathy was a new intensive care unit (ICU) nurse caring for two patients. Eight hours into her shift, she had checked on a 54-year-old male patient suffering from a severe respiratory condition. His intravenous medications were infusing properly, and he appeared clinically stable.

As Kathy turned, she noted that her patient had stopped breathing. Immediately, she summoned help by calling a Code Blue. Momentarily, more than a dozen doctors, nurses, respiratory technicians, and a pharmacist filled the room and hallway and resuscitated the patient.

Kathy froze, standing near the head of the bed. However, the patient was successfully revived, and his vital signs became stable.

At the end of her first shift on the ICU, Kathy went to her supervisor and said, "I cannot do this work. I panicked after I signaled for the Code Blue today. I just froze and could not move."

Her nursing supervisor said, "Kathy, it happens to all of us. You did exactly what you were supposed to do, and we got a great outcome for our patient. I will not let you quit after just one day. Please work with me the rest of the week. Then we can decide what you want to do."

The next day, Kathy returned to work at the ICU to care for the patient who had stopped breathing the day before. As she walked into room 2218, her patient said, "You are my nurse. You saved my life yesterday! You were my emotional rock. Yesterday was almost like an out of body experience for me. I could feel the medicine that they gave me, and I could feel and see the nurses, doctors, and others touching me and doing different things. It was like I was watching them work on someone else. And you were standing over there near the head of my bed. I could see your face. You appeared calm. You helped me believe that everything was going to turn out all right. Thank you for saving my life!"

### Case Analysis

Kathy still works in an ICU as a caring, skilled, and capable nurse. She knows that healthcare embodies a team effort. She enjoys working in an environment where she feels supported and can thrive.

In a report on a survey of nurses working in a magnet hospital, the essential elements of a good working environment were[4]:

- coworkers who are clinically competent;
- a healthy nurse-doctor relationships characterized by two-way dialogue; and
- a paramount concern for patient welfare.

Holistic care, encompassing the patient's body, mind, and spirit, continues to be a theme for top hospitals that have applied for and received magnet nursing status.

## Case Presentation: Physician Burnout

Dr. J had been an emergency physician for more than 20 years. He had saved hundreds of lives with his skill and compassion, but he began to describe himself as "burned out, completely fried." Yet, he had no desire to change professions.

An ambulance brought in a female patient who was in labor. Dr. J phoned her obstetrician, who replied, "It will be at least an hour before I can get to the hospital." Dr. J told the patient, "Your doctor is on the way. However, if you need a doctor before he gets here, I will assist you. I have delivered babies for over 20 years."

Five minutes later, the head of the baby was crowning, and Dr. J delivered a dark-haired baby girl with blue eyes. Carefully, he placed the baby's head in the palm of his hand, and laid her body on his left forearm as he clamped and cut the umbilical cord. Gently, he cleansed her face. Her blue eyes locked onto him. In that moment, he thought, "I am the first human being she has ever seen. It is my job to welcome her." Suddenly, he was reminded why he was an emergency room doctor. He felt that he was standing on sacred ground.

### Case Analysis

Burnout occurs when work and/or personal demands exceed one's ability to cope. It can result in psychological distress, physical symptoms, clinical errors, and increased patient morbidity and mortality.[5] A brief encounter renewed Dr. J's calling and gave him back his reason for living and working. He never forgot the patient encounter of the dark-haired baby girl with the blue eyes. Being renewed helped him recover from burnout.

## CONCLUSION

Pastoral medicine combines spirituality, healing, and science in an environment that encourages and enriches caregivers and promotes caregiving. It creates a nurturing base that provides a healthy, healing place for patients, families, and staff.

Key Concepts

- Caregivers have used pastoral medicine for centuries to promote holistic care.
- Modern scientific technology is enhanced by principles of pastoral medicine that help patients, families, and staff find meaning and purpose in their lives.

## NOTES

1. Gundersen, L. 2000. "Faith and Healing." *Annals of Internal Medicine* 132 (2): 169–172.

2. McBride, J. L., G. Arthur, R. Brooks, and L. Pilkington. 1998. "The Relationship between a Patient's Spirituality and Health Experiences." *Family Medicine* 30 (2): 122–126.

3. Vandecreek, Larry. 1995. *Spiritual Needs and Pastoral Services: Readings In Research*. Decatur, GA: Journal of Pastoral Care Publications, Inc.

4. Studer, Q. 2003. *Hardwiring Excellence*. Gulf Breeze, FL: Fire Starter Publishing.

5. Cohn, K. H., D. B. Panasuk, and J. C. Holland. 2005. "Workplace Burnout." In *Better Communication for Better Care: Mastering Physician-Administrator Collaboration*, ed. K. H. Cohn, 57. Chicago: Health Administration Press.

# About the Editors and Contributors

KENNETH H. COHN, MD, MBA, FACS, is a board-certified general surgeon. He obtained his medical degree from Columbia College of Physicians Medical School, completed his residency at the Harvard-Deaconess Surgical Service, and performed fellowships in endocrine and oncologic surgery at the Karolinska Hospital and at Memorial Sloan-Kettering Cancer Center, respectively. He was assistant professor of surgery at State University of New York Health Science Center at Brooklyn, and later moved to Dartmouth-Hitchcock Medical Center as associate professor of surgery and chief of surgical oncology at the Veterans Administration Hospital at White River Junction. With the change in the medical economic climate, Dr. Cohn entered the MBA program of the Tuck School at Dartmouth and graduated in June 1998. He worked initially as a consultant at Health Advances, assisting six firms to commercialize new products. Since joining the Cambridge Management Group, he has led change-management initiatives for physicians at affiliated hospitals within the Yale, New Haven; Banner, Colorado;, Cottage, Santa Barbara; and Sutter, Sacramento Health Systems. He remains clinically active, covering surgical practices in New Hampshire and Vermont. Dr. Cohn has written 40 articles published in peer-reviewed medical journals and two books, *Better Communication for Better Care: Mastering Physician-Administration Collaboration*, and *Collaborate for Success! Breakthrough Strategies for Engaging Physicians, Nurses, and Hospital Executives*. His Web site is http://www.healthcarecollaboration.com.

DOUGLAS E. HOUGH, PhD, is associate professor and chair, the Department of Business of Health, at the Carey Business School of Johns Hopkins University. He is responsible for eight programs, including the innovative Hopkins Business of Medicine, a four-course graduate certificate program and an MBA program with concentration in medical services management, designed for experienced physicians (offered in partnership with the Johns Hopkins University School of Medicine). Dr. Hough has over 25 years of experience in industry and academia. He has been a research economist at the American Medical Association, a manager in the healthcare consulting division of Coopers and Lybrand, and a partner in two healthcare strategy consulting firms. His research interests are in identifying the optimal size and structure of a physician practice and in determining the impact of changing physician demographics on the structure of medical practices. His consulting interests focus on methods of strengthening hospital-physician relations (e.g., the development of integrated delivery systems, physician-hospital initiatives, and management service organizations), as well as the organization and strategic direction of physician practices. Dr. Hough is a frequent speaker and author on healthcare issues related to physicians. His research has been published in such professional journals as the *Journal of the American Medical Association,* the *Journal of Human Resources,* and the *Journal of Medical Practice Management.* Dr. Hough earned his MS and PhD in economics from the University of Wisconsin. He received his BS in economics from the Massachusetts Institute of Technology. He is a member of Academy Health, the American Economic Association, the International Health Economics Association, and the Medical Group Management Association.

NEIL J. CAMPBELL, MA, MBA, is currently the founder, chairman, and chief executive officer (CEO) for Mosaigen, Inc., a biotechnology development corporation located in Rockville, Maryland. Mr. Campbell is also a member of the Adjunct/Practitioner Faculty of the Carey Business School at Johns Hopkins University. Mr. Campbell was formerly president and chief operating officer/CEO for EntreMed, Inc., where he led the turnaround and transformation of the biopharmaceutical company. Prior to joining EntreMed, he served as senior director of commercial development for Celera Genomics, where he led U.S. and international efforts to develop the e-commerce markets for medical high-performance computing and bioinformatic software tools. With over 20 years of industry experience, Mr. Campbell has held executive management, business development, and sales and marketing positions with Life Technologies, Inc., IGEN, Inc., and Abbott Laboratories. During his career, Mr. Campbell has successfully developed and/or introduced over 170 products and services in the areas of high-performance computing, medical software, e-commerce, pharmaceuticals, medical devices, clinical diagnostics, consumer healthcare products, research products, bioinformatics, and nanotechnology. He cofounded Quanta Biosciences of Gaithersburg, Maryland, and currently serves as an advisor to the company. He's also on the board of directors for a number of organizations. Mr. Campbell earned his MBA and MA in management systems from Webster University in St. Louis, Missouri, and his BS-BA from Norwich University in Northfield, Vermont.

DIANE L. DIXON, EdD is managing principal of D. Dixon & Associates, LLC, an independent leadership and organization development consulting practice specializing in healthcare and human services. She has taught leadership and organizational behavior in the Business of Medicine Program at Johns Hopkins University-Carey Business School. Ms. Dixon writes a leadership column for *Caring for the Ages,* an official publication of the American Medical Directors Association published by Elsevier Medical News Group. A chapter, "Successfully Surviving Culture Change," was included in the book, *Culture Change in Long-Term Care.* Ms. Dixon holds a doctorate in education from George Washington University's Executive Leadership in Human Resource Development Program. The focus of her research was transformational leadership and hospital chief executives.

ANAND S. JOSHI, MD, MBA, is currently the director of clinical procurement for New York Presbyterian Hospital, an academic medical center of 2,300 beds and up in New York City, that was most recently ranked sixth in the *US News and World Report* honor roll of U.S. hospitals. Having published and presented numerous times on the topic of strategic sourcing of hospital supplies and, specifically, sourcing physician preference items, Dr. Joshi has established himself as a recognized authority in hospital supply chain management.

EDWIN E. LEWIS, Jr., is senior security advisor, information systems manager, and an adjunct instructor for the Johns Hopkins University, Carey Business School. He has extensive experience in supporting federal, state, and commercial clients over a wide range of defense, intelligence, and healthcare programs. Within the healthcare market, he has supported the deployment of large commercial and state-run systems, as well as managed security operations for the centers for Medicare and Medicaid services payment processing system. He also has extensive experience as a graduate school instructor, having developed and taught courses ranging from medical informatics to information technology economics. Mr. Lewis received his graduate degrees from Loyola University in Baltimore and from the Johns Hopkins University. He also holds multiple certifications in information security and related technologies.

CHRIS D. MELETIS, ND, is past dean of naturopathic medicine/chief medical officer and is now professor of natural pharmacology at the Oregon-based National College of Naturopathic Medicine (NCNM). He has also served as dean of clinical affairs at NCNM. Earlier, he was medical director for Outside In, a clinic in Oregon offering complementary and alternative medicine (CAM), and staffed by NCNM residents/interns working in partnership with allopathic residents from the Oregon Health and Science University. He has been a licensed naturopath since 1992 and has his own private practice. Dr. Meletis is principal investigator leading a Consortium Oregon CAM study with a $1.5 million grant. He has contributed to five books, including *The Natural Pharmacy*, and has authored nine books for major publishers, including *The Complete Guide to Safe Herbs*, *Enhancing Fertility Naturally*, and *Better Sex Naturally*. He has been extensively interviewed in popular media, including magazines like *Body and Soul,*

*Working Mother*, *Mademoiselle*, *Self*, *Heart & Soul*, and *Good Health Keeping*. He's also been interviewed on Internet sites and radio and television.

SAMUEL MILLER, a professional hospital chaplain, is director of mission and ministry at Porter Adventist Hospital in Denver, Colorado. A resident of Colorado Springs, Colorado, he holds a BA in theology from Southwestern Adventist University and a master of divinity degree from Andrews University.

JAYNE OLIVA, MBA, is principal with the Croes Oliva Group, a team of medical group management diagnosticians. The Croes Oliva Group works with healthcare organizations and their affiliated physicians, as well as private practices, to improve front-line operations and boost performance in profitability, productivity, patient access, and patient-care coordination. She also coaches and mentors physicians for optimum leadership performance. Ms. Oliva holds an MBA from the Kellogg Graduate School of Management at Northwestern University. She teaches graduate-level courses in outpatient care delivery and physician practice management, speaks nationally, and appears frequently in regional and national publications.

MARY TOTTEN, MBA, president, Totten & Associates, is a speaker and consultant to hospitals and health systems and other health-related organizations on quality of care and medical staff credentialing, strategic planning and mission development, governing board orientation, and board self-evaluation and governance restructuring. She conducts board retreats and education programs and writes and publishes books, articles, and newsletters for healthcare leaders. Her publications include the American Hospital Association's *Guide to Governance for Hospital and Health System Trustees*, first and second editions, *The Board's Role in Quality of Care: A Practical Guide for Hospital Trustees*, *The Future of Health Care Governance: Redesigning Boards for a New Era*, and *The Trustee Handbook for Health Care Governance*, first and second editions. Ms. Totten holds an MBA from the Kellogg Graduate School of Management at Northwestern University and has served on several hospital, health-system, and educational institution governing boards.

J. DEANE WALDMAN, MD, MBA, is a practicing pediatric cardiologist and pathologist, as well as a principal in ADM Healthcare Consulting. He is professor of pediatrics and pathology, University of New Mexico Health Sciences Center, and professor of healthcare strategy, R. O. Anderson Graduate Schools of Management in Albuquerque, New Mexico. He has published over 100 citations on medical topics in pediatric cardiology and more than 25 citations on the strategy and management of healthcare, with emphasis on the application of systems thinking. He has deep experience in healthcare culture, turnover/retention of the healthcare workforce, and physician-manager relations.

KATHRYN K. WIRE, JD, MBA, CPHRM, is a healthcare risk management consultant, author, educator, and certified civil mediator. She actively participates in risk-management and health law organizations, contributing articles and programs on claim and outcome management, conflict management, and long-term care. She wrote a chapter, "Embracing Poor Outcomes: A Comprehensive Claim Reduction Strategy," for the 2004 edition of West's *Health Law Handbook*. She has lectured for local graduate healthcare programs on risk management, conflict management, and negotiation.

# Index